BERNARD DARWIN ON GOLF

BERNARD DARWIN

Edited and with a New Preface by
JEFF SILVERMAN

NEW FOREWORD BY BRAD FAXON

Essex, Connecticut

To Nick Lyons . . .
. . . for showing the way

An imprint of The Globe Pequot Publishing Group, Inc.
64 South Main Street
Essex, CT 06426
www.globepequot.com

Distributed by NATIONAL BOOK NETWORK

First edition published by The Lyons Press in 2003
First Lyons Press paperback edition 2005
Updated Lyons Press paperback edition 2024

British Library Cataloguing in Publication Information available

Library of Congress Cataloging-in-Publication Data Available

ISBN 9781493084258 (paperback : alk. paper)

∞™ The paper used in this publication meets the minimum requirements of American National Standard for Information Sciences—Permanence of Paper for Printed Library Materials, ANSI/NISO Z39.48-1992.

Contents

IV

The Players, Ridiculous and *Sublime*

V

A Golfer's Almanac

VI

Fields of Play

VII

Crossing the Pond: The Atlantic Monthly *Dispatches*

VIII

Valedictory

Foreword

Growing up not far from Rhode Island Country Club, I began my golfing adventures as a young caddie. Of course, I loved playing first and foremost, but I was pulled into the game by more than that. The course itself, one of the many designed in the state by Golden Age master Donald Ross—he summered in nearby Sakonnet—was a puzzle that fascinated me every day. So I began to learn about golf architecture. And history. I couldn't miss it at RICC; the club was one of the golfing homes of the great Glenna Collett-Vare, the only golfer, female or male, to win six US Amateur championships.

Amazingly, golf kept opening its doors, inviting me in and teaching me history. On my high school golf team, I got to play at places like Newport Country Club, host of the first US Open and the first US Amateur Championship, and one of the most beautiful golfing sites I've ever seen. And a little farther away, across the border into Massachusetts, I was able to walk the fairways of The Country Club in Brookline, and what young caddie doesn't get chills at hearing the story of how another young caddie, Francis Ouimet, his bag carried by an even younger caddie—ten-year-old Eddie Lowery—improbably took on the best and bested them all there? The first amateur to hoist the Open trophy, Ouimet won the 1913 championship in a playoff over a pair of British golfing legends, Harry Vardon and Ted Ray. Another Brit happened to be on hand to verify Ouimet's scorecard. His name was Bernard Darwin. I had no idea who he was. I later found out that he was a legend, too.

The more golf I played, the more golf's history grabbed me, and by the time I was playing college golf, I was reading everything I could get my hands on: biography, history, fiction, architecture, instruction, game stories, and essays—and have never stopped. Not that long into my career on the PGA Tour, I met a book collector named George Lewis who handed me an old volume by a writer versatile enough to do it all—and do it in a way that dazzled: Bernard Darwin. The same Bernard Darwin who walked beside Ouimet at Brookline and signed that revered scorecard. He wasn't just a signature on an artifact from golf's past anymore. His words and ideas shined a light on what was then for me golf's living present. All these years later, that light continues to illuminate the game I love.

Which is why *Bernard Darwin on Golf* has become one of the cornerstones of my golf library. Sure, there have been other fine collections of Darwin's essays and columns, but no other editor compiling a book about Darwin's long lifetime of work and play—Darwin himself was an accomplished golfer—managed to bring together so much material from so many places as Jeff Silverman managed to do in assembling this anthology.

From profiling Bobby Jones and, naturally, Ouimet, to simply lying in bed and musing over the variety of golf holes he could create in the covers with each twitch of his legs, Darwin, as a writer, covered the waterfront—and I can say this from experience: Darwin's shoreline is a good bit longer than Rhode Island's. Along the route, his prose captures the enchantment and complexity of a game that drew me in when I was just a kid looking for a loop. On every page, *Bernard Darwin on Golf* reinforces why, in the half century or so since, I've never left.

—Brad Faxon
Barrington, Rhode Island
February 2024

Preface

Shortly after *Bernard Darwin on Golf* was published in 2003, I received a note from its publicist telling me that one of the then big-three national golf magazines had named the book the best—let me repeat: the BEST—golf book of all time. I paid no attention. The guy's pulling my leg. I mean, there are an awful lot of golf books in the world, right? Then the magazine's editor called me directly. This time I listened.

Travel & Leisure Golf, regrettably no longer among the living, was a publication less interested in improving our swings than in encouraging us to appreciate the many good things that go into the game itself. Golf literature was one of them. But, again, there's been so much of it. And consider, too, the great typists who've let their fancies wander across fairways and greens real and imagined: John Updike, Herbert Warren Wind, P. G. Wodehouse, George Plimpton, Dan Jenkins, Henry Longhurst—and that's barely a start. I hold them in awe. They have all stood the test of time. *Bernard Darwin on Golf* hadn't been on the shelves for six months yet, but somehow it jumped the lot of them. Hmmm . . .

To narrow tens of thousands of volumes down to the twenty-five that would make up its final assemblage, the magazine convened a panel of nine distinguished sages of the sport—sadly, Plimpton himself, who would have been the tenth, died as the project got underway—and gave them the titles of one hundred worthy books from which to anoint their roster. All the writers previously mentioned were naturally included. So were Bobby Jones. And Ben Hogan. And Michael Murphy. And Peter Dobereiner. And on. And on.

And amazingly, leading their final roll call was—drumroll, please—me and my anthology.

But, of course, it wasn't me at all, and it wasn't my anthology, either.

It was all Bernard Darwin.

His friends called him Bernardo—and all who appreciate great writing on the game are his friends—and the only plausible explanation I can come up with for what continues to connect Charles Darwin's grandson with the grandson of a couple of immigrant tailors is that some rare ebullience in the universe thought it might be fun to nudge me toward hitching my wagon to his star. His prose—the most engaging, perceptive, insightful, enduring, and sprightly ever to waltz across the golfing page—was his superpower. I fell under its thrall the first time I read it, and by the time I assembled *Bernard Darwin on Golf*, I was even more beguiled. Two decades later, the pleasures have grown ever deeper. Still, why *this* book?

Let's go back in time. The last decade of the twentieth century and the early days of the twenty-first were still pretty much the dark ages vis-à-vis the internet; newspaper and magazine databases were embryonic at best. So when I began looking for more and more Darwin to read for myself—no easy enterprise in the early nineties—my avenue was used bookstores—mostly located across the Pond—and searched the old-fashioned way: by mail.

Books began arriving. I read them. Then I trolled for uncollected columns and stories in library stacks of old magazines. Again, bingo. I suddenly had hundreds and hundreds of pieces of Darwiniana.

And it hit me. If I encountered so much in reading Bernardo, mightn't other golfers too? Since there was no single, comprehensive and sweeping compendium of his work readily available, I pitched the folks at Lyons Press about assembling this anthology, and they said sure. From there, my job was simple. All I had to do, really, was stack all the pieces I'd collected into a pile, throw them in the air, and the six dozen or so that landed closest to my fingertips would form the collection.

Darwin is *that* good.

I wrapped the package and mailed it off. Anybody could have done it really. Right place, right time.

And that, essentially, is how *Travel & Leisure Golf*'s best golf book of all time came to be. Bernardo, over the course of a blessedly long and productive working life, did the heavy lifting—and did it beautifully. As the book's editor, I just got out of his way.

As I said, Bernard Darwin is *that* good.

I trust you'll agree.

—Jeff Silverman
Chadds Ford, Pennsylvania
February 2024

Introduction

I

In 1993, an editor at the *Los Angeles Times Magazine* who had no idea that I knew nothing about golf asked if I'd like to profile Fred Couples. I said sure. For reasons that had nothing to do with Freddie, this turned out to be a pretty good decision on my part.

The truth is that I did know a few things about golf—like what an exercise in self-mortification it can be to play, especially when I'm the one who's playing. I even knew a few things about Couples. What I really didn't know was enough about either to feel comfortable writing about them with authority. I began asking friends more up on their golf than I was for the name of the best golf writer they'd ever read; whoever it turned out to be, I wanted to pick his prose. The answer was unanimous: Herbert Warren Wind.

At my local bookstore, I found a single copy, sadly overlooked in the six or seven years it had been sitting there, of Wind's magnificent collection of *New Yorker* magazine golf pieces, *Following Through*. The front cover was creased. Several pages were bent. The back cover had a small tear. I bought it anyway.

On page 153, I bumped into Bernard Darwin.

In 1976, Wind marked the centenary of Darwin's birth with a lovely encomium—part ode, part profile—to the man and his work. Though I had no idea who Darwin was yet, I was—through the 152 preceding pages—getting to know Wind pretty well, and if *he* thought the guy was worth writing about, I assumed he'd be the gold standard.

I can quote the first sentence of "Bernard Darwin" by heart: "There is little disagreement that the best golf writer of all time was an Englishman named Bernard Richard Meirion Darwin."

When the best writer you know of on a subject tells you there's someone better still, it's prudent to pay attention. I did. And though I never committed the second sentence to memory, it goes like so, and brims with promise: "Beyond this there is a large body of readers made up not only of golf addicts but of addicts of other sports, who believe that Bernard Darwin may well be the finest talent who has ever written about sports, not excluding such towering figures as William Hazlitt, Leo Tolstoy, William Faulkner, Siegfried Sassoon, and Ernest Hemingway, all of whom occasionally wandered into the field, or such regular writers on sports as Pierce Egan, Robert Surtees, Ring Lardner, . . . A.J. Liebling, and Joe Palmer—to name some of those who come most quickly to mind."

Who *is* this guy, and where's he been all my life? By the end of the piece, I was fully prepared to jump into the relationship that's now gratefully entering its second decade. I admit that as relationships go this one hasn't always hasn't been easy sailing. Darwin—and I can't really blame *him* for this—played hard-to-get from the start.

It was almost impossible to find his work. He wasn't on the shelves in the library, nor was he listed in *Books in Print.* I began scouring used-book stores. I'd write friends in England. One by one, volumes dawdled my direction, each a little testament to perseverance and a lot of luck. Golf essays. Biographies. A children's book. Golf histories. A study of Dickens. Non-golf essays. More golf essays. Elegies to the leathery British club and the exclusive British public school. Memoirs. Anthologies he'd assembled. And more golf essays. Some thirty hard-covered treasures in all. He'd left behind quite a legacy.

Like the accomplished golfer Darwin was, he had those two requisites for good game—length and touch—at the typewriter, too. Prolific he certainly was. And his prose danced with style and grace.

While the internet's made my search for the complete Darwin easier, the sad truth is that with the exception of a few specialized golf book-club reprints directed at those addicts Wind alluded to—like the one I've happily turned into—no sampling of Darwin's wonders has found an American tee time before. *Bernard Darwin on Golf* is a swing at that oversight.

II

First, some background.

Though no one needs a Charles Darwin to suggest we golfers are a species unto our own, the origin of the sub-species of human being whose function on this earth would be to dissect, explore, ruminate over, and explain why we golfers are who we are and do what we do indeed shimmied down a limb of that selfsame family tree. Bernard Darwin was the Great Man's grandson.

Understandably, given the world that he was born into, Bernard Darwin didn't set out to write about golf—or any other sport for that matter. He himself proposed that chronicling sports was a job "into which men drift, since no properly constituted parent would agree to his son starting his career in that way. Having tried something else which bores them they take to this thing which is lightly esteemed by the outside world but which satisfies them in some possibly childish but certainly romantic feeling." Considering his lineage, "drift" might be less fitting a verb than "evolved." Unlike most of us, Darwin appeared, by all accounts, to be a remarkably satisfied man.

His evolution began early. His mother died giving birth to him, and his father, Francis, one of Charles's five accomplished sons—a doctor by training but a botanist by choice—moved himself and Bernard back into his parents' house in Kent. While Charles Darwin was a constant and apparently kindly presence, Bernard's memories of the man who changed the way we look at our humanity and its beginnings are hazy, though this much is clear: Bernard called his grandfather Babba, and recalls holding his hand when they walked. When Charles himself died in 1882—Bernard was almost six—Francis and son moved again, this time to Cambridge, where Bernard would grow up, and, after Eton, attend Trinity College, studying classics and law.

And—yes—golf.

Darwin was already well schooled in the game by then. He wasn't sure quite when he began to play, but his best guess was that he was 8, and the course was Felixstowe, near Ipswich in Sussex, where the imposing Willie Fernie, winner of the 1883 British Open, was the pro. "I only know that there was a time when I did not play golf," Darwin recounts, at 52, in *Green Memories,* his first volume of memoirs, "and then after a blurred interval came the time when I played it with a fire of enthusiasm not yet extinguished."

It was a fire that his family stoked. As a lad, Bernard joined his father on the links, and, in time, both became regulars at Aberdovey, a course in Wales conceived and constructed by Bernard's uncles on his mother's side. Throughout his life, Aberdovey would have a particular hold over Bernard's golfing imagination; though, in time, he'd be welcome anywhere, even ascending to the captaincy of the Royal and Ancient at St. Andrews, Aberdovey was the one course to which he'd return annually to play for sheer joy.

At Cambridge, he captained an excellent golf team—tall and thin, he was built to swing a club—and, through time, kept his skills honed enough to represent England in several international team competitions, including the first Walker Cup match (an event so improbable he recounts it with subtle glee in "My Second Trip to America"). Twice—in 1909 and 1921—he reached the semi-finals of the British Amateur, each time losing to the eventual champion. Bernardo—as friends called him—had game.

Yet, when he set off to make his way in the world, the idea of earning a living through this game he loved and burned with was out of the question. Professional golfers were considered an unseemly lot; it would be decades before they were allowed entry into clubhouses and grillrooms on either side of the ocean. And the job description of "Golf Writer"—at least the way it would (that word again) "evolve" through Darwin's pen—had yet to be imagined. To be sure, others had been writing, and writing quite stirringly, about golf—Horace Hutchinson, Arthur Balfour, and W. G. Simpson come quickest to mind—but none considered it an occupation. (Indeed, Balfour's better known for his day job; from 1902 to 1905, he was England's Prime Minister.) So Darwin took the prudent path and worked at what he'd been trained for. He became a lawyer.

And didn't like it. As a solicitor, he found the paperwork boring. He trained further as a barrister, and was duly admitted to the bar, but as much as he liked the drama and brio surrounding murder trials, he didn't much like arguing cases. In 1907, a friend who'd been weighing in on golf for London's *Evening Standard* moved on to another paper, recommending Darwin as an apt replacement. Now 30, this was was the life mulligan Darwin was waiting for, and he was savvy enough to use his shot well. In 1908, he happily hung his wig up for good.

That was the year that he left the *Standard* for *The Times*, to write the weekly golf column—"Tee Shots"—that would appear on Saturdays until his retirement from the paper forty-seven years later. At the same time, he also began to pen a weekly golf column for *Country Life* magazine. Golfers on the western shore of the Atlantic would have to wait more than a decade for Darwin's prose to reach the U.S. with any regularity. He became a fixture in *The American Golfer* from 1922 until the monthly's demise in the late '30s, and contributed a handful of longer essays to *The Atlantic Monthly.*

Meanwhile, back in Britain, golfers would be able to set their clocks by Darwin's stunning reliability right into the late 1950s. (He died in 1961.) Darwin understood that showing up was half the battle, and one of his great strengths of character was showing up without fail. Over the half century that his work appeared in *Country Life,* Darwin found himself absent only once—*once!*—and he was quick to defend the aberration. It seems the ship he was crossing the Atlantic on ran into weather and couldn't wire off his words in time to meet their deadline. As journalism streaks go, this one's nonpareil.

As a writer, Darwin cared.

III

Darwin cared so much as a writer because he cared so much as a golfer. Put another way, the tremendous passion, competitive spirit, and quest for perfection that fueled him on the course propelled him to ever-higher achievement off it, though, not surprisingly, these passions manifested themselves in different ways in each arena.

As a player, he was not immune to the twin plagues—tantrum and outburst—that seep into most of our games following particularly egregious flubs and foozles, and those he played with deemed him a world-class mutterer with a biting and not always temperate wit. His eruptions could be volcanic, and though they embarrassed him to no end, his unwavering sense of perfection made them as much a part of what he brought to the course as his mashie and his spoon. How different he comes across in print! On the page, he was every hacker's doting uncle—kind, welcoming, inclusive, funny, self-effacing, ever the gentleman, and really a quite charming and generous story-teller. By all accounts, the personality that greets us in the writing was very much the disposition of the man when his fingers weren't wrapped around a niblick with the pressure of a few bob on the line.

Darwin, the all-embracing golfer, understood golf from inside the inside, and it was from that innermost sanctum that he sought to think about the game and set down his thoughts. He had an epic grasp of golf history and a hail-fellow intimacy with its great characters and true heroes. Consider his sweep: He grew up in the days of the gutty ball and Old Tom Morris and lived long enough to witness Palmer, Nicklaus, and Hogan slug it out down the stretch at Cherry Hills. He knew Vardon, Braid, and Taylor well, and wrote with gusto and appreciation about Ray, Ouimet, Jones, Sarazen, and Hogan, as well as the best women players of his day, such as Glenna Collett Vare and Joyce Wethered. He especially liked Wethered, whom Jones considered swing for swing the greatest golfer on the planet. Darwin even teamed with her once to win the storied Worplesdon Mixed Foursomes, referring to himself, in his account of the 1933 match, as "the elderly gentleman whose name for the moment escapes me."

He had an uncanny knack for being in the right place at the right time when legends were forming down the fairway. Look no further than the 1913 U.S. Open. Not only was Darwin on hand to see young Francis Ouimet's unlikely victory, he was integral to the proceedings. To his great surprise—and personal delight—officials tapped him to serve as Ouimet's official scorer in the play-off round against Vardon and Ray. Thus, his signature is forever fixed on the scorecard marking one of the most magical moments in the annals of the game.

All of which is why we golfers *should* be reading him, but there's something else about his work that makes it impossible to *stop* reading him once we've started, and it's this: Bernard Darwin had an amazing gift for wringing wonderful, enduring, uncontestable truths about golf and human nature out of the small and seemingly irrelevant. Like a cigarette. His dog playing with a ball. A crossword puzzle. Whether it's best to clean your irons after every round or let them darken. Even his own bed sheets. They all wove their way into memorable newspaper and magazine columns; their permanence has earned them the right to be called essays. Had he been alive in the '90s—the 1990s that is—I imagine the producers of "Seinfeld" would have tossed buckets of money his way to lure him onto their staff. Of course, Bernardo would have demurred, the way he demurred when some American Barnum tried to coax him over to lecture on his grandfather while the Scopes monkey trial was the talk of the town. Besides, given the treadmill of television, it would have interfered with his golf.

And nothing interfered with Darwin's golf. Nothing, sadly, except the arthritis that would eventually twist his fingers and the gout that would blow up his toes. In his 60s, these debilitating conditions forced golf's finest essayist to lay down his clubs. He still followed the game, of course, and he still wrote about it with the same passion that etched his work from the start. But he couldn't play anymore. Naturally, Darwin found the majesty in his loss and made it universal, marking this aspect of the game's passing from his life with one of his most beautiful efforts. The essay is called, simply, "Giving Up the Game." Wrenching and bittersweet, it holes out this volume.

IV

A few short notes about all that follows.

First, the sourcing. Most of the pieces included in *Bernard Darwin on Golf* first appeared in one of his four primary homes: *The Times, Country Life, The American Golfer*, and *The Atlantic Monthly*. A few selections arrive from *The Golf Courses of the British Isles* (1910), his first book, and from his 1928 reminiscences, *Green Memories*. The long look at Bobby Jones is culled from his chronicle *Golf Between Two Wars* (1944). Throughout his career, Darwin regularly gathered together his work from *Country Life* and *The Times* between hard covers; pieces that could be sourced back to the original periodical and year receive attribution that way, otherwise I've credited them to the collection – *Tee Shots and Others* (1911), *Out of the Rough* (1932), *Playing the Like* (1934), and *Rubs of the Green* (1936). *Every Idle Dream* (1945), home of this volume's valedictory, was, except for that essay, a potpourri of Darwin's musings on subjects other than golf, and is thoroughly delightful from start to finish.

Darwin was an obsessive reader throughout his life, and a revered expert on Dickens. He loved sharing his reading pleasures; he peppers his essays with literary references and quotations from the books he loved, especially Dickens. Recognizing his allusions is certainly a bonus, but Darwin was a genial enough writer to include us on the ramble whether or not we happen to share his literary enthusiasms. He was also prone to slipping in contemporary and historical references. He expected readers to be educated, inquisitive, and up on the world around them; he never wrote down. Again, though, his words alone will cheerfully carry us along.

Finally, like all obsessive golfers, Darwin enjoyed dispensing his share of good and bad advice through the years, and I've included a section of these semi-instructionals in the mix. Though I doubt any of his tips will help make you a better player, simply leafing through as much Darwin as possible will, without question, make you a better golfer by far. It might not show up on your scorecard, but I promise that you'll feel it in your heart.

—Jeff Silverman
January, 2003

Bernard Darwin on Golf

I

On Himself

On Being a Darwin

Green Memories
1928

There was in the Salonica Army an officer of enormous stature. I never met him, but I heard a story of him, very likely apocryphal, which pleased me. It was said that he was so well accustomed to being asked his height that when he saw a perfect stranger preparing to accost him, he merely said "Six feet ten inches" and passed on his way. I quote that story because I have all my life been in the same boat with him, though in a different way. When anybody begins a sentence "What relation———?" or "Was the great————?" I at once know what he, or she, is going to ask, and answer "Grandfather." In the circumstances I may presumably hold myself lucky in that only two old friends of mine call me "Monkey," or words to that effect. Moreover, they do not often do it before my face, whatever they may do behind my back.

That first question I can answer. Subsequent ones I often cannot. I only wish that I could remember my grandfather better, that I had been a little older or he a little younger, for he would, I know, have been the most heavenly possible grandfather to have. I was in effect, though not actually in fact, the only one of his grandchildren who ever saw him. I lived and was brought up in his house at Downe, in Kent, since my father came back there when I was born and my mother died. I was, however, only five and a half at his death—and a five-year-old's memories are very, very dim, at least in my case. Moreover, in the case of somebody, of whom one has subsequently heard and read much, genuine memories are so hard to disentangle from fictitious ones. In fact there is only one thing about him that I can remember clearly and unaided. We were returning from a family journey, and when we got out at Orpington Station my grandfather said that he and I would walk down by the shortcut and the carriage would pick us up on the road. So we did walk all alone along a little footpath across a plowed field, where there is now a broad road with hideous villas, and it was all very secret, romantic and exciting. That small memory is in itself so entirely trivial that no one can have invented it for me and I know it is my very own. I often feel as if I could remember the sound of my grandfather's iron-shod stick as he walked his appointed number of rounds of the path round the little wood called the Sandwalk, but I am suspicious in this case: I think I have imagined it because it is mentioned in my father's biography, and because I was familiar with the stick, or others like it in the hall at Downe. I do remember the day on which he died, because I know that I was rather awe-stricken and picked lords and ladies in the Sandwalk and that is really all. I had no notion that he was a person of any save domestic considerations. As far as I knew he did nothing in particular. If I had been old enough to consider the question I might have shared the views of a nurse who had come to us from the Thackerays and said that it was a pity that Mr. Darwin had not something to do like Mr. Thackeray; she had seen him watching an ant-heap for a whole hour.

When my grandfather died we moved to Cambridge, but the house at Downe was still kept and my grandmother, who lived until I was grown-up, went there every spring and stayed till the autumn.

My grandmother was, I think, the wisest person I ever knew and had a beautiful serenity that belonged to no one else. It would be idle for me to describe her since it has been done much better than I could do it by my aunt, Mrs. Litchfield, in *Emma Darwin, A Century of Family Letters*. She said things that had alike in matter and manner a flavor of their own, and yet if I try to set any of them down they will probably convey no impression whatever except to those who knew her. Only the other day an old friend quoted one to me that seemed to me entirely characteristic. It was the morning of some kind of garden party at our house at Cambridge and my grandmother observed, "I don't think we shall have anybody today but the humble and the dull." Another that has always stuck in my head was her greeting to me when I came home for the holidays after the winter half at Eton where, as I suppose, I had been having a cold: "You look very green and ugly." Yet another that always pleases me was her comment on a little book, mostly made up of quotations, that had attained great popularity: "It is the kind of book that some women think it does them good to read." As my mother was dead my grandmother had a good deal to do with bringing me up. Some of her methods were rather singular, for they consisted in the offering of small bribes. Thus I was given sixpence or a shilling to learn to write without inking my fingers. I was also bribed to come indoors when I was sitting out on the lawn in broiling sunshine assiduously making a sketch of the house. I do not know if this nipped a talent in the bud, for I never sketch now and nobody pays me not to do so. Odder still were bribes to eat pie crust with my apple tart and to like cheese and mustard. I suppose these small heterodoxies on my part bothered her in some indefinable manner. I suppose also that she based this system of education on a belief in the way of least resistance in trivial matters. Most certainly she never would have adopted it in the case of anything that did matter.

As long as my grandmother was alive I went to Downe often and it remained my real home, compared with which Cambridge did not count. I have now come to live there again, though not in the old house, and the coming back has been a great romance. It is still wonderfully peaceful and pleasant. Hardly anyone knows where it is, and I hope they will remain in ignorance. Almost the only people who do know appear to be a few pious Americans who, at long intervals, make a pilgrimage to see the house. There have always been a few pilgrims, and I remember our delightful old butler, Parslow, who took care of the house in winter time, inscribing in the visitor's book, in his shaky old handwriting, "Two Germans. One Russian." Incidentally, I have spelled it "Downe." This is contrary to all my bringing up, for there was a tradition in the family that only the basest outcast spelled it otherwise than "Down." Why this arose I do not know. At any rate today everyone spells it with an "e," and I have ceased to kick against the pricks. I have a horrid notion, too, that in this case everybody is right. The house, at the moment of writing, is apparently going to be bought and given to the nation. It is a girls' school, and my younger daughter went to school there—as it were in my old nursery that looks down in the mulberry tree. I play golf on a new course that has been made close to it, in a valley where I used often to practice driving in my holidays, and from it I can see the Sandwalk.

I said, at the beginning of this chapter, that the subsequent questions I was asked were often hard to answer. There is one, however, which is easy, namely, "Are you scientific, too?" To this I can answer with an unequivocal and not even, I am afraid, a very regretful "No." I sometimes supplement it by quoting a remark of my great-uncle Ras, who said to his brother: "My dear fellow, I don't give a damn for the whole kingdom of Nature." In my second half at Eton my instructor wrote at the end of a "Science abstract"—some stuff about molecules—"Quite unworthy of a K.S., still more of one called Darwin"; I have been living up to his verdict ever since. I should like to add in gratitude to those who brought me up that none of them ever tried for a moment to thrust natural history down my throat. There was a member of another scientific family who was presumably not so fortunate, for he expressed, when a boy, the wish that, whatever else he might become, he might not be a distinguished man of science. His prayer has, I believe, been answered, not merely in the letter, but in the spirit. The scientific strain persists, however, in my generation, and when eugenicists make pedigrees of us, some of my cousins have special asterisks denoting "able" or "very able." These I observe, as I hope, without envy. My father was, I must suppose, unlucky in this respect. He was scientific himself, though he also loved books and wrote, as I think at least, quite admirably and with a particular charm of his own. He was, however, the father of two children incapable either of understanding or wishing to understand any scientific fact. My sister Frances (Mrs. Cornford) and I are, if we are anything, by way of being "littery." She certainly is, as she writes excellent poetry, and I have earned a living by writing prose, in the sense at any rate in which M. Jourdain talked prose. The only trace that I can find in myself of a scientific ancestry is that I hate like poison the modern word "scientist." I have been brought up to consider it a vulgar abomination and shall continue to do so. "Naturalist" is the word I learned to use, though for the life of me I cannot see on what ground, philological or otherwise, it is a penny the better.

I once had a chance of making some money—for me quite a lot of money—out of being a Darwin, and I am glad to say that a combination of self-respect and self-preservation made me refuse it. An enterprising lecture agent in America asked me to come over to the United States and deliver lectures on Darwinism. I refused politely but firmly. He asked me again and yet again when the tomfoolery of Dayton was at its height. Like Mr. Harold Skimpole I cannot remember exactly how large was the bribe I was offered, but it seemed to me a very big one. Being by now rather weary of this gentleman's importunities, I answered that the State of Tennessee appeared to be making a fool of itself by talking about matters which it did not understand and I did not want to emulate it. However it was not I but the enterprising gentleman who scored, for he sent the whole correspondence to a leading New York paper, where it appeared with the memorable headline: "Darwin Kin Finds Scopes Trial Folly." I have often wondered whether he got paid for it, and if so, how much? I have also wondered what sort of time I should have had lecturing on Darwinism in the Middle West. My friend "Ian Hay" tells me that a large part of the audience only comes to see what the lecturer looks like and having said, "Oh, so that's him, is it?" departs at once. If that was the worst that had happened to me it would not have been so bad, but I think I chose the wiser part.

Those who have married members of my generation of Darwins unite in stating that we are all extremely arrogant about our ancestry. It is not a subject, perhaps, on which I am competent to judge. I can only say that I am personally not conscious of this vice. If one is disposed to be arrogant on such a subject, it is a very good antidote to go to Somerset House and see, for instance, how many other Darwins there are in the world. When I was an articled clerk I had one day to go to Somerset House to look up somebody's birth, and thought that I might as well look up my own at the same time and for the same fee. I discovered that there were seven other Darwins born in the same quarter of the year as myself. That makes thirty-two Darwins born every year, and the total number alive mounts with hideous rapidity, "like the nails in the horse's shoe, Sammy." I have always remembered the name of a young lady who came next to me in the list. She was born, if I remember rightly, near Rotherham, and her name was Venus Victoria Darwin. How Queen Victoria would have liked to find herself in such deplorable company as Venus and my grandfather is a subject for pleasing if irreverent speculation.

If I make mild jokes about my family, it does not follow that I am not proud of it. It has incidentally contributed to my meeting interesting people, and I wish I could remember more about them. When I was about fifteen or sixteen, we used to go, during my summer holidays, to Eastbourne, and my father and I used to go on walks with Professor Huxley on the downs. He was most friendly and stimulating, and I listened hard, but I cannot remember nor even invent anything that he said. Mrs. Huxley I remember well, because she lived to be a very old lady. She came to the Darwin centenary celebrations in 1909, and had the unique honor of a seat on the floor of the Senate House during the giving of honorary degrees. No woman had ever sat there before. I recollect one little story of her girlhood that Ms. Huxley told me at that time. She was a little girl in a country town and was sent on an errand to buy a piece of ribbon "either pink or blue," said some elder person. "It's quite immaterial." She visited many shops. They had ribbons both pink and blue; but after she had inspected the ribbons and chosen one of them she always asked, "Is it immaterial?" and the shopman could never give a satisfactory answer. And so she trudged on and on, weary and despairing, and came home at last to report that in the whole town there was no ribbon that was immaterial. It is a touching little story and has an excellent moral, not to use long words to children.

To the centenary there also came Sir Joseph Hooker, who had been a great friend of my grandfather's, and was by this time, I think, ninety-one. Yet he went through the whole series of festivities, soirées, garden-parties, degree-givings and all, and only most reluctantly drew the line at the dinner. My kinsman, Sir Francis Galton, who was then about ninety, had not felt equal to the effort of coming, and Sir Joseph spoke of him with the tenderest pity: "Ah! he's very infirm, poor fellow!" My daughter, aged one, then the only great-grandchild, came to a party, which was given by the family in Nevile's Court at Trinity, in her perambulator, and Sir Joseph chucked her under the chin with a very charming gallantry. It was when she was only a little older that Dr. W. G. Grace waved his hand to her as she flattened her nose on the window. So she will have something to boast of,

Quand elle sera bien vieille, au soir, à la chandelle.

Francis Galton I did know a little, but not nearly so well as I should like to have done. The stories of his endless and ingenious experiments are probably too well known for repetition—how, for example, he wanted to discover in what form his words would penetrate most quickly to the brain of a cabman. In the case of the first cab he took he would say, "Twenty-eight, Rutland Gate" (I have forgotten if this was the right number of his house), to the second "Rutland Gate, twenty-eight," to the third, "Two eight," and so on through I do not know how many variations. He made elaborate tests to discover at exactly what temperature the water should be in making tea, but the experiment I like best to remember was that which ascertained which town in Great Britain had the prettiest and which the plainest women. He had some form of machine which he carried in his pocket and at each lady he met he pressed the appropriate button to record his verdict. I am privileged to know the jealously guarded secret as to which town has the plainest ladies, but I am pledged by a solemn oath not to divulge it.

The centenary will always be a pleasantly memorable event for all who took part in it. The coming of so many distinguished representatives of science from all parts of the world was obviously memorable, and to descend to more trivial things, never was such a gorgeous array of gowns seen in Cambridge or in all the world. The doctors of foreign universities vied with one another in the splendor of their purples and golds. Our English Doctors, in their scarlet, looked but poor creatures, and as for the ladies in their best frocks, they were drab indeed. The various functions culminated in a dinner, at which my eldest Uncle William made, I think, the simplest and most moving speech I ever heard. Although Mr. Arthur Balfour made the first speech and one worthy of the occasion, I think that with all respect to him and those that followed him, my uncle played them all off the stage. He was not a man of science, being a country banker, but I remember when his speech was over the late Mr. Marlborough Pryor saying, with an intense zest of appreciation, "He's as good as any of them."

What my Great-Uncle Ras has been to my father and his brothers and sisters, my Uncle William was, I think, to the nephews and nieces of my generation. Nobody could tip more nobly or more delightfully. He had the sweetest smile and the trimmest and tidiest appearance, enhanced, if possible, by small white whiskers, that I ever saw. Uncle Ras had said of him that "William looked so clean that you could eat a mutton chop off him anywhere." He had a passion for reading, and was always supposed to be "finishing a paragraph," so that he was late for luncheon. He was also very fond of music, and could laboriously pick out tunes on the piano with one finger to his own great satisfaction. Whether it was to anyone else's satisfaction was a thought that probably never occurred to him, for he was the least self-conscious man in the world. At his father's funeral in Westminster Abbey, he was observed to have his black gloves on the top of his bald head. He had simply felt a draught and adopted the obvious remedy. I have seen him walking across a high road between the garden and the house, with the long cushion of a cane chair balanced neatly on the top of his head and depending on either side. He presented a truly singular spectacle, but this would never have entered his head. There never was a more entirely beloved person.

For that matter all my uncles—and my aunts, too—have been angelic to me, and have set me an example which I am quite incapable of living up to in respect of my own nephews and nieces. There is a particular glamour and romance about what uncles do and say that belongs to no other human relationship. I have still an intense relish in remembering a certain walk that my Uncle George took with me, when I was very small, to Westerham. It is an honest trudge from Downe to Westerham, and I think I must have come back in the wagonette, possibly asleep. At any rate we walked there and had cherry tart for lunch at the inn. There was a stranger also having lunch at the inn, and my uncle, in asking him to pass the bread, called him "Sir." This made an abiding impression on my mind, presumably because I thought that gardeners call people "Sir," but uncles did not.

My Uncle George had a most devoted adoration for Downe and everything to do with it. He knew the woods and the fields and their names better than anyone else, and always seemed to be the organizer of walks, just as when a boy he had organized the wooden lances and uniforms and coats of arms of his younger brothers, among whom was my father. About 1909 or 1910 he and Uncle William took Downs House from their own tenants and had almost the whole family to stay with them. It was a most touching thing to see his happiness there. It pleases me to fancy that I have inherited a little of this devotion, even though the "Big Woods" have now turned into the woods behind the seventh green, and I shall never go or know the walks as he did.

My Earliest Golfing Days

Green Memories
1928

On which course I actually began I do not know, because I cannot remember beginning at all. I only know that there was a time when I did not play golf, and then after a blurred interval came the time when I played it with a fire of enthusiasm not yet extinguished. My earliest memories are, I think, of Felixstowe, and I believe myself to have been eight years old.

We stayed sometimes in lodgings, sometimes in the Clubhouse itself. This was heavenly, for one could dash out on to the course early and late. There was also a particularly engaging and friendly steward, an old sailor. He had been present, or at any rate near at hand, when Lord Mayo was murdered, and his description of the event passed into a family proverb: "Her ladyship and all the ladies and gents aboard were very much put out."

With all respect to the Felixstowe course as it is today, I think it was a better and pleasanter one then. There were but nine holes, but they were very good ones and all on the most beautiful, delicate seaside turf—turf of a fineness rarely to be seen today; and I am saying this not on the strength of childish memories, but from subsequent and grown-up recollections.

The greatest hero there was the professional Willie Fernie, who had quite lately won the Open Championship. It seems to me still that no man hit the ball quite so easily and quite so cleanly as he did. His shop was close to the second tee opposite the Martello tower. It had the peculiar and beautiful smell—I suppose pitch is one of the ingredients—which all professionals' shops have, a smell as entrancing in its way as that of Mr. Twinning's shop in the Strand. I have a clear picture of Fernie standing in the doorway, an apron round his waist, a kind of yachting cap with a shiny peak on his head and in his hands a half-finished club which quivered beneath his fierce and knowing waggle. I doubt if I ever had the honor of speaking to him, though I hung in a fawning manner round his shop door looking at him with an adoring and dog-like eye. Certainly I had no lessons from him and I have often wished since that I had been given some. The only lesson I ever did have was from his successor, Thompson. He was a man of some penetration, for the only thing he said was that I bent my knees too much, and they have remained far too flexible to this day. The golfing Ethiopian cannot change his skin.

Among the members of the club the outstanding figure was Mr. Mure Fergusson, and my recollections of his play have become uncertain, because I have so often watched him and played with him as a grown-up. I only know that he was great and god-like, and if I saw him coming behind me in the distance I got out of the way. For that matter, I got out of everybody's way as well as I could. I was an outlaw allowed to exist as long as I did not harm. In the morning and afternoon I played by myself, a small figure in a flannel shirt, brown holland knickerbockers, and bare legs burned to a painful redness by the sun, carrying three clubs and dodging in and out between grown-up couples, where I could see a clear space.

Sometimes, when the course was crowded, I played only the second hole over and over again, sheltering in between whiles behind the Martello tower. It was—for grownups—a one-shot hole and had a kindly green with shelving sides, and I once did it in three.

Occasionally people spoke to me as they passed; some were very kind, but I can only remember clearly one such scene. Some enormous boys passed me, they must have been at least fifteen; one said that I "did not play badly for a kid," and the other replied in a disparaging tone, "H'm! too much swagger swing for me." I can see the place where it happened; I remember the boys' names, and two or three years ago I played against one of them in a foursome competition. He turned out to be a most agreeable middle-aged gentleman, but I felt a friendly but nonetheless quite perceptible desire for revenge, and I am glad to say we beat him.

In the evening, when the crowd had thinned, came the crowning joy of the day, for my father used angelically to come out and play with me. We played one ball between us, a foursome against nobody, and I think we tried to keep our score. At any rate I am certain that we once did the nine holes in 56. My own individual record was supposed to be 70, but I do not feel so certain about that; there may have been some laxity in holing out. At any rate I am sure of this, that were I now to play a round by myself, I could not keep my score without untruthfulness, and I believe the same remark applies to many golfers of unimpeachable honor.

My First Open

Country Life
1942

I have no desire to be cast upon the scrap heap, but the notion of watching an Open just once as an idle spectator with nothing to do is, I admit, a seductive one. Let people believe it or not, the reporting of that last day in particular is no joke, especially if you have two accounts to write and a broadcast or two thrown in. In my ears, as I think of it, is a confused sound of the rushing of crowds, the pattering of rain, the shouting of stewards, and the clicking of typewriters. I see myself, covering in a shelter, asking imbecile onlookers for information which is never true, staggering back to the clubhouse for dry clothes, writing on my knee under the lee of a sandhill and having the paper blown out of my hand by a playful wind, looking at the cars pinned up in the Press tent and trying to invent some interesting manner in which the scores may have been arrived at. When a friend with nothing to do but relapse into a drink asks me how I "get my stuff off," and whether I post it, I could do anything to him that is sufficiently malignant and has for choice boiling oil in it.

It seems to have become harder work since I first embarked upon it, partly because I have grown older and lamer, partly because championships have grown bigger. My mind goes back with yearning to the first Open that I ever saw and reported, that at Prestwick in 1908. I have forgotten the writing about it, which I took in my comparatively youthful stride, and remember only the fun of it. It seems to me, perhaps inevitably, the pleasantest championship I ever watched. The weather was fine and hot and sunny, the course green and lovely after a deluge of rain on the Saturday before; I stayed with kind friends right on the course, looking out on the Goose-Dubs from my bedroom window. It was ten years since I had first played in an amateur championship, but this was my first Open (I never was so rash as to play in it); it was all fresh and exhilarating; I was still rejoicing in a new life and in a new freedom from thralldom of the law. Finally I saw golf played as well as I have ever seen it played since and, as it then appeared, incredibly well, for that was the year in which Braid won with 291, and only once before had the winner's score been under 300.

Apart from the tremendous nature of that score I suppose this could not be called an exciting championship, because Braid was winning easily all the time. Even when he took his famous or infamous eight at the Cardinal in the third round he finished in 77, and his nearest pursuers, already faint and far away, scarcely closed the gap at all; some of them even fell farther behind. Apart from that eight and the general magnificence of the winner I have grown rather hazy and, even though I have just read the account in the *Golf Year Book* of 1909, I do not remember as much as I ought, though certain things do come back.

James started in such a way as to make it perfectly clear that he was going to win. He began with two threes, went out in 33 without the ghost of a slip, and finished in 70. When we came back to the club, open-mouthed from watching this round, we found that it did not lead the field, for Ernest Gray of Littlehampton had done a still more astonishing 68. Gray was a fine player and on his day really brilliant but, with all possible respect to him, we felt that he was one of those who would "come back to his horses," and in fact that was a sound prophecy, since the next best of his four rounds was 79. Those who were assumed to be Braid's most dangerous competitors, Vardon and Taylor, were already nine strokes behind him after one round; so was Ray, and though Sandy Herd had played very finely he was four behind; Tom Ball, ultimately destined to be second, had taken 76. In short, it seemed as the Americans say, "in the bag," and Scottish patriotism rejoiced accordingly. It had still further cause for rejoicing after the second round. This time Braid began quietly 4, 5, 5, letting a shot slip at the tiny little 2nd hole. After that he went sedately mad with four threes in a row; he was once more out in 33, home in 39, round in 72, and five strokes ahead of all the world.

Looking at the figures, I observe that in this second round he has a three at the 12th hole, and that brings something back to me; in fact it brings two things, a tremendous brassie shot followed by a long putt, and the only occasion on which I ever saw the sage of Walton so far demean himself as to run. The long since departed stone wall then guarded the 12th green and ordinary mortals played their seconds short of it and so home with a pitch. This time Braid had hit a very fine tee shot, rather to the left as I see it in my mind's eye, and took a long reconnoitering walk forward. It was then that, having made up his mind, he trotted or ambled gently and with no lack of dignity back to his ball and lashed it home. Oddly enough this desperate feat had, as its immediate reaction, the only serious mistake that he made throughout the four rounds, apart of course from the eight at the Cardinal. He frittered away the spoils of that three by taking a six at the Sea Hedrig. How he did it I do not remember, but accidents can always happen on that fascinating little pocket-handkerchief of a green perched among the hilltops.

Immediately after that he got another three, at the Goose-Dubs. No doubt he holed a putt; the number of middle-length putts which he holed was appalling.

It was next morning in the third round, which is generally deemed the most crucial, that the eight happened, and by this time every earnest student knows how it happened—a second from a not very promising spot into the Cardinal and then two mashie shots, over-bold perhaps and striving for distance, which sent the ball glancing off the boards and out of bounds into the Pow Burn.

Apart from the horrid spectacle, I remember, or I think I remember, two things clearly. The only sign that James was a little shaken came at the 4th hole; he put his second on to the green and took three putts. At the Himalayas came glorious amends, a putt holed for two. I see it a little downhill and from the right, but I daresay I am wrong; James doubtless recalls it with perfect accuracy. What I remember beyond all question is how we all broke into rapturous clapping. The crisis, in so far as there had been any crisis, was past. He was out in 39, home in 38; he was six strokes in front, and the eight had done no more than keep his pursuers just within sight of him. His last round was a model of confidence and steadiness combined and he beat Tom Ball, who ended with a 74, by eight shots.

The looking back at the scores has perhaps swept me a little off my feet into reminiscence. If I have been tiresome I apologize on the inadequate ground that I have myself enjoyed it. I have felt once more in imagination the Ayrshire sun on my back, climbed with eager steps the Himalayas, sat on the soft dry turf, behind the Alps green, and watched Braid moving stately and processional toward inevitable victory.

A Second Visit to America

Green Memories
1928

In 1922 I went to America again, this time as a camp follower of the team that was to play in the first match for the Walker Cup. I went there for *The Times*, but traveled and spent my time with the team and was treated as a member of it. All the friendly and hospitable things that were done to the team were also done to me. And it so chanced that in the end I became an actual member, because Mr. Harris, the Captain, fell ill; I had to play in his stead and became Captain of the team in the field.

The team was, I think, just about as good a one as we could send, considering that Mr. Holderness could not make the journey. Other people, of course, did not agree, and those who always attribute complex and underhand motives to selectors did not forget to do so. That it was not good enough to win was generally recognized, since we knew by this time how very good the American amateurs were. They had come to Hoylake the year before, and, though they had failed in the Championship, they had shown what they could do in the International match. In their own country they were likely to be invincible, and so they proved.

The eight who set out on the adventure were Robert Harris (Captain), C. J. H. Tolley, R. H. Wethered, C. C. Aylmer, C. V. L. Hooman, W. B. Torrance, John Caven and Willis Mackenzie. It is the invariable rule to describe any touring side at any game as "having been a very happy family." It is a detestable phrase and somewhat suspect in my ears. When I hear it applied to a cricket team I expect, later, to hear from someone who knows that in fact the members of it fought like cats and dogs. Therefore I shall not use it in this case, but I will declare notwithstanding that we all got on very well together and never had any sort of a quarrel. What our hosts thought of us I do not know, but we liked them immensely, and so I can only hope that they liked us reasonably well.

We landed in New York in the middle of what I call a heat wave. Whether it was legitimately entitled to be so called, I am not sure, but it was immensely and steamily hot, and looking back I think we made a mistake in not going at once to Southampton and playing tranquilly amid the sea breezes at the National Golf Links. There was some little time to spare before the match, and it seemed then that we were likely to get stale if we went to the National too soon. Moreover, the prospect of staying in New York for a few days was very tempting. So we stayed and were looked after with endless thoughtfulness by Mr. Fritz Byers, the then president of the U.S.G.A. and an old friend of some of us, and various other kind and pleasant people. We played on different courses round New York—the Links Club, Piping Rock, Westchester—Biltmore, Oakland and Lido. It was rather a strenuous life. It involved a fairly long drive into the country, for the courses are farther away than corresponding courses are from London. When we got there we generally ate a large lunch and then went out to play in the heat of the day. We tried with but moderate success to play in shirtsleeves.

It is at first a bewildering experience, and I shall not forget Mr. Harris's first coatless drive. It was one of the grandest hooks it has ever been my fortune to see. Lido struck me as on the whole the most difficult course I had ever seen. As most people know, it was made under the eye of Mr. C. B. Macdonald out of a piece of perfectly flat marshy land near the sea. The sea sand was sucked up by gigantic engines which I cannot describe, and spread in waving layers upon the marsh. On it were grown turf and bents, and thus there arose a true seaside course on the most magnificent scale. Next door to it can be seen the original marshy country, and the contrast is wonderful. Unfortunately mosquitoes live in the original marsh and do not fully realize that they are not supposed to live on the reformed marsh also. It was amusing to find in the last hole one to which I had originally given a prize. Mr. Macdonald offered through *Country Life* some prizes for the best designs of holes of various lengths. Mr. Horace Hutchinson, Mr. Fowler and I were the judges, and we gave the prize to a design of Dr. Mackenzie's, and now I saw the hole in actual being as the eighteenth hole at the Lido. A very good one it was and uncommonly difficult.

Whether the Lido is really more difficult than Pine Valley, I am not sure. We made a raid on Philadelphia to see that famous course, stayed a night there and played in a competition which none of us won. That was not surprising, since Mr. George Rotan went round in 69, quite one of the best medal rounds that ever was played. Personally I did rather well till I got to the eighth hole, where there is a very small green entirely surrounded by a wilderness of sand. I think my score was an average of fours till I reached it and I never finished it. Whenever an American friend writes to me he generally has something to say about the eighth hole at Pine Valley, and only the other day one of them sent me a photograph of it. When I look at it my surprise is not that I did not hole out, but that anybody else has ever done so.

Pine Valley is a very wonderful and very beautiful course, a little like our own St. George's Hill at Weybridge, but on a grander and far more terrific scale. It has everything—lovely white sand, thousands of fir trees, and formidable water hazards. There is one green jutting out into a lake which looks from the high tee above it infinitely alarming. There is another where we drive across a deep gorge, with water at the bottom of it, to a plateau green surrounded on all sides by a forest. No doubt familiarity with the course would breed never contempt, but a certain measure of philosophy. However well one knew it, it must remain a great and awe-inspiring course.

At the end of these excursions our golf was worse than when we had first landed, and when we got to the National the team had to settle down and begin all over again. The members of the team stayed at the clubhouse, and I being only a free-lance was allowed to occupy my old and delightful quarters with Mr. and Mrs. Macdonald. The golf soon grew better in these more tranquil surroundings, not that my own did; it remained atrocious, but that did not matter until Mr. Harris, by great ill luck, fell sick. Some of us played in an invitation tournament which Mr. Tolley won, playing extremely well and beating Mr. Hooman in the final. Then on the day before the match there came a terrific thunderstorm. American thunderstorms are not like ours. They go away and then they come back and yet back again. Consequently the course was almost drowned. It stood the ordeal very well, but even so some of the greens were soft, and in the foursomes one ball stuck fast in the green of the "Cape" hole. Mr. Bobby Jones tried to play it with his niblick and the ball jumped back and hit him on the foot.

It will not describe the match at any great length. We lost three foursomes out of four and five singles out of eight, and so the whole match by eight points to four. Mr. Wethered and Mr. Aylmer did very well in beating Mr. Evans and Mr. Gardner, and our last three men in the singles—Mr. Hooman, Mr. Mackenzie and I—managed to beat Mr. Sweetser, Mr. Marston and Mr. Fownes respectively. As Mr. Sweetser soon afterwards won the Championship, Mr. Hooman did a great thing in beating him at the thirty-seventh hole. It was rather odd that Mr. Mackenzie and I should win our matches, because I do not think he will resent the statement that he had up till then been playing villainously, not quite as badly as I had, but still wonderfully ill. However, he rose to the occasion like a hero and beat his man handsomely.

As this is an egotistical book, and as moreover I have only played in one Walker Cup match (and that by an accident) and shall never play in another, I shall say a little about my own match against Mr. Fownes. It had an odd beginning in that, while I was out playing some practice shots, a ball hit by another practicer, hidden from sight, hit me on the breastbone. I thought for a moment that here was a state of things if the only available substitute was killed. Then I realized that I was none the worse, and that the ball had been spent and lifeless. Another odd thing about that match was that I owed the fact of my winning it to a man with a cinematographic camera. I had begun playing very badly and very nervously. Mr. Fownes had gone off at his top speed with 3, 3, 4, for the first three holes, winning them all. At this point Mr. Dunn, who is famous all over the world as Mr. Dooley, could bear it no more. He had kindly come to look on and give me a little encouragement, but seeing no reason why I should not be eighteen down he fled in silence and sorrow. The fourth hole is a very difficult short hole copied, as I said elsewhere, from the Redan at North Berwick. Mr. Fownes ruthlessly put his ball bang on to the green, and as I was about to play my tee shot, in a state of semi-collapse, the man with the camera began to make it whirr at me. This seemed the last straw and yet it saved me. I tried to blot him and his noises out of my mind. I could not think of any more new styles, but merely of the ball, and so, by the grace of Heaven, I hit it and put it on the green. I halved that hole in three and stopped the rot. I won the fifth, and at the next my adversary, trying to get round a half-stymie, knocked my ball in. Everything was now going right instead of wrong, and after having lost the first three holes I was miraculously two up at the turn. One of these holes I still kept at lunch, and in the afternoon playing—for me—very steadily and well with just one bad lapse near the finish, when victory was at hand, I managed to win by three and one.

Two or three odds and ends of things stick in my head from this match. In the morning round Mr. Fownes and I had a gallery of two very pretty young ladies as we drove from the seventeenth tee. Mr. Fownes is, in fact, a few months younger than I am, but he is, if I may say so, of a more venerable aspect. There is a good long carry over a cross-bunker from the seventeenth tee, and when both he and I hit our very best shots well over it, the young ladies burst into rapturous applause. They deemed it no doubt a very gallant effort on the part of two such very old gentlemen. I also remember well the demeanor of our umpire, Mr. John Ward, once a famous baseball player, and a good golfer too. I was driving with one of the oldest and most battered even of my clubs: a spoon-like brassy, with no paint on the head, the grip in tatters and some string depending from the shaft. Mr. Ward had hardly said a word until he asked if he might look at my club. He examined it carefully and remarked, "No one would ever believe that any man every played with that club in an International match."

The seventeenth hole in the second round is also—for me—memorable. I was dormy two and had hit a drive not very good but comparatively safe. Mr. Fownes, without the young ladies to cheer him, was in the cross-bunker. I put my ball somewhere on the green and he left his in the bunker. I turned to my black caddie and said, "I believe I really am going to win a match," and I can still see the beautiful and seraphic grin that spread gradually across his countenance from ear to ear. In fact, Mr. Fownes played so tremendous a third out of that bunker that the grin was soon wiped from my own face. It came back in the end, however, and stayed there for the rest of the day, even though I had to make an open-air speech to the assembled multitude at the presentation of the Cup . . .

After two visits to America one necessarily forms some views, however nebulous, on the difference between British and American golf. There obviously are a good many differences, though it should be added that none of them matter a straw, as far as harmony in match playing between the two countries is concerned. I have seen all but one of the International matches, and they are the most perfectly and genuinely friendly matches imaginable. The climate makes one difference between the two games. The Americans play their best when we are feeling limp with the heat, and they are cramped and shriveled with cold when we think it a nice fresh golfing day. We used at one time to cherish an illusion that the Americans could not play in a wind because they were not used to it. That this is an illusion has been abundantly proved, so long as the wind is not too cold. When it is, they are naturally affected as we are by the heat. I will not say it has been an unlucky thing, but it has been an odd thing that in both the Walker Cup matches at St. Andrews the weather has been, for that rather bleak spot, unusually balmy.

There is a difference in style, for the American golfers have now a very distinct style of their own. And a most graceful and serviceable one it is, with a certain lithe movement of the hips and a reliance on the swing rather than the hit as its two most obvious features. There is some small difference in language, as that they call traps what we call bunkers, and they "make" a hole in four and we "do" it in four—or perhaps more often in five. There is a difference in courses, in that the American courses are a little more cut-and-dried than some of our own. There is always, or nearly always, in America a clear-cut division between the rough and the fairway, and the player has to drive down an avenue, as he does on our heathery courses. There are not in America—or at least I have not seen them—courses such as St. Andrews and Rye, where at certain holes the player appears to have a whole parish to drive into and will be penalized for his errors, not so much directly by getting into rough or bunkers, as indirectly by finding his next shot made exceedingly difficult. The game also tends to be more cut-and-dried on American courses because of the absence of wind. It is more possible, I think, for a man to play the same shots day after day at the same holes than it would be here.

The differences, however, which are really the more interesting, and certainly the more difficult to analyze, are those of temperament and of general outlook on the game. One remark I should like to make, although I have probably often made it before: Because American golfers are intensely keen and have a wonderful power of painstaking, some Britons picture them as dour and gloomy enemies with their thoughts set wholly on victory. Nothing could be farther from the truth, and if anyone wants to see an example of good golfing manners, combining a proper keenness to win with consideration for the adversary and a friendly enjoyment of the fight, let him watch a match between two American champions. I only wish we had half their complaint.

That they are keener than we are admits of no doubt. Be they good, bad or indifferent players, they are keener to improve themselves. The fattest and most middle-aged American golfer wants, if he can, to hit the ball in the right way, and there are far fewer grotesque swings and more good ones to be seen among the rank and file of players than there are here. They take more lessons; they practice more. A friend of mine, who has been much in America, made what I thought an astute observation on this point. When the Briton goes out to practice, he said, he stops when he has hit some good shots. The American, on the other hand, regards that as the moment to go on practicing, in order, so to speak, to nail down the improvement to the counter and keep it. He quoted as an example his meeting with Mr. Chick Evans on a Chicago course. Mr. Evans had just come home in triumph from winning the Western Championship, and was asked to make one in a four-ball match. He excused himself on the grounds that his iron play had not been quite up to the mark and that he must go out and put it right. So out he went with a caddie and a clothesbasket full of balls. What is more, when my friend had finished his match and had tea, there was Mr. Evans still at it, pitching a perfect snowstorm of balls all around his caddie's feet. No British champion would be capable of that. If he were, he would be deemed on the borderland of insanity; but there is a greatness of soul about it.

It is this keenness and this perpetual itch to improve which makes the American, as I suppose, so much interested in his score. He is a more honest counter than we are, because he will hole out a putt having no bearing on the match in order to keep his score, whereas we are apt to give ourselves the putt and assume that we should have holed it. This habit of holing out irrelevant putts, together with a preference for four-ball matches, makes for a rather slow general progress round the course, and personally I prefer our laxer British ways. At the same time I cannot doubt that the resulting holing out and recording of a score, the always having something to aim at, beyond the winning of the hole, must keep a player up to the mark and be good for his golf. Whether it is so good for other people's golf is another question, but if everyone does it that question does not arise.

If an Englishman betrays so earnest an interest in his score, he is set down, and generally not without reason, as a selfish golfer. But it is impossible to call the American golfer selfish, because he is, in fact, an extraordinarily social golfer. He is so sociable that he does not want to play a single against just one adversary. He wants at least three other people to play with, and even so he is not satisfied, but will match cards and have small friendly side bets with various other people playing in other matches.

To so sociable a man one might have thought that the foursome would appeal, but it is very, very seldom played, as far as my experience goes. It is presumably not energetic enough. The American golfer wants to be living every moment of his time on the links. It should be added that when the Americans do play foursomes they play them uncommonly well, and in the Walker Cup matches have done better in the foursomes than they have in the singles. This ought to be rather a blow to those who hold that foursome playing is a sacred mystery and only those who have long been initiated can hope to shine.

The four-ball match in which everybody holes out is apt to be rather exhausting to the less enthusiastic Briton. At the same time the four-ball match as played by the best American players is a very good game, a much better one, as it seems to me, than as it is played in England. I speak as one who does not, as a rule, like four-ball matches, but I must admit to have enjoyed them very much in America. When we play four balls here the game is apt to be too slapdash; everybody slogs lightheartedly, bangs his long putts at the hole and plays generally without a due sense of responsibility to his side and his partner. That is not the way the American plays in such a game. He is trying his hardest all the time, not taking ridiculous risks or trying fancy shots, playing seriously and carefully, although not too solemnly, the best game that is in him, and the result is a thoroughly good match, which can do nothing but good to the player's golf.

Confessions of a Practicer

Country Life
1919

At a certain pleasant house where I have spent year after year a winter golfing holiday there is an ancient Scottish retainer. He is now, alas! past work, but for many successive winters he used to greet me with a hardy annual joke: "We've put you in the big room, Mr. Darwin, so that you can play golf when you have a mind to it." I had just once, after a day of peculiarly gross errors on the green, taken a putter to bed with me and practiced against the legs of the chairs, and I was never afterwards allowed to forget it. It is the sort of reputation that one can never lose, and, indeed, I am afraid I have deserved it during most of my golfing life. It has probably done more harm than good, given more pain than pleasure, but the habit is almost impossible to break, and I must still confess myself an inveterate and almost unrepentant indoor practicer.

In my rooms at Cambridge I wore two holes through the carpet by means of my stance, to the great distress of my bed-maker, so that I had to get a piece of linoleum to cover up the eyesore and so propitiate her. I have putted, till my back ached, over the floor of a verandah at a small hole between two slabs of slate. I have even putted on the floor boards of a bell tent at the pole. I have played short pitches into a capacious armchair. I have tethered myself by the leg to a bedpost in order to prevent my body from swaying or my knee from bending. I have employed a strange device, blessed by Harry Vardon, whereby a string was fastened at one end to the player's cap and at the other to a piece of metal that slid up and down a groove in a post. If the player moved his head ever so slightly that confounded piece of metal began to slide up the post before his eyes; I am not sure that it did not even ring a bell. In short, if there is any folly which any reader has committed he may be sure that I, too, have committed it.

Moreover, your true practicing lunatic does not confine himself to places where he can use a real club and a real ball. If he cannot swing a club he will swing the fire irons; if there is no room even for a poker, then a paper knife: nay, he will swing away vigorously without any weapon at all. A golfer of my acquaintance was one day holding forth at some length on this subject, declaring that the proper way to practice was to take out all your clubs, without any balls, and practice swinging them one after the other. "I don't agree with you at all," said another golfer, growing perhaps a little restive under the discourse. "The proper way is to take out no clubs, but a box of balls, and practice keeping your eye on the ball." His remark had the desired effect; nevertheless, I would not utterly condemn the theories that he found so tedious. Certainly I can recall many occasions when I have swung myself into what Sam Weller called an "appleplexy" with no compensating benefits whatever, but there have also been just a few when I have hit upon the secret. One in particular was at Sandwich just before the Bar *versus* Stock Exchange match—a very good match it was incidentally, and it is a pity that it was given up. On that Friday evening I was slicing so contemptibly and continuously that ten down with eight to play seemed to stare me in the face for next day's match. I rushed desperately back to the Bell and swung away in my room—it may have been with an umbrella, or it may have been with a toothbrush—until the last available moment before dressing for dinner. When I had tried everything in vain and was beginning to think that I should have to miss the soup, a sudden inspiration sent my arms whirling freely away after the imaginary ball. I dashed down to dinner with hair unbrushed, but filled with a new and satisfying creed. Next day I drove, as you may say, like a printed book and defeated a doughty opponent by an agreeably large margin.

It must be admitted, however, that this comes near to being the exception that proves the rule, and these overnight inspirations more often than not prove sadly disillusioning in the morning. They have an extremely disturbing effect, so that you know no peace of mind until you have actually tested the new theory with club and ball. If the first two or three shots are successful a blessed calm settles down upon you: the restless craving is appeased and you are probably in for a spell of decent play—until the next breakdown; but if, which is more likely, the ball does not go as you have hoped, why then you have wearied your brain and body to no purpose and your last state is much worse than your first.

I have one particularly tragic memory of indoor practicing, not my own, but somebody else's. He was a gentleman well advanced in middle life, but of a youthful and passionate keenness. We stayed together at a hotel for a meeting and as he had never before played in a team match his eagerness was almost painful. He lost his match by six holes. Nobody dared to condole, and he shut himself up in his room to swing away the memory of that black disgrace. For some time those listening without heard only the recurrent swish of the club. Then came a fearful crash and he was discovered plucking himself of bits of glass amid the ruins of a chandelier. He went to bed at eight, caught the half-past six train next morning and the meeting knew him no more.

To turn for a moment from the lighter and more ridiculous aspects of the subject, there is no doubt that many a golfer who thinks that he is practicing most virtuously is really doing nothing of the sort. He takes out a caddie, half a dozen balls and a club of which he is particularly fond. The caddie goes out into the long field, the player tees his six balls in a row and slogs them merrily away and then the caddie brings them back again. This may be excellent fun or exercise, though personally I like to do my practicing in secret; but it can rarely do any good. You can scarcely grow more than confident in a club, and you can waste good shots. The only practice that is really beneficial is with a club or of a stroke of which you are not the master, and in that case you must determine to take out only that recalcitrant club or to play only that particular shot. I have sometimes gone out having solemnly vowed to struggle with nothing but half-iron shots, and then yielded to the temptation to take a favorite brassie with me as well. When twilight has at last fallen, or all my balls have been lost in the heather, I have found to my extreme mortification that I have done nothing but slash gaily with the brassie, and those confounded half-iron shots have been postponed once more. Again, even if you do harden your heart and toil away at the iron shots, there is a temptation to do so in some pleasantly open spot and at no particular mark. But a half-iron shot in the abstract is of very little use. In a real game it has to be played up to a flag, and it is the fact of there being bunkers to right and left of that flag that makes your shots so crooked. If you are in a very bad way indeed the nice open space may be allowable for a stroke or two, but you must not pamper yourself too long. Sooner or later you must put it to the touch of the bunkers.

A Golf Writer's Revenge

American Golfer
1935

I am writing this article a little before its time because I am going for my holiday. I don't want to work more than I can help on a holiday; I do want to gloat about it beforehand. Just once a year seems to me a not excessive allowance in the matter of gloating. Moreover, though I may seem to be selfish, am I not putting myself in sympathy with all the world because all the world has a holiday.

At this moment I am thinking about a train from Kings Cross Station, about Berwick and the silvery Tweed far before us. Thinking about the Forth Bridge and the change at Leuchars Junction and finally the last little bit of the journey in the little local train which will bring me curving into St. Andrews, right along the edge of the links. Well, my readers, if I have any, can translate that heavenly journey of mine into their own language. Their journey will have different landmarks and will take them to a different paradise, but it will be essentially the same and at the end of it they will find, just as I hope to do, their own familiar friends plying their niblicks in familiar bunkers.

There is, indeed, one aspect of a golfing holiday which does not appeal to all but does to this poor golfing writer. That is the blissful thought that he is going to play golf without having to write about it. I suppose all of us, who are not saints and angels but reasonably malignant human beings, habitually heighten the joys of a holiday by thinking about other people who have already had theirs and gone back to work. As we loaf gently down to the clubhouse after a late breakfast with the prospect of two good rounds before us, we reflect, not in a wholly Christian spirit, that they are at the moment catching their daily-bread trains to their offices. I am going to revel in this discreditable delight in its most poignant form.

During my fist two weeks at St. Andrews there will be two competitions, the Jubilee Vase and the Calcutta Cup. Not only shall I not have to report them but I shall, with my own eyes, see somebody else having to do so. When I have finished playing or watching I shall be able to take my ease and my drink while I watch the other poor fellow button-holing competitors, asking them how they fared, listening to their tales of woe, making hasty notes which he will not afterwards be able to read and ultimately retiring to a corner laboriously to write his story. Could anything be more maliciously agreeable than that? It is as if the office worker on a holiday could, but means of television, actually see his fellows toiling in black coats and hot cities. At such a moment I could almost exclaim to the rest of the world "Envy me, sirs, I am a golfing writer!"

It is of course a sad commonplace about a golfing holiday that the best part of it is the looking forward to it, the second best the packing for it, and the third best the journey, and the fourth best the holiday itself. Can any perfectly truthful man lay his hand on his heart and say that he has ever played as well on his holiday as in his dreams he thought he was going to play? Disappointment begins, as a rule, on the very first blissful day of all. We may not have been playing much beforehand, but we have practiced putting on the domestic course on the lawn, pitching over the flowerbeds and driving in the neighboring meadow.

For each of those arts we have got a new theory and new theories are wonderfully effective on a lawn or in a field with nobody to look at us. The moment we come on to a real course there is a subtle but definite change in the atmosphere; light, wind, turf, everything is different. We imagine that we shall be perfectly at home and in fact we feel perfectly strange. We realize yet once more that domestic practice is better than none at all but not a substitute for practice in a game and on a links. The disappointment is the keener because our hopes have been so absurdly high, and we shall be fortunate if every one of those theories has not been abandoned before the first nine holes are out.

This anguish does pass off. For a day or two we are like the small child, who, because he is not allowed a particular piece of cake, thinks drearily that there will never be any cake again in the world. Then just because we are getting familiar with the feel of the club we find ourselves playing rather well and then comes the really crucial moment—are we going to get stale? Judiciously to ease off just when we are as we say "coming on to it" requires sometimes a fierce effort of will, but if we do not make that effort we shall probably have sad things to suffer. It will be harder to play well later on because the dreadful part of staleness is this, that we hate the game and yet cannot bear to give it up. It becomes a deadly drug from which we cannot refrain even though we know it is destroying us. Even if we do succeed in taking a day off our mind is occupied with new and complicated theories for the next morning. The time to take it easy is when we have a system, however fallible, which is producing satisfactory results. Then our mind is at peace, we can spend a whole day vacantly throwing stones into the sea and return to the links genuinely refreshed.

I have preached a sermon of this sort to myself before many holidays and seldom conformed with my own doctrines. What will happen this time? Meanwhile I have a theory, and it is high time that I went out into the field and tried it.

II

The Spirit of the Game

Golfing Reveries

The American Golfer
APRIL 1930

I wish I could enjoy the game of golf as much as Johnnie enjoys his game of ball. Johnnie, I ought to explain, is a black cocker spaniel. The game is demanded every evening after dinner by a series of restless squeaks, superficially resembling but yet clearly distinguishable from the squeaks which demand the opening of a door. If the word "ball" is mentioned the squeaks become so passionate in their intensity that any prospective player must say, "Do you know where Johnnie's sphere is? I can't find it."

The game itself is simple. One player throws the ball, and the other rushes after it, judges to a nicety the angle from which it will come off any piece of furniture which may act as a pepper-box, and brings it back again. Sometimes he brings it back at once, sometimes he cannot resist pausing to chaw it, and must be spoken to in a stern voice. When the throwing player grows weary of the game the retiring player tees the ball on the floor between his front paw and putts it with his nose in a gentle and appealing manner.

The game is clearly an admirable one, for the player never grows weary of it, but I should very much like to know which part of it he enjoys the most. There is the primitive joy of the exercise; the wild stampede after the ball across the slippery floor, which leaves the room a wreck of crumpled rugs; there is the technical skill of the fielding it as it bounces off the side wall, and there is the afterglow of the chawing. What is the peculiarly poignant satisfaction in the chawing? I wish I knew. There were once in Germany some wonderful dogs that could rap out messages with their tails, but Johnnie is not a typtological dog and cannot tell me.

It may be simply that the ball has a succulent flavor, or it may be something rather more subtle, a licking of the chops of memory. He may be saying to himself with every bite, "Ha ha! They thought they could deceive me by pretending to throw it into the far corner and then dropping it into that chair, but I saw what they were at: I put my long black nose in behind the cushion, and there it was."

These three different joys belong also to the golfer. As to the exercise, the honorable name of golfer cannot be given to him who plays purely with that object, though it can afford legitimate consolation in pouring rain on a flooded course with the prospect of a well-earned sleep after luncheon. As to the technical skill, few of us have really enough of that, though we can occasionally produce results which we can attribute to it. But we can all enjoy the chawing. This can be quite a harmless pleasure if we only remember gloatingly what happened and do not worry our heads about the how or why.

The sight of the ball just disappearing into the hole with the winning putt, the six-foot stride with which we danced forward as if on air to pick it out, the dismay on our enemy's face and the smirk on our caddie's—these things it is pure bliss to recall and there is no danger. I have two such memories from one and the same tournament which I must set down again; one, that of being two up with three to play on an eminent person and seeing his ball go into a bunker which I knew to be full of snow; the other, of being all square with one to play, playing the one off four with no bunkers in the way and a socketless iron with which to knock the ball along the ground on an inglorious installment system.

It is another matter, however, and a highly dangerous one: if we recall the physical sensations that accompanied some particular shot. Such sensations do occasionally persist in a remarkable way. We recollect how beautifully and exactly poised we were at the end of the shot-on the right toe and the left heel, as in a certain familiar photograph of Freddie Tait—or how the shaft seemed to quiver and thrill in our hands or how we looked so long at the place where the ball had been that we had positively to be told where it had gone—straight as an arrow for the pin.

These are entrancing memories but what perilous ones! It is too much to ask of erring human golfers that they should not try to reproduce those sensations and to do that is fatal. Our retrospections must never be, in Mrs. Malaprop's words, "all to the future."

It would be a privilege to know whether the great ones of the earth indulge in this habit of metaphorical chawing, and if so which are the supreme shots that they remember. I was reading the other day something that Vardon had written about the best shot he had ever played, a niblick shot from under the clubhouse railings, at Northwood, right over the clubhouse itself to within a yard of the hole. Doubtless it was a wonderful shot, and yet he must surely have some equally ecstatic memory in a rather more romantic setting.

What do the other champions think about as they lie in bed deliciously half asleep or sit looking at the pictures in the fire? Does Mr. John Ball see again his ball pitching safely over the Dun bunker from his great brassie shot against Mr. Mure Fergusson? What do the glowing coals show to Braid? Perhaps the shaft of his cleek snapping, the head flashing and hustling along the turf, and the ball safely alighting on the last green at Muirfield to make him champion for the first time. There is a certain brassie shot, too, over the wall at Prestwick and the putt that went in afterwards for a 3. That must haunt him pleasantly now and then.

Mr. Tolley must see his ball going into the hole for a 2 at the thirty-seventh against Mr. Gardner and himself walking after it long before it has dropped. So one might go on forever, thinking enviously how happy all great men must be. And yet it is barely possible that they indulge in none of these beautiful retrospective dreams any more than Johnnie is doing now, as he lies camouflaged on a black rug before the fire snoring placidly. Perhaps that is one of the reasons why they are so great.

The Sounds of Golf

Out of the Rough
1932

In golf, as in everything else, there are certain characteristic sounds with which our ears grow familiar. We know them so well that we hardly realize their existence until we hear them again after an absence from the links or until, owing to some change in the game, we come to miss them. To these old familiar golfing sounds a new one has been added in the course of the last few years. It is the metallic clank caused by one steel shaft touching another as the caddie takes a club out of the bag. Perhaps clank is not quite the right word, for there is also something of purring in the sound. At any rate, though my vocabulary is vague and inadequate, the sound is perfectly distinct, and we shall soon know it so well that we shall hardly notice it any more than we do the roar of an airplane which once set us staring at the heavens.

For myself I first noticed it while playing in a foursome, all four members of which had gone worshipping after the strange new gods of steel. It set me trying to enumerate the other sounds characteristic of our game. Steel may fairly be said, I think, to have added another new one in the unmistakable "swish" of the shaft through the air. I have already grown accustomed to it, but when I first bought a particularly engaging little spoon, its music seemed infinitely exciting and romantic. Old Tom Morris used to talk of the music of a shaft, meaning the spring or whip in it. It was a charming and poetical thought which has now come to be a comparatively prosaic and everyday fact. It is comforting that the modern game should bring some pleasant sound with it, because the old game had beautiful ones that are not gone forever. Some melody went out of golf when the rubber-core replaced the gutty. The ring of a gutty struck quite cleanly with an iron club was a twofold joy; it was cheerful and pretty in itself and spoke of a stroke perfectly made. It is only when we play a shot with a gutty and hear it again that we realize what we have lost. The gutty rang even off an iron putter. I have a feeling—no doubt quite fantastic and due to ancient hero worship—that the ball struck by that lofted putting cleek of Freddie Tait's sang a clearer, louder song than anyone else's. I am sure that one did know instantly and certainly whether a putt had been struck or not, and on rare red-letter days one felt sure the ball was doing down merely from the click with which it left one's club.

"Crack after crack rings out cleanly as every ounce of youthful muscle is thrown into the blow." I quote from memory, but I trust with reasonable accuracy, a passage which I love in Mr. Hutchinson's description of the young professionals and university students driving off at St. Andrews while Old Tom looks on to see that they do not trespass on the home green. That was written of the gutty, which I am prepared to say made a pleasanter noise than the rubber-core off any club, but I will admit that the new ball does make a very satisfactory one when struck by a driver. The big hitters make a much bigger noise than ordinary people. I know no more terrific crack than that of a perfectly stuck drive by Mr.

Wethered; it is like a pistol shot. It amuses me to harbor the belief that I could, with my eyes shut, tell the sound of his drive from anyone else's. Of course I could not, but I shall continue to say that I could. Similarly I feel as if I could tell by ear his sister's drive from that of all the other ladies.

These are the pleasant sounds of golf. There are others equally familiar but less pleasant. There is, for instance, the rattling and bumping of iron clubs one against the other as a small caddie who has been lingering behind tries to overtake his irate master. It is generally accompanied by loud hiccups—an affliction so common among caddies as to demand scientific research—and ends with a terrific crash as the luckless child trips over a hummock and falls prostrate. Then there is the sound of our foursome partner missing a crucial mashie shot by digging too deeply into the turf. The stroke sometimes known as a "grumph" makes a horrid, heavy, dead noise, quite unmistakable. We look in another direction, perhaps, in an agony of apprehension, as he plays his shot, and then "Hello," we say, "I didn't like the sound of that one." Our ear has been all too true a monitor, for, sure enough, as we look round there is the ball climbing feebly into the air to fall into the cross-bunker over which it should have soared. A splash is, I suppose, only a splash, whether made by a golf ball or any other falling body; yet is there not something peculiarly and characteristically ominous about the splash of our own ball in a pond which we thought we had carried by the skin of our teeth? I feel almost inclined to say that the sound of splashing is quite different according as the water is casual or in a bunker, but that is to be too imaginative. Another watery sound that we know all too well in winter golf is the purring of the ball on a waterlogged putting green. We have examined the green minutely in the hope of finding something that we could call a puddle, however tiny, and so be able to lift. Honesty compels us to play the ball where it lies, and then—*p-rrr!* and the ball sends a small fountain spouting into the air and sits sulkily down after traveling exactly halfway to the hole. When I think of that sound one particular and tragic scene comes before me. It is the third green at Worplesdon; the final of the Mixed Foursomes has come to the thirty-ninth hole in such a deluge of rain as I hope never to see again, and poor Miss Joy Winn and Mr. Longstaffe, who have fought so heroically, are trying in vain to force their ball with their putters over the sodden grass. Three times running they try, and still the ball is not in the hole. That was the cruelest ending to a good match that ever was seen and the wettest even at Worplesdon, where the pattering of rain on umbrellas, the swishing of macintoshes in the wind and the squelching of water in the shoes make inevitable music.

Finally, the custom of various eminent golfers of carrying a shooting stick and sitting down between strokes will soon add a new sound and a new terror to golf. I was playing with one of these illustrious heavyweights at Rye in January and our game was haunted by a peculiar eerie and melancholy piping. One of our four grew exceedingly restive under this affliction, but no culprit could be discovered; at length it was found to be the wind whistling through some joint of Mr. John Morrison's shooting stick while he sat poised in placid majesty. I don't know whether this is a matter for a new rule or is only a question of etiquette.

The Humor of It

Playing the Like
1934

Perhaps much writing about golf makes one inclined to talk about something else. At any rate, I only realized the other day what a long time it was since I had had a good square, sit-down talk about golf. Let me add at once that I enjoyed it immensely.

By a lucky chance I met an old friend, a very great golfer of an epoch that is now, alas! beginning to pass away. Our conversation was possibly a little reminiscent and historical and dealt with those who were heroic names rather than flesh and blood heroes to the other people in the room. It was, however, a remark of one of them that produced from the sage a memorable reply. I could not help thinking of the young clergyman who asked that single question of Dr. Johnson about Dr. Dodd's sermons. . . . We had been discussing the fighting qualities of various champions, how one would fight from love of revenge and another like a rat in a trap because he could not help it. Then said one of the company, "You could fight pretty well too, couldn't you?" The answer was not one of Johnsonian thunder; it was rather with a wistful ghost of a smile that the sage answered, "Sometimes—when I could see the humor of it."

Into those few words there is packed nearly all the wisdom of all the volumes that have been written upon the "psychological" side of golf. Moreover, the example by which this truth was illustrated was a striking one. The great man had played the seventeenth hole at St. Andrews on a crucial occasion. The match was all even and he had the best of the hole, having reached the foot of the green in two wooden club shots. Then he putted—a little too gently, a little too much, perhaps, to the left—and the ball took that familiar and malignant curve and ended in the Road bunker. I myself saw the dreadful thing happen and, having no sense of humor, still shudder at the recollection. Everybody sooner or later putts into that bunker. The boast of never having done so would justify a retort such as "W. G." is supposed to have made to the young man who said he had never made a duck: "Then you go in last—you can't have played much cricket." Still, it is not on the face of it an amusing thing to do in a tight place in a championship, and my friend was not at first amused. However, in an auspicious moment he heard a Scottish spectator call on his Maker in a tone of poignant solemnity; he laughed, played a carefree niblick shot out of the bunker, halved the hole, and in the end won the match.

If my friend's wisdom needed any confirmation, which it did not, it soon came to me from another distinguished source—I was reading Miss Joyce Wethered's new book, and here is her recipe for developing a measure of philosophy against all the horrid things that are bound to happen. "I know quite well," she says, "the two qualities that have helped me most, although I realize that they may not help everyone. The first is honesty with oneself, allowing for no excuses; and the other—which may appear an odd choice—a sense of humor." O infinitely great and fortunate lady! A sentence or two farther on she declares—and I believe her from my heart—"I have been able to laugh at myself for the absurdity of such intense feelings and the perversity of one's thoughts."

One of the difficulties in acquiring this quality is the same which besets us in the merely physical part of the game—namely, timing. If we could hit the ball at the right moment we should hit it much straighter and farther than, in fact, we do, and similarly, we want to see the absurdity of our conduct or our situation at the precise moment. Years, or it may be days or even hours, afterwards we are most of us capable of reflecting how supremely laughable was the circumstance of our having laid ourselves a dead stymie when we had two for the match. We may think leniently of that beast in the gallery who sniggered aloud; we may come to see his point of view. But this is not enough; if it is to do us any good we have got to deem it funny there and then, even as we lay aside our putter and take our mashie niblick to pitch the stymie. That demands an almost morbid sense of humor, and yet there is still a further step, for suppose that in trying to pitch the stymie we knock the enemy in and lose hole, match, and all. Can you laugh then? Personally I make not the faintest pretension to being able to do so, but if you can, why then you will be, in Mr. Kipling's inspiring words, "a man, my son."

If we cannot see the joke we may yet pretend that we do and "grin horribly a ghastly smile." We shall not deceive ourselves nor, probably, anybody else, but still we shall have made, in our modern jargon, a "gesture," and on the whole it is better than foaming at the mouth or breaking a club.

By way of a modest beginning I have been trying to put my precepts into practice. In a fit of March madness I had bought two new super-clubs, at a price which I dare not reveal even on the counterfoil of my checkbook. On the loveliest of spring mornings I dashed off to try them in a state of tremulous absurdity. How truly ludicrous I was in thinking that a new club, or indeed anything but the silent tomb, could benefit my game! I called myself every kind of preposterous old idiot, and yet, as I teed my first ball, my hand was a little unsteady with excitement. I sliced once, I sliced twice. This was my chance for coming out strong. I made the woods ring with loud and bitter laughter. Oh, yes, I had a sense of humor; there could be no doubt about that. Was it not the very quintessence of fun that I should spend that unmentionable amount of money on these ridiculous clubs, decked out with a little red stripe here and a little white stripe there, and then puff the ball gently over mid-off's head? When I had partially recovered from my fit of merriment I teed another ball and hit it, comparatively speaking, miles down the course. I teed another and yet one more: I marched up and down hitting five at a time.

On the whole I hit them rather well. I almost forgot to see the exquisite joke of my imagining that I should hit them well next time.

The People in Front

Playing the Like
1934

Hazlitt thought it one of the best things in life to be known only as "the gentleman in the parlor," and certainly it is a pleasant title. There is something so respectable about its anonymity, and yet it suggests all the romance of wayfaring. Other titles formed on somewhat similar lines suggest nothing but feelings of hatred and contempt. Such is that of the large class of golfers whom we call simply "the people in front." When the clocks have been put back and darkness falls prematurely on the links, they are more than ever detestable.

It is true that they are not, as a rule, in the least to blame for the delay; so much we grudgingly admit, but it does not make their little ways the less irritating. They waggle for hours; they stroll rather than walk; they dive into their monstrous bags in search of the right club and then it is the wrong number, but they are not sorry that we have been troubled; their putting is a kind of funereal ping-pong. We could forgive them all these tricks, from which we ourselves are conspicuously free, if it were not for the absurd punctilio with which they observe the rules. They will insist on waiting for the people in front of them when it must be palpable even to their intellects that the best shot they ever hit in their lives would be fifty yards short.

The one thing to be said for them is that when they are in front of somebody else they can give us a little malicious gaiety. Some while ago I was playing on the same course as was an eminent person. My partner and I started in front of him, but others of our party were less fortunate. For some time we could not quite understand why there were several empty fairways behind us. Then we noticed that on the tees couples were rapidly silting up. It was as if a river had flowed placidly on until there was thrown a mighty dam right across it. As in our old friend, "Horatius,"

The furious river struggled hard
And tossed his tawny mane,

but the dam held; in front, steadily, methodically on went the eminent person, studying both ends of his putts with all that intense power of forgetting for the moment the affairs of State which is the hallmark of his class. And I am bound to confess that we laughed, like Mr. Manzalini, "demnably."

Generally, as was said before, the people in front are not the real culprits. "I know it's not their fault," we say in the tone of the man who, as he broke his putter across his knee, exclaimed, "I know it's only a d——d game." That being so, it ought to make no difference to us who are the people for whom we have to wait. We should go no faster and no slower if Bobby Jones and Harry Vardon were playing in front of us instead of that old lady who scoops the ball along with a club that goes up so obviously faster than it can ever come down. I suppose we must be golfing snobs, because it does make a great difference. To be kept waiting by the eminent (I mean the eminent in golf) is to be reconciled to the inevitability of things, whereas we always believe that the scooping lady could get along faster if she tried. Moreover, there is the disquieting hope that she may lose her ball. It would be of no real help to us if she did, but instinct is too strong for us. Every time her ball is seen heading for a gorse bush our heartfelt prayers go with it, and though attainment will swiftly prove disenchanting, it is a great moment when at last she waves us on and we stampede courteously past.

It is at that precise moment that we are most likely to hit our own ball into a gorse bush, for it is a law of nature that everybody plays a hole badly when going through. To be there and then repassed is one of the bitterest humiliations that golf can bring; it must be akin to that of being rebumped by the boat so gloriously bumped the night before. But, of course, no rational being will endure it; far rather would we surrender the hole and make a rapid though undignified rush towards the next teeing ground. By this time, it is true, we are hot, flustered, and angry, and wish that the woman had kept her ball on the course. Nevertheless, we shall soon be wishing that the new people in front will lose theirs. What fools we are! and in nothing more foolish than in this matter of passing.

My original list by no means exhausted the crimes that can be committed by the people in front. They can call us on and then, finding their ball in the nick of time, go on themselves, but that is an offense so black and repulsive that I cannot write about it. They can try over again the putt they have just missed, and this crime has become more fashionable since we have been taught to admire American assiduity in the practicing of putts. They can take out a horrid little card and pencil, and, immobile in the middle of the green, write down their horrid little score. In that case, however, there is compensation, for there is no law of God or man that can prevent us from letting out a blaring yell of "Fore!" To see them duck and cower beneath the imaginary assault may not be much, but it is something. They may think us ill-mannered, but what does that matter? The worst they can do is write an article about the people behind.

On Being Dormy

Playing the Like
1934

It is doubtful whether golf, or indeed life, has any sensation to offer equal to that of becoming dormy. It may be that we experience only a blessed relaxation after strain and feel comparatively good-natured towards the enemy, or again we may want to turn on him in savage exultation and shout, as Andrew Kirkaldy once did when he holed his putt at the Corner of the Dyke, "The door's shut now." In either case it is a moment of almost delicious bliss.

I have been racking my brains to think of anything corresponding to it in other games. I can only discover one example. In the fourth innings at cricket, when the batting side have made the match a tie with one or more wickets to fall, they may be said to be dormy. No other game or sport can produce that defiant certainty, that absolute of immunity. A man may be leading by a hundred yards in a mile race with but ten yards to go, but he *may* fall down in a fit. If I were to play Mr. Newman or Mr. Davis at billiards and my score were blank, as it inevitably would be, and the champion's was 9,999 and I were left with a double balk, the chances of my ultimate success would be negligible, and yet the impish fates might have something up their sleeves. But if (of course in receipt of a stroke a hole) I am dormy one on Mr. Bobby Jones, I am impregnable; I need not even touch wood to avert the evil chance; there is the exquisite rub.

If these emotions appear excessive, I can best make my defense in the words of Mr. Malthus, the honorary member of the Suicide Club, "Fear is the strong passion; it is with fear that you must trifle if you wish to taste the intensest joys of living. Envy me—envy me, sir," he added with a chuckle. "I am a coward!" Every time the ace of spades was dealt to another player, Mr. Malthus enjoyed the quintessence of being dormy; he found the relief so intoxicating that, as we know, he "trifled once too often with his terrors" and drew the card of death at last.

It is one of the most ruthless things about almost every match-play tournament that there is no dormy. We may be five up with five holes to play, but there always looms the hideous possibility of all the five dropping away one by one, so that we have to totter out again to the nineteenth under the gaze of gloating eyes. To this rule of cruelty there is one blessed exception. If a match is halved in the Jubilee Vase or the Calcutta Cup at St. Andrews, there is no prolonging of the misery, and both sides pass through into the next round. So in these kindly competitions we do not greatly care what happens so long as we avoid defeat; if we have a four-foot putt for the match on the home green, we bend all our faculties to the task of laying the ball dead; if we are as many holes up as there are holes left to play we light a pipe and assume, without affectation, an air of almost inconceivable jauntiness. There have even been cases in which charitable persons have lain under suspicion of not trying to win, and only the most malignant feel seriously annoyed if they let victory slip. At any rate, they have lived to fight another day.

In these peculiar circumstances we attain to the ultimate poignancy of dorminess and can really, as the word implies, go to sleep if we have a mind to. For that very reason we are likely to finish with a modest steadiness, for the plain fact is that as a rule we are not sleepy enough. For the first hole after we have become dormy a pleasant drowsiness sets in, and that will very likely enable us to get the half we want; but if we lose one hole we are apt to get restive, and if we lose two or three, terror seizes us by the throat. We come to feel that nothing but a mistake by the other side will save us, and despite our prayers it is just at that moment that the beasts will not make a mistake. Sometimes, but not often, luck comes to our aid, and I am still fondly hugging to myself the memory of a certain rot-stopping long putt. I don't think the ball deserved to go in; it was struck only with the courage of despair; if it had not hit the exact back of the hole it must have jumped out again, but—ha! ha!—it stayed in, and once again the sky was blue and the larks were singing.

Other epicures in sensation may not agree, but I am disposed to think that the instant of sudden realization that we are going to be dormy is sometimes better than that in which the impossible has really happened. A foursome of a few days ago comes gratefully to mind. After toiling and struggling and being down, we had by some incredible means become all square with two to go, and then my partner played a second shot of a quality so dazzling that my eyes are still blinded by the glory of it. I knew where the foe was—an agreeably horrid place—but I could not see our ball upon the green. "Where is it?" I cried in an agony, and a trusty friend walking with me replied, "It's so near the hole that even you can't help putting it dead." That was the supreme moment, and not the later one in which the ball, tremulously pushed towards the hole, did actually lie dead.

By some mischance this lovely word "dormy" has become partially corrupted in its passage across the Atlantic. I judge so at least, because I have now and again read in American golfing magazines that *A* was dormy three, when it appears from internal evidence that, in fact, *B* was three up on him with three holes to play. How this inversion arose I cannot explain, but those who are guilty of it have wholly failed to grasp the beauty of the word. It is the only one in our language which signifies that for one transcendent moment we can snap our fingers under the very nose of Fate.

Down Memory Lane

Country Life
1936

The keeping of a diary is a matter on which people are as a rule rather reticent. Perhaps they are merely afraid of being thought to be bores who will pitilessly inflict pages of trivialities on their friends, and that is an admirable motive. Perhaps they cherish the hope that when they die they will blossom into an unexpected and posthumous fame as so many Pepyses. Whatever their reason, they are generally shy about admitting to anything of the kind, and so it happens that I have no notion how many of my friends keep golfing diaries and in how many books is some such entry as this: "Beat B. Darwin by 6 and 5. He was perfectly hopeless, but I played rather well."

I once kept a diary, and I wish I had gone on. Why I gave it up I hardly know, save that I reached the end of one book and, just as I was going to begin another, I had such a devastating and disastrous time on the links that I could not bear to record it. I solemnly and sincerely advise other people to keep one, not because it will necessarily become an historic document, but because just once or twice a year, a good many years hence, it will give them a sudden thrill to look at it, just as once in a very long while we enjoy turning up some ancient collection of stamps or the picture books of our childhood. My one day comes about Christmas time because—it is a shameful confession—I generally find there is not enough to do on Christmas Day. When all presents have been given and received and looked at and thanked for, when you have eaten your turkey and plum pudding and taken a walk to get rid of some of their effects, there is still time to spare, and it is then that I retire surreptitiously to my room and read my old diary with a certain melancholy pleasure.

This diary of mine began in 1899 and ended in 1903, so that I can look back at my matches of—to take a good round number—thirty-five years ago. One thing that strikes me in the retrospect is that while I have, of course, clean forgotten most of the games recorded, I have hardly forgotten a single one of my partners or opponents. It is only at very long intervals that I have to scratch my head and say: "Snooks—who the deuce was Snooks? Anyhow, he can't have been much good, since I had to give him a half"; or else: "Snooks must have been a good player, since he seems to have beaten me pretty comfortably—only, who the devil was he?" Almost the only occasions on which I have to puzzle my head over Snooks are those of a single visit to a course previously unknown to me. Then I imagine that he was the captain of the local club, and perhaps I may be pardoned for having forgotten him. At Aberdovey or Woking or Chiswick or Mid-Surrey or some other course on which I played regularly during those four years, I find no Snookses; I can remember all my opponents, sometimes vaguely and sometimes quite clearly, even down to the eccentricities of their respective swings. The mere writing down of their names in the book must have helped to grave them on my memory, and that is one advantage of keeping a diary.

Incidentally, how the writing does change from page to page during four years! It was not that my handwriting (many printers would deny that it deserved to be so called) was in a state of flux during that period. It is rather that the writer's mood changed constantly. When I see a beautifully neat and tidy page I feel pretty sure that things were going well with me, and that I enjoyed recording every night the modest triumph of the day. I am the more sure of this when I examine the page carefully and see that it is dotted here and there with nice little scores in nice little brackets with plenty of fours and threes and not too many sixes. There are, on the other hand, pages on which the doings of five or six days were clearly recorded at one and the same time. The writing becomes hurried and slovenly; there are no tidy little scores and only one or two despairing comments such as "Driving unspeakable" or "Putting too awful." Then I know that, as one day of bad golf followed another, I put off each night the task of setting down the results, until at last, being forced to do my duty, I did it as perfunctorily as possible.

One would think that after thirty-five years defeat would have lost its bitterness, whereas the pleasure of victory would remain, but I am not sure that this is so; *surgit amari aliquid* even to this day. The reason is, perhaps, that I am, as I read, in the position of one knowing the future. As I see some good score, evidently recorded with pride and gratification, I know that it was but a flash in the pan; far from inaugurating a new and happier epoch, it was, in fact, the precursor of some major disaster. There is one springtime, for instance, towards the end of the gutty era, when everything appears rosy-colored. It begins at Aberdovey, and there is a flamboyant entry followed by exclamation marks: "Great field day. Three pots in one day." When I look at it now I only say: "Ha ha, my boy, you didn't know what was coming to you." The calamity does not come at once. On the contrary, I proceed to St. Anne's and, according to my statement, equal the amateur record, but as I had not a card and pencil this was very likely a lie. Once more at the present moment I laugh cynically, but at the time it was "all wery capital," and the entry that follows at Formby is cheerful enough. Then the page turns over; I get to Hoylake and suffer a complete collapse and a horrible double-figure defeat. What a good thing it is that the future is hid from us!

While a great many of the entries fail altogether to revive the memory, others stimulate it to an extraordinary degree. The sight of a particular patch of handwriting makes me remember exactly what new style or dodge I as cultivating at the time. It may be that the fine nib brings back the temporary triumph over an elbow or the fact that I was crouching less than usual; the fat nib suggests visions of a particular wooden club with a yellow head, and a dreadful fit of tumbling backwards, even without the note "Something must be done about this driving."

There are some pages, again, that strike me dumb with admiration at my own and my companion's energy, or perhaps I should rather say, with envy of our youth. Some six and thirty years ago I was staying at the same hospitable house by the same course from which I have but lately returned, and I find that for five consecutive days we played not only two singles each day but a nine-hole foursome afterwards. Just think how early we must have started to play five and forty holes on a January day, how quickly we must have walked and lunched, and, even so, how dark it must have been when we finally holed out. Just think, too, any of you who know the scene of those labors, that we had a very steep hill to climb afterwards, with no cars to carry us back after our one round as we have now. However, if I go on in this sad strain I shall induce people not to keep diaries, whereas I set out to persuade them to do so. So let me end by assuring them on my honor that the pleasure is really much greater than the pain.

Golf as a Soporific

Playing the Like
1934

A friend who has been ill, but is now, I am glad to say, on the mend, writes to me that he has been putting himself to sleep by playing imaginary rounds of golf. He has formed a high opinion of this device; indeed, he seems to think, as Sam did of Mr. Roker's narcotic bedstead, that "poppies is nothing to it."

Those that lie awake may like to hear how he does it. First of all he chooses a course he knows well, since, as I suppose, he wants to make no effort in recalling the exact scenery. Next, he always assumes that his tee shot is a good one. This is not because he always does hit a good one in real life—I have seen him miss them—but because he has found that the missing of drives has some subtly wakeful influence. "After that," he says, with an engaging modesty, "I play to form and allow for many lapses from grace." He adds that he has found it great fun and that only very seldom has he had to play a second round before sleep comes to his rescue.

One odd thing is that there is a particular course which is more successful than any other. Rarely has he got past the ninth hole there; that tremendous hole, the seventeenth, he has never played. The late Sir Francis Galton, among his many and ingenious statistical inquiries, discovered which town in Britain possessed the plainest ladies, but he would never reveal its name. Similarly I will not reveal which is the most blessedly drowsy of all courses. Why it should possess these properties I cannot for the life of me understand, for it is a great course. It may be the wind that sweeps across that noble heath, and so blows, even in make-believe, a kindly dust into the eyes.

On second thought perhaps my friend's testimony is really a high compliment to it. Take the analogy of reading in bed. The shoddiest, most vapid detective story is a dangerous companion if it be new; but the great detective stories of the world, of which we know not only the plot but the very words by heart, are infinitely soothing. For my part I could get to the very point in "The Moonstone" when Franklin Blake is going to read the name on the nightgown, and then cease upon the midnight without pain. Sherlock Holmes may cry, "You see it, Watson, you see it!" and, even as he lashes furiously at the bell rope, I turn out the light. So it may be with courses; what we need is a beautiful familiarity.

We all have our own ways of wooing sleep, and, as a rule, keep them coyly hidden in a secret chamber of the imagination. I know one whose method is more romantic than golf; it belongs to the dim days when for him there was no golf. Lovely cuirassiers and dragoons, hussars and lancers surround the Napoleonic traveling carriage in which he lies, a legacy, as I suspect, from a first visit to Madame Tussaud's. Ah! how their breastplates shine, their pennons wave! They have new uniforms every night, and are gilded and befurred even as was the Grand Army in *Le Conscrit.* They clatter away with their Emperor in the darkness, making him feel deliciously safe, and the sound of their horses' hoofs grows fainter and fainter till it dies away in the distance; they have turned the corner and so has he.

Sometimes that phantom cavalry cannot escort him within the merciful gates, and golf has to be tried, but it is seldom a success. This is due, I fear, to a most unlovely quality in him: he has not the humility of my sick friend; a horrid vanity prevents him from making the appropriate number of bad shots; thus the round maintains altogether too high and so too exciting a level. Clearly, it would be a pity to start with a bad hole, and gradually the mistakes get put off again and again. A four at the third! Why, it is unthinkable! It is the easiest thing in the world to put the ball on to that big green—with a side-wall, too; he could not be frightened of a blind shot over a sandhill.

A five at the seventh—well, that may pass, but even that is a concession; he could almost get up in two with a wind behind, and who ever could or did take more than four at the eighth—a mere drive and a pitch? Then the vain creature declines to take three imaginary putts; he doesn't ask much, he doesn't want to hole any long ones, but three putts would be most disturbing. And so it goes on till before he knows where he is he has got a four for sixty-nine, and it would be a pity to break down so near the end. So a sixty-nine it is, with cheering crowd round the home green, and who could go to sleep after such a round?

A far better plan would be to go to bed and then give audience, one at a time, to a series of players who have had bad luck in a medal round. There were in "Erewhon," if I remember rightly, some luckless persons who were official or professional "borees"; but it may be doubted if they ever had to endure anything quite so terrific as the man who has been hitting all his shots perfectly and yet took ninety to get round.

Surely such a narrative ought to numb the too active senses if anything can, and yet even here there lurks a danger. As the creature goes maundering on about his tee shot ruled on the guide flag and the iron shot that by all the laws of everything ought to have taken the slope and come curling round to the pin, there is an irresistible temptation to cut him short and say, "Yes, but what did you take to the hole?" Speaking from a long and bitter experience, I can say that it does no good at all; it does not stop him, but it does stop one from going to sleep. I had thought of going to see my sick friend and telling him about one or two of my recent rounds, but perhaps I had better not.

Lovelock's Mile

The Times
1934

There is no doubt where I ought to have been last Saturday; I ought to have been at Wentworth watching the match at golf between England and France. I shirked it unashamedly and went to watch something which I deemed, with all respect to the golfers, better worth the seeing: the mile race at the White City between Lovelock and Bonthron.

Nothing in this life, not even our next holiday, is ever quite so good as we think it is going to be, and, apart from the glorious circumstance that the right man won, I suppose that this great mile was just the least bit disappointing. Yet I would not have missed it for any earthly consideration. Why, the buzz of excitement when the men came out was alone worth all the money; one could have wished for a false start or two to prolong it. So of course was that supreme instant that comes in every race, when we could shout

"He's got him!" with defiant conviction, with no timid thought of propitiating the Fates. So most of all in this undemonstrative country was the genuinely emotional rush of dark and light blue blazers to embrace the victor.

Then, almost as good as any of these things in a less agitating way was the talk afterwards. I stood silent and awestricken among the heroes of old. There was one whose record had stood for seven and forty years and still stood at the end of the day, though it had a nasty shake; I swear I saw his jaw drop when the artist on the loud-speaker announced forty-eight and paused a second before coming to the four-fifths. There was another whose half-mile is immortal and I shook his revered hand. There was a third whom I had seen as a schoolboy when he won his first mile at Queen's Club, looking very prim and young with very large, round spectacles, and Oxford thought they could beat him and found themselves deliciously wrong. There was, to mention just one more, he who I had seen nearly forty years ago rolling down the straight at the end of a famous quarter with a famous red head behind him. These, and "such great men as these," had much to say of the tactics of the race. Ought the Cornell pacemaker to have gone faster for the first two laps? Why, when with Leach in close attendance he did draw some eight yards ahead, did Bonthron seem disinclined to go up and stayed behind with that pattering dark blue Nemesis at his heels? There was one there, a great ally of Cambridge and I think the shrewdest of them all, who when those first two laps were done foretold the end. The Americans, he said, were playing into Lovelock's hands, for if it was going to come to a finish, there was only one man who could win it.

What fun it all was! I could not help feeling that, exciting and agonizing as golf can be, it lacks a little something in that element of tactics. Perhaps it would be more than we could endure if it had it, and we ought to be thankful. At any rate, say what we will, it does lack it. Golf is a contest of temperament, but not of wits. We may be tactical in playing short of a bunker or taking a particular line, but that is only with the view of doing the hole as well as we think we can, not in order to outwit or bamboozle the enemy. We cannot say to ourselves, "All right, if he wants to do fives we will do fives too and come with a rush of fours at the end." If we attempted any such insanity we should be far more likely to come with a rush of sixes. Even in a qualifying round in score play the golfer cannot save up his best efforts for the real test to come; he cannot keep the ball out of the hole if it wants to go in, although he knows that, against his will, he is using up the ration of putts which is all the grudging Fates allow a mortal. No; all we can do at golf is to play as well as we can from the very start and to the very end. That is a very dull remark, perhaps, but it may be nearly the whole truth.

I remember a rather bombastic young gentleman, a very fine golfer, coming in much pleased with himself after the first round of a championship. He had been drawn against one who had beaten him in another tournament and he had had his revenge. "I was determined to have no nonsense about it this time," he proclaimed. "I went all out from the very start," and proceeded to reel off an imposing list of fours. "That's all very well," commented an eminent and long-suffering personage, "but suppose he had gone all out from the start too." The young gentleman was a little damped and could make no answer. Indeed there is no answer to make, for, as I said, there is nothing to do but to start as well as possible and keep it up as long as possible. A golfer is sometimes said to spurt and the word is permissible, for it conveys a picture, but his spurt is not like that of a runner, deliberately kept back waiting for the right moment. What, in fact, happened was that, having played badly, he began to play better; he would have liked to have done those fours and threes earlier in the round if he could and then he would not have needed them at the finish; there would not have been a finish because he would have been walking in triumphantly from the 14th green.

There are, to be sure, tactical methods of harassing the enemy, but our fellows do not think very well of us if we employ them. We must not walk fast if our opponent does not like being hurried—a method sometimes recommended by the older race of Scottish caddies; we must not lie on our stomachs interminably contemplating the line of the putt against one who is notoriously impatient of delay. We must not—perhaps most criminal of all—say that we should like to give our adversary a short putt but feel regretfully bound to see him hole it. There is something else in that matter of short putts which we ought not to do to him and yet I am sure we often do it, though not of malice aforethought. We concede with an airy grace a couple of short ones and then when he has a rather shorter one to tackle we stand silent, like graven images, contemplating the distant horizon. I have seen this highly effective course of conduct, but it is not a laudable one, and if we never gave short putts the question would not arise.

I heard the other day of a case of rather greater subtlety. *B* had two for it on the first green from a moderate distance and *A* at once gave him the hole. Said a friend to *A:* "That was rather a lot to give. I should have let him putt." *A* replied: "He might have holed in one and that would have given him confidence in his putting." Was this a permissible piece of tactics or was *A* rather too deep a dog? I am not prepared to give a verdict, but I am sure of this: that the oftener I am given the hole when I have two for it the better I shall be pleased.

Crime or Folly

The Times
1937

One day last week I was reading, perhaps with rather a drowsy eye, the account of a match at squash rackets when suddenly an arresting phrase woke me up. I gathered that So-and-so might have won but for making "shots of almost unbelievable folly at moments of great importance." I experienced an instant feeling of sympathy for the poor fellow. I also thought that here was a writer who could enrich my limited vocabulary against the next time when I had to describe the missing of a putt. So I read on to find the same player accused of "egregious error" and "ill-timed eccentricities." By now I was almost to tears on his behalf, but still I persisted. I wanted to discover, however painful it might be, what were the dreadful things he had done. Furthermore, since I have a bad habit of translating everything into terms of golf, there might be some analogy between his crimes and those which the more black-hearted of golfers commit.

His chief offenses appeared to have been two; the first that he tried to take a ball when he ought to have asked for a let; the second that being in one game within a stroke of victory he served—my pen falters in the transcription—"straight on to the tin." Heaven forbid that I should endeavor to excuse one of such palpably criminal instincts. Doubtless he deserved his fate, and yet in other ways he may be a most respectable man and I am still sorry for him.

When I come to turning this sad story into golfing language I am not sure that everything can be explained by "unbelievable folly." There seems to be a distinction between the two mistakes, to use a miserably small word. To serve the ball on the tin at game-ball is like topping the ball into a bunker in front of our noses at dormy one when the other fellow is really in trouble. It is the most deplorable stroke and one which the Fates will not forgive, but is it, strictly speaking, an act of folly? Poor wretches that we are, we do not do it on purpose, and not even our foursome partner, justly incensed though he be, can think that. It was simply that we would not act up to our doubtless admirable intentions. On the other hand, the not asking for a let was a deliberate act. A possible golfing equivalent is the playing of a ball out of a puddle when we might lift it out instead. That would be a folly, even if of an heroic nature.

Golf being a cold, calculating sort of game gives perhaps more scope for folly than any other. We have all the time in the world to make up our minds as to what is the wise thing to do and then we do the foolish one. Yet even so it is often hard to say exactly how foolish it was. We see a man go out for a long carry over a bunker or burn when he is playing the one off two, and we say in a furious whisper, "The man's a fool! Play short, you idiot!" We do not know, however, what is going on inside his head nor how frightened he may be of a short pitch. He may have coolly calculated all the chances and decided that he was more likely to get over with a brassie than with a mashie. I once saw a player at Westward Ho! who was dormy one in the semi-final of the championship; although his enemy had been in all manner of trouble, he lashed out at his second with a brassie and he jumped the burn! That looked an incredibly rash action, and yet he thought before he did it, and who shall say that he did not think rightly? He knew himself and the spectator did not.

Last year in a championship at Deal I saw a respected and illustrious friend of mine apparently take leave of his wits. He too was dormy one; both he and his enemy were at the foot of the bank in two, and a five would in all probability be good enough for the half and the match. Every individual hair on my head stood straight on end when I saw him, instead of knocking the ball up the slope with a putter or a straight-faced iron, take out his mashie niblick. It was a horrid little pitch to play at such a moment, and, sure enough, he fluffed it and lost the hole. When he had ultimately won the match at the 21st I ventured with infinite delicacy to ask what on earth had possessed him. He answered that he had had such bad "jitters" on the green that he felt as if he would miss the globe if he took his putter. Only those who have suffered from that fearful complaint can fully appreciate his action, which, though unsuccessful, may yet have been the wisest in the circumstances.

Last summer at St. Andrews I was very properly rebuked by another eminent friend while watching the final of the Amateur championship. In the first round Ferrier held a good lead from Hector Thomson after the 13th hole. Then he cut his tee shot over the wall out of bounds at the Long-hole-in and so gave his hardly pressed adversary a needed and heartening opportunity. I stigmatized it as a foolish shot at such a moment, but my friend would not have it. A man, he said, playing as well as Ferrier was then, got into a frame of mind of such concentrated confidence that he never thought of the possibility of going out of bounds. To do so might admittedly be disastrous, but even so it was much more than worth the risk to attain so happy a state. Being myself of a timorous and pessimistic frame of mind I could not speak from experience, but there was at any rate a good deal to be said for the contention and I withdrew the "foolish."

It is a shameful thing to confess, but I once very nearly called a Major-General foolish. He and I were partners in a wartime match—not a very important one—played by foursomes, and on the first green he was left with a putt of between two-foot and three-foot for the half. Our opponents, as all well-disciplined young soldiers should, exclaimed smartly in chorus, "That will do, Sir"; but the General insisted on trying that putt, and he missed it by several inches. His was a noble action, worthy of the best traditions of the British Army, but from a base commercial standpoint it was not a wise one, for the enemy could offer to give us no more putts and we missed all the ones that we were not given.

Bad Useful Golf

American Golfer
1924

I do not know what anonymous genius invented the expression "Good useless golf," but he said in three words what we most of us say in far too many when we have just lost a match. Indeed, I fancy that he said it, not with any conscious desire of turning a phrase, but in the hope of checking a flood of lamentable explanation that did not interest him.

Those three words generally imply an essential futility in the neighborhood of the green and an incapacity to take chances. We may spurt, but we always wait just too long before doing so. We are never beaten by much, but we are always beaten.

The opposite of this admirable phrase is less often heard, and yet "bad useful golf" conveys just as pithily and distinctly a common state of affairs. No single tee shot is clearly hit: the ball is, as a rule, smothered or half-topped, and has a touch of slice on it, and yet it always evades the bunker by inches. The iron shots are poor things, mistimed and pushed out; still they scramble onto the green somehow; generally by means of a lucky kick. And the putting and chipping from off the edge of the green are, of course, beyond reproach. The doubtful putts are all holed, and two or three long ones stagger into the cup.

In fact, our game is a long drawn out series of "two of those and one of them" followed by a "plop" or "plunk"—or any other agreeable onomatopoeic word—against the back of the tin, the whole making up what is humorously called a par four. Par indeed! And yet a succession of such fours are undeniably and horribly useful, not merely for their intrinsic merits, such as they are, but because they are apt to impair the enemy's courage more effectually than the most flawless golf.

I played just such a round only the other day, and my feelings alternated throughout between an impish glee and utter shame. I was the more ashamed because my young adversary bore it all, not merely with a stoical courtesy but with a smiling face, whereas I knew that, had we changed places, I should have been either tearful, or apoplectic, or both.

If this bad useful golf is to be as useful as possible we should observe certain rules of conduct. We should accept it for what it is, and not try for the moment to improve upon it. We should say with somebody in the Battle of Lake Regillus, "The gods, who live forever, are on our side today," and leave the matter in their hands accordingly. If we take thought about the drives, they may possibly go a little farther, but they will lose their invulnerable quality. The ball will then go "plop" into the bunker, not into the hole. The kind of golf we are playing may be of a very poor kind, but it is better than none at all, and we must recognize this as quickly as possible.

On the other hand we must also recognize the fact that it will not happen next time and, before we play again, we must physic ourselves, in a golfing sense, severely. There is only the difference of about a quarter of an inch on the putting green between the "bad useful" and the "bad useless," which is the lowest stage of all.

Although we acknowledge in our inmost hearts that we are for this one round under heavenly protection, we must never say so aloud; no, not even if we follow what we say with some superstitious safeguard such as "knock on wood." We must never assert the plain truth of the matter: that it makes no difference how we stroke the ball since a pitch is sure to be close and a putt sure to go in. The Gods of Golf simply will not tolerate any impiety. To say "I have been putting well" is blasphemous; "I am putting well" is fatal.

The other day I was playing in a friendly team match, and at luncheon one of the other side, who had won his single, explained his victory by the statement that he was not much good at anything else, but he *could* hole putts. He said this with the utmost modesty; it was in truth not a boast but an apology, and yet I could not help feeling that here was a man defying lightning. When I found that he was to be one of my opponents in the foursomes after lunch, my hopes rose high, nor were they disappointed. The poor soul could hardly ever lay the ball dead. It was a truly pathetic sight. His partner became infected with the same microbe. Worse, neither could hole it even when it was dead. It was an awful warning.

In Mr. Eric Parker's Eton Anthology, there is a pleasant story of a member of the cricket eleven who declared that he was put out because he omitted some particular, superstitious formula of his before the ball was pitched. Mr. R. A. H. Mitchell replied—and one can hear the uncompromising tone in which he said it—"You'll be put out with that stroke no matter what you do."

That, no doubt, represents the braver and more commonsense view, but for myself I prefer to remain a slave to my own heathenish beliefs. Indeed, this article is only a humble thanksgiving to the hidden powers that befriended me last week, and a plea for further favors on the next occasion—it will come all too soon—when I am driving like an old lady and pitching like a small child.

Absit Omen

Country Life
1941

Golfers will do anything in reason to avert the evil chance. If we meet a friend, whom we suspect of doing well, in the course of a medal round and are so indiscreet or so inhuman as to ask his score, it is ten to one that he will answer us with vague generalities and conjectures that he is sure to come to grief before he has done. Similarly, no one who is playing a match in a tournament willingly says that he is three up; the most that he will admit is that he is "doing pretty well at present." Nor is this said from any desire to spare his adversary's feelings; it springs wholly from a fear of provoking some terrible Nemesis. These phenomena are indeed so well known that I should be almost ashamed to mention them again did they not lead up to a rather different and singular instance of "touch-woodishness," if I may so term it.

I have just received a long and pleasant letter from a young friend of mine, a very good golfer, who, having been till lately playing in Trinidad, is now, when he gets the chance, struggling with the sand greens of Nigeria. He, too, wants to avert the evil chance, but it is, as will be seen, an altruistic desire. He has developed a habit of doing holes in one, and as sure as ever he does it some frightful public catastrophe ensues. The first time was in the meeting at Westward Ho! before he went abroad. That was on September 1, 1939. He had never achieved the feat before, but his pleasure was short-lived; a passing caddie told him that the Germans had invaded Poland. In the following year he was playing on a short course in Trinidad, and again holed his tee shot. It was the very day that the German hordes poured into Holland and Belgium. So now he is frightened of playing golf lest the malignancy of Fate should not yet have worked itself out and a third one should produce something still worse.

I have endeavored to exorcise these fears by telling him that the third time is lucky, and further that I did a hole in one during the last war, in Macedonia, without producing any visible effect on the campaign one way or the other. It was a beautiful hole (I laid it out myself), and it was in a way unique. It was played twice in the round from diametrically opposite tees, and was at once the first hole and the last of the round. A better natural green I never saw, for it consisted of a small hollow, very shallow, set on a low hilltop, with the ground falling away on every side. The first hole was comparatively simple, since only a mashie-niblick pitch was needed and there was nothing worse than broken ground in the way. The last, as was only proper, was more testing; the tee shot was considerably longer, and the bank guarding the green steeper, while between tee and green stretched an oozy and ominous piece of marsh. It was a lovely green, with one engaging little tree casting a patch of starveling shade upon its verge, and I have never either forgotten or forgiven the RE's who, in the watches of the night, cut down the tree and stripped off the turf for their own base purposes. My only consolation was and is that no one else could ever again do it in one.

When, by the way, I did it, it was at the last hole and not the first, so that there was no fear of any personal golfing disaster overwhelming me. Fate could not harm me; the round was ended, and that, for most ordinarily excitable people, is a not unimportant point. These flukes in the grand manner are apt to have a disturbing effect, and therefore it is well that they should come as late in the round as possible. If they happen early, we are rather light-headed for a hole or two afterwards, and before we settle down again Fate will take its chance.

Not many courses have a last hole that can be done in one, but a notable exception is Prestwick, where the last green is within reach of a modern full shot; the books set it down as 283 yards long. I remember that on one occasion in the Army Championship a gallant officer holed his tee shot there, and that must have been a thoroughly dramatic occasion, with the seats outside the clubhouse filled with spectators. However, as he had taken, if I remember rightly, ten to the first hole, perhaps his transports were modified. There was a very famous one done at Prestwick at the seventeenth in the days of the old twelve-hole course. That was in the Open Championship, by Jamie Anderson in his last round; so he had not much time in which to lose his head. In any case he had given sufficient proofs of imperturbability, for at the fifteenth he had holed a full iron shot and at the sixteenth a very long putt. I have always felt sorry for the man who was second in that Championship; I think he had very good cause to complain of destiny, for after that series of outrages Jamie Anderson won by one single shot.

We should be better golfers than we are if we could overcome the feeling that the Fates, after favoring us grossly, are sure to turn against us. It is much too strong for most of us. To hole one or two good putts is eminently encouraging, for we think, truly enough, that we are hitting the ball well and we have confidence in our latest new method, whatever may be. But when the putts are too long or too frequent, then we grow afraid and make perhaps the most lethal of remarks, that we must have had our ration. I have heard something like it said by one of the calmest and sanest, as he is one of the best, of golfers, Mr. Francis Ouimet. It was in the Amateur Championship at Deal in 1923. In the morning he had to play one very fine player—I think it was Mr. Tolley, but I am away from books. At any rate, the putts went in from everywhere and Mr. Ouimet won easily. In the afternoon it was the semi-final and he met Mr. Wethered. Now the ball obstinately refused to go in and he was more or less easily beaten, and said afterwards that he could not get away from feeling that he had had his full day's allowance in the morning.

One of the wonderful things, as I remember it, of the late Mr. W. J. Travis's win at Sandwich in 1904 was that he holed some really long putts in every round, certainly in every round after he had begun to attract attention and the American terror had spread across the links. If he ever allowed himself to think that he had had his ration, he showed no signs of it. Indeed, the vision, as I recall it, of that slight, serious figure, black cigar in mouth, watching the ball as it ran towards the hole, rather conveyed that he expected it to drop every time. He was not only a superb putter, but he had a new club, the Schenectade, and faith in a new putter can sometimes endure for a considerable spell. I rather hope my young friend in Nigeria will not buy a new iron. If he does he is sure to hole another tee shot with catastrophic results.

Silence Is Golden

Country Life
1949

There is no rule of golf laying down what one may or may not say to one's opponent, but I gather from a paragraph that I have just read that it is otherwise at Association football. No referee can insist upon the game being played in absolute silence, and a player can call out to one of his own side "so long as he uses no ungentlemanly expression." On the other hand, if he calls out to one of the other side, and so causes his attention to be distracted, dire things can befall him. He may be deemed guilty of ungentlemanly conduct, he may be cautioned and finally "an indirect free kick" (I am not learned enough to know what that means) may be ordered. Here is an example which will make an instant appeal to a friend of mine. The one rule of all rules of golf that he really wants made is to deal with the opponent who says, "I am afraid that at this stage of the match I must ask you to hole that one." I am not sure what the penalty is to be, probably "something lingering, with boiling oil." Generally speaking he wants the wretch to lose the hole and match, to be disqualified, kicked out of the club, blackballed for all other clubs, and in short, wiped off the face of the earth.

I agree with him that the offense is a heinous one, but I think that perhaps he underestimates the difficulty of drafting a rule to meet it. What, for instance, is the exact form of words to be penalized? "I should like to give you that one, but I mustn't," is, for instance, a variant equally criminal. I remember it, sad to say, being used on the last green in a championship, and with the natural—I refrain from saying the desired—result: the putt was ruined, and the villain, unconscious or deliberate, went on to win at the nineteenth or twentieth. To hole the first of two short putts and exclaim in an ecstasy of relief "First half," is another action wholly to be deprecated, and it is conceivable that some form of words might be devised against such remarks, or indeed against any remark at all made before the opponent plays his putt. I do not think it would be wise, though it would no doubt be possible.

There is, however, a good deal to be done without any speech at all, and I have a shameful feeling that I may have done it myself. The mere looking at the other fellow's putt, as if debating whether to give it to him or not, does not improve his frame of mind or his chances of holing it, and yet we have most of us probably been guilty. I remember that in wartime some evacuees insisted on leaving their comfortable place of refuge and returning to the danger zone on the ground that they did not like "the way the butler looked," and the way some people look at our putts is in the highest degree objectionable. I have seen people of the most incontestable honor hole their own putt, extend a club to the enemy's ball as if about to knock it away, and then think better of this generous impulse. There is no legislation possible against such deeds, which are indeed done quite unconsciously. For that matter the really dreadful remark which I began by quoting may proceed from the agitation of the moment, or a sadly mistaken notion of politeness. There is, I am afraid, nothing to be done save to try hard not to do these things ourselves, and never again to play with anybody who does them more than once. As with a dog, a first bite may be allowed, but that is all.

I recall the late sir Ernley Blackwell, a great stickler for the observation of rules, and a man of the most perfect golfing manners, saying "If a man looks to see whether he has laid me a stymie I consider it an impertinence." That is a truly formidable expression, but there are occasions on which it is justified. I suppose there is no one who, as he sees his ball apparently blocking his opponent's way, has not taken a mere passing glance to discover how effective is the blockade. That is only human, but if an opponent, having laid us a stymie, takes a prolonged survey of the situation, perhaps going down on hands and knees to that end, he is fully worthy of Sir Ernley's condemnation. There is only one further offense that he can commit: he can say, "I don't think it's a stymie. I've left you room." For that it seems to us at the moment that even his heart's blood would not atone.

The putting green is the most prolific scene of what those so scrupulous football players would call ungentlemanly conduct, but there are other occasions. To stand too closely over an opponent in a bunker is either an act of utter ghoulishness or implies an offensive doubt of his veracity. As Horace Hutchinson once very properly wrote, "There is no justification for the audible enumeration one by one of his strokes," and in this matter of enumeration there is no one that I have more whole-heartedly desired to kill than he who, in a friendly match, insists on writing down my score in a horrid little book. If he wants to keep his own he must be allowed to do so, but why should he unasked keep mine? He is the kind of man of whom it was once said, "When I play with So-and-so I always leave my niblick behind." Well, well, that is one of the things that can never happen to me again. A very famous judge once said to a friend of mine: "I am afraid when I was at the Bar I must have done many improper things; in fact, I know I did." So I know I did many improper and highly irritating things when I played golf, and it is some little comfort for playing no more that I cannot now be guilty.

There still remains, however, the risk of saying improper things as a spectator, and that I shall doubtless continue to do. One who once played for Oxford and is now a distinguished KC still reproaches me with something I said when he put his second shot at the home hole through the clubhouse window at Rye in the University match. Upon the honor of a poor gentleman I did not mean him to hear it, but I doubt if he quite believes me, and at any rate that is no excuse; he did hear me. Some spectators' voices (mine no doubt among them) have an unfortunate power of carrying. The thought of Rye brings back to me the sound of Arthur Croome's voice growling away in the distance as I am trying to play a critical shot. He was wholly unconscious and he spoke low, but the carry of his voice was immense. How pleasant if only one could hear it again.

There is nothing to be done to spectators, not even a free kick. I remember some long time ago that in a professional tournament, I think at Gleneagles, the marker made a mistake in the cards of two eminent players, putting down a four to *X* and a five to *Y* at a particular hole instead of vice-versa. Everybody, players, spectators and all, were certain as to the fact and there arose some question as to what was to be done. Then up spoke one who was, incidentally, a member of the Rules of Golf Committee. "Its perfectly simple," he said. "You disqualify the marker." On the same principle you might no doubt disqualify the spectator. More effective than that, you might warn him off the course, as delinquents in the world of horses are warned off Newmarket Heath. That is an alarming thought. I must mind my "p's" and "q's" and maintain the most discreet silence, lest I be escorted off the links by a guard armed with blasters. I really shall try to behave myself.

The Golfer and the Crossword

Playing the Like
1934

The early stages of a new year almost inevitably bring to many golfers the reflection that the time of improvement is for them past and over.

It is a saddening thought, because whatever the pastime, there is no fun comparable with that of improving at it. Take the humblest possible instance, that of bicycling. Can we not even now remember the first unaided wobble? At any rate, I can do so with the most exquisite thrill. Throughout one whole, hot Sunday afternoon a kind father had propped me up as I swayed hither and thither across the lawn. Suddenly, almost without my knowing it, the prop had been withdrawn and was mopping its brow, and there I was "sailing," so to speak, "with supreme dominion" by myself. And there followed an even more poignant experience, the fist venture on the road. It was the Huntingdon road at Cambridge, and it is not in any way a beautiful one, being straight, flat, and hemmed in on one side by rather ignominious houses. Fierce old Cobbett might have called it "as vile a spot as ever I saw." Yet on that shining September evening, as I rode my new bicycle then (second-hand *Grand Modèle de Luxe*), palm trees appeared to bloom along its borders, while jeweled birds sang in the branches.

The moral would appear to be that we should periodically begin a new game so as to taste the supreme joy of emerging from abject dufferdom. Alas! the supply of suitable games is apt to run out. Were some of us, for instance, to take up the noble game of rackets, we should doubtless improve at it for about a quarter of an hour, but our improvement would be cut short by apoplexy. About this time last year I believed during the space of one whole, happy day that I was improving at a somewhat less exactingly athletic game, Corinthian bagatelle, and then the meteor of my enthusiasm "dropped and in a flash expired." This January a purely intellectual and therefore sedentary sport has given me the longed-for sensation; I have been improving at crossword puzzles.

Most people have, I know, played the game so long by this time that they know and can confound all the knavish tricks of those who devise such devilries, but I had always stood out. It chanced, however, last week, that I was staying in a holiday house, and after we struggled round the golf course we did the crossword puzzle in committee. One of our number—not I—wielded the pencil and read out the clues, and the rest made suggestions. Let not "grandeur hear with a disdainful smile" of our laborious plodding; we took a long time over it; we were not, I suppose, very good; indeed I know I was not, but I did improve, and how heavenly that was!

Gradually and imperceptibly the beginner's wits sharpen; he comes to understand the mind, if I may so term it, of his adversary; he even admires those stratagems which at first he has regarded as not being cricket. The men who set crossword puzzles do not "play cricket," but once allowance is made for that fact it must be acknowledged that they are clever, if rather dirty, dogs. The beginner ceases gradually to hate them and enjoys the encounter as a kind of all-in wrestling, in which everything is permissible. Now and again he is almost sorry for them, so quickly and easily does he circumvent their wiles. Inspiration comes to him in brilliant spurts. There was one evening last week when we went in to dinner having four problems still unsolved, and with the preliminary glass of sherry I—*moi qui vous parle*—had, unaided and after a long period of utter sterility, solved three of them in one gorgeous rush. And then the foe turned like a rat in a trap and defied us for hours.

It was only after we had given our poor brains a good long rest by means of bridge or billiards that in one last desperate sitting we won the match. Certainly it was a vast relief to go to bed knowing that no horrid imp would perch on the pillow and wake us, saying, "Ha, ha! I am twenty-three across and you can't guess me"; but it was impossible not to feel that the moral victory rested with the setter of the problem.

The childish ups and downs of joy and sorrow are not for the mature golfer. He realizes it in the fullness of time all too clearly and envies, not without bitterness, those who are so young, either in actual years or in golfing years, that they can look forward to a genuine and lasting improvement. The world has few things better to give. There was a certain bunker at the home hole on the old nine-hole course at Felixstowe, and once upon a time with the last tee shot of the last round on the last day of a summer holiday, I carried it for the first time—carried it by at least two yards. I can still see that ball flying, and I declare that it seems to have angel's wings. The next summer I could carry the bunker easily and every time, and that is the beauty of improvement in its earlier stages; there is no heart-breaking going back. Memory skips on seven years or so to another occasion to be marked with a white stone—a scratch medal won on one day with eighty-six (I don't know what the other people were about), and on the very next day, in a Bogey competition, a seventy-six and the proud colonel in the dust, seven holes down.

This egotism must be forgiven. I only set down these memories in order to stimulate others to recall with a joyful sadness their own doubtless far more glorious ones. And now the immediate question I have to decide is whether or not to embark on crossword puzzles all by my little self. It is one thing to be a member of a band of brothers all engaged in the adventure, and quite another to face unsupported that grim, uncompromising pattern of blacks and whites. When one is in company there is always the chance of a little innocent dishonesty; one can shout a fraction of a second after somebody else and pretend that one shouted first, but now I am alone.

On the whole it would perhaps be wisest to be an epicure in delightful sensations, to save them up. I do not think I shall do any more puzzles till I visit again, supposing that I am bidden, that pleasant house set on a hill. Then once again I shall be able to delude myself into the heavenly belief that I am getting better and better.

The Golfer's Cigarette

Country Life
1947

At this time, when we are exhorted on patriotic grounds or compelled on economic ones to reduce our smoking, it may be appropriate to consider the question in relation to the golfer. The average golfer has acquired the habit of smoking a good deal in the course of his round. Sometimes in moments of crisis to soothe his agitated feelings, sometimes in exquisite surcease when the crisis is over; and, if he makes good resolutions, he will feel the want of tobacco fully as poignantly as any other man. I am not yet prepared to say from the evidence of my own eyes whether he has made, or rather whether he has kept, those resolutions. I am writing some little time after St. Andrews and Carnoustie and trying to remember how much the players smoked.

Some of the American victors certainly seemed to me to light a good many cigarettes, but I am not sure that they smoked them to the end. I thought rather that they lighted them at crucial instants and then threw them away after a few relieving puffs as the illustrious Bobby Jones used to do. In any case, I fancy they had brought their own native brands with them and so could not lacerate Mr. Dalton's feelings. I know that my old friend, Francis Ouimet, gave me several which did not emanate from this country. They were not Lucky Strikes, such as I had smoked in 1922, but they had much the same flavor and reminded me pleasantly of the National and the Country Club and the now remote days of the first match. As to our own players, they certainly had an occasional cigarette, but I would not go further than that in any generalization. I can provide no damning evidence either for the Chancellor of the Exchequer or for those who are forever trying to discover some reason, such as the lack of calories, why we lost, beyond the fact that the other side played just a bit better.

It is curious to remember that once upon a time, and not really so very long ago, it was not deemed the right thing to smoke in a match of importance. Freddie Tait was very fond of his pipe, but on a great occasion he would give it to a friend in the crowd to carry and take every now and then a few surreptitious puffs. I recall a story told me by an old friend now dead and a good Hoylake golfer in his day, Edmund Spencer, who was an inveterate smoker. He reached the last eight of the Amateur Championship at Muirfield in 1897, and while playing his final match heard an indignant Scottish spectator exclaim, "I should like to knock his cigarette out of his mouth." That was certainly an extreme view and already, I should have thought, a little out of date because another Hoylake golfer, Harold Hilton, had by that time become a familiar spectacle with his perpetual cigarette. At any rate, it is a good many years since smoking could be held to show any disrespect for an occasion or an opponent. If anything, it shows too great a respect rather than frivolity or lightness of heart.

There have been many great golfers who have been great smokers, but if I had to choose the three most famous and most typical, I should say Harold Hilton for cigarettes, Ted Ray for pipes and Walter Travis for cigars. Ray's pipes were incidentally always a source of interest to me because they had, if I may so express it, curly shafts. I do not know how it may be with other people, but when I have tried to play with a pipe in my mouth I have always been afraid of hitting it with my arm, and with grave danger to my teeth, in the act of following through. That was with an ordinary straight pipe, and the danger would seem to be greater with a bent one. However, it did not seem to trouble Ray, who never took his pipe out of his mouth, and there was certainly no lack of rude vigor in his follow through. The cigar-smoking golfer has always been a comparative rarity, and Walter Travis's cigar created a great impression at Sandwich in 1904. It was such a very black and formidable cigar and accorded so perfectly with his rather sinister air. There seemed something as calculated and devilish about it as there was about those long putts that nothing could keep out of the hole. It made him look what he was, a killer.

For the ordinary mortal—and I am thinking of happier and cheaper days—a cigar has just the opposite significance. It stands for a jovial, post-prandial foursome, in which nothing greatly matters. There is about it an essential lack of seriousness. Either all is well with the world, or, if it is ill, it is so very ill that it is vain to repine. In an old article on golf at St. Andrews (it was published in the *Cornhill* in 1867), there is an account of a foursome, in which two partners, Browne and Gurney by name, are not hitting it off very well, owing to Browne's habit of sending wild tee shots into the whins. There is "another search, another ineffectual uprooting of a whin, and Gurney again emerges, but this time, wonderful to relate, with a comparatively cheerful countenance. He takes out his cigar-case, lights a cigar, and walks along contentedly smoking it, and apparently enjoying the scenery. This is a fatal sign. When a man smokes, he is either winning very easily or has given up all hope of winning." Today that last statement may still be applied to cigars but not to smoking in general and assuredly not to a cigarette.

There is a great variety of golfing cigarettes. There is the one that a man lights on the tee just to steady him and help him over the first hole. There is the one, particularly applicable to medal rounds, which follows a disaster in a bunker leading to a six or a seven. There is, in a match, the one that is felt to be absolutely necessary when a nice little winning lead of three up or so has suddenly been reduced to a single hole. There is the cigarette to be smoked at the turn, irrespective of the state of the game, but because the turn is a definite occasion and an occasion calls for tobacco. Finally and most blissful is the dormy cigarette, when the player feels that

> . . . *nor steel, nor poison,*
> *Malice domestic, foreign levy, nothing,*
> *Can touch him further.*

There are doubtless many other kinds, for I have enumerated only five, and I heard a golfer of distinction admit the other day that he had smoked nine and twenty—and done a 74—before lunch. Let me hasten to add that it was also before the Budget. It is very hard to prove whether tobacco does us any good, but we think it does. Similarly those who have acquired, as I have, the habit of smoking while we write, think it helps us to find the right word. It may, in fact, be quite the wrong word, but we get along with the sentence which is hanging fire. We are like Charles Surface who said he never lost if he threw on a bottle of champagne, or at least that he never felt his losses. But today these are all academic questions since we are, of course, doing what Mr. Dalton tells us.

A Fresh Start

Playing the Like
1934

A kind correspondent has written telling me of something that has lately befallen him, and suggesting that I make an article out of the event. I am delighted to try, but the difficulty is that while setting me the exercise he does not tell me precisely how he wishes it treated. It is not quite clear whether I am to be sorry for him or to envy him. Both methods of treatment are possible, and readers must judge for themselves which is the more appropriate.

The facts are that he plays golf on a course of which the club-house was lately burned down. He and some hundred other golfers have thus lost their clubs and their club bags and their golfing garments; even their very boots have been consumed by the devouring element, and with the aid of the insurance company they have got to begin life all over again.

A golfer's first instinct is to be dreadfully sorry for his fellow thus bereft. I picture him searching disconsolate amid the still smoldering ruins, coming across some twisted mass of metal, unrecognizable save by affection's eye and saying with bitter frivolity, "Alas, poor Yorick! I knew it, Horatio, a niblick of infinite jest." Even the charred toe of an ancient boot may awaken in his mind beautiful memories of monthly Bogeys. Boots have a poetry of their own. I was once lent a pair in which to play a game of football, when old enough to know better, and as I reflected that those very boots had, while covering immortal feet, kicked a ball for the Old Carthusians against proud Preston, tears came into my eyes. Think, too, of a coat (for I like to believe that my correspondent plays in the habit of an old-fashioned gentleman), an aged coat pleasantly wrinkled, its ragged cuffs bound, perhaps, with leather, with all its grays turned green, and a comfortable rent under one of the armpits. Not all Savile Row's horses and Savile Row's men can set up such a coat as that again.

That is the pathetic side of the picture, and the pathos of it could only be more unbearable than it is if these were the days of wooden shafts before the coming of matched sets of clubs. In those happy, far-off times the collecting of a pack of clubs was the work of years; one had been picked up here and one there, and every club had its own history; a shaft was a living thing with an individuality of its own, and when it died it left a gap in society. Today complacent owners do not ask you to waggle reverentially a particular shaft; they bid you admire a whole numbered series. If, as I assume, the victim of the flames uses steel-shafted clubs, his bereavement is not what it might once have been, for there are as good shafts in the shop as ever came out of it; the widower will soon be able to console himself, not for the loss of one, but for that of a whole seraglio. "Wot 'ud become of the undertakers vithout it, Sammy?" said Mr. Weller, senior, when philosophizing about the death of his wife, and perhaps my correspondent may find comfort in reflecting on what would become of the club-makers.

Having tried gradually to induce in him a mood of pious resignation, I think I may now open fire (if he will forgive the use of that word) with the full batteries of my cheerfulness. The fact is that I am rather jealous of him than otherwise. What fun he will have roaming through the shops weighing, waggling, and appraising! And he will be able to do it with a clear conscience at somebody else's expense. It may be that for a long time he had felt that some of his clubs were not quite what they ought to be, but had been held back by a tenderness for his wife or his children or even for the poor tax collector. I knew a man once who, in a moment of fury (I think he had lost by 9 and 8), made a bonfire of all his clubs, with his boots on the top of it. He enjoyed himself very much in replacing them, and he had a bad conscience and no insurance company at his back. What magic wands my correspondent will be able to buy without a qualm! How silver-shining will be their shafts, and how sweet a clangor will they make in that new bag complete with "zip" fasteners! Why, the man ought to have danced round the blazing clubhouse with maniacal glee.

Nor is the question of clothes wholly unworthy of his consideration. I said that I hoped he played in a coat, and so I do, but I cannot conceal from myself that it is more probable that he wears woollies of many colors, and leather jerkins. If so, he will be able to peacock it in such finery that he will be taken, until he swings his club, for an American professional on a visit. His knickerbockers will be plus anything he pleases, and his feet will be shod not in somber black, but in the chastest white creations over which meander glistening little rivulets of brown leather or perchance even of blue.

Clubs do not make the player, neither do clothes, but at least it will be given to him to do what very few other golfers have ever done—namely, to start again with a completely clean sheet, with nothing to remind him of past failures. As I write about him I begin to feel a certain incendiary itch coming over me. There stand my clubs, with which I lost innumerable holes only the other day; there is my old coat, which has been repeatedly condemned by the domestic authorities, and here, at my very elbow, is a box of matches. It is only with an effort that I restrain myself.

The Black Flag

Country Life
1933

A kind correspondent has lately written to me about a golf match played for a unique stake, which could not offend those holding the most tremendous views on the wickedness of gambling. As a guarantee of good faith he has told me the name of one of the players, the course where they play, and the town where they live; but these, as Dr. Watson used to say, "for obvious reasons I suppress."

Every Sunday these four players play two four-ball matches, in which the sides are always the same. No filthy lucre changes hands, but if either couple ever lose both matches they are bound under the most solemn oath to appear at their work on the following morning each wearing a black tie. So singular a vow has, naturally, not escaped the notice of their friends, who scan the Monday morning's neckwear of the combatants with the closest scrutiny, and if the black banner of defeat is seen it is hailed with heartless and uproarious merriment.

The case of the losers is fully as hard as that of our old friends of 1651, James Rodger, Johne Rodger, Johne Howdan and George Patersone, who were "complained upon for playing at the golf upon ane Lord's day," and, having confessed their "prophaning," were "ordained to make their public repentance the next day." No penitent, I am told, ever donned the white sheet with more sensible shrinking than they do their black, and they have even tried to avoid the extreme disgrace by the most transparent subterfuges, such as the putting on of a tie bearing the minutest white spots. Instant discovery has, however, always ensued, to be followed by the exaction of heavy though nameless penalties.

Black is obviously the right color, in so far as it suggests mourning for lost holes, and yet I can conceive ties which might cause the wearers far greater agonies. As it is now, they are the victims only of their immediate circle. The ordinary citizen who sits opposite them in the train or passes them in the street is not a penny the wiser; but supposing they had to wear ties bearing a horribly garish combination of stripes; then everybody that met them would, as De Quincey said in *Murder as a Fine Art*, "ogle their throats." It is true that the said everybody would not know what they had done; he would only deem them insane, but that would be hard to bear. I have myself a drawer which is a moraine of ties ancient and modern. There are one or two that occasionally come to the surface, as I search feverishly for the one I want, and whenever I see them a shudder goes through me. There is one in particular that I ought to have worn when representing a distinguished club last year. By a strong effort I actually put it on, but I found that I really could not face my breakfast in it, and had to substitute something a little more peaceful. If those four golfers would like the recipe I shall send it them, and I can assure them that they will be glad to return to their present badge of defeat.

It would be interesting to have some statistics of how often this black flag has to be hoisted. Perhaps it is not very often. It may be that the pair who win in the morning are overcome by an agreeable "dormy" sensation and luxuriate in their lunch accordingly, to the detriment of their afternoon's play. They may even feel sorry for the other side and let them off easily, but I scarcely think they do that; I believe, rather, that they apply themselves to the second round with a certain jovial malignity and a desire to have their prowess well advertised to their friends on the Monday morning. Here, however, I am only guessing, and that is a crime that as a schoolboy one was always told not to commit under the direst impositions.

How many matches these four golfers have played altogether, history does not record, but, at any rate, they still keep their reckoning by holes. I have heard of two old friends and regular opponents who thought holes too small and niggling a method of scoring and reckoned their gains and losses purely by matches. They played together nearly every day, and towards the end of the year the tension became great, since one or other of them might be five or six matches up with only twenty or so to play. To be dormy on the year's play was a glorious moment. In one year, if I remember rightly, one of the parties, finding himself a serious number of matches down, took a holiday, went to the seaside and had a series of lessons from a distinguished professional. Thus fortified, he came back and soon turned his deficit of matches into a profit.

In America golfers seem to have the habit of belonging to regular "foursomes" (I am afraid they are really four-ball matches) and playing the same match together at weekend after weekend. If this habit is growing in England, then it may be the result of the motor car. This interesting piece of speculation is not mine, but belong to Colonel A. N. Lee, who is this year the captain of the Notts Golf Club. He has revived the cheerful custom of a club dinner, which had fallen into desuetude since the war, and I had the pleasure of being a guest. In his speech Colonel Lee pointed out that in old days all the golfers went out to Hollinwell by one of two morning trains, according to their laziness or their industry, and returned by the same train in the evening. Thus everybody knew everybody else, and the man who had no match could pick one up in the train.

Today everybody goes to golf in a car, and the same four players are apt to go and come back together, to the loss of general sociability. I had not thought of it before, but I expect he is right. No doubt the car is a blessed invention. Nevertheless, what fun it used to be, in dim ages past, going down to Woking in a slow and early train from Waterloo, stampeding down the platform at the other end for a good place in the wagonette, stampeding again up the path to the clubhouse to get a good place on the tee. The journey back, too, had its charms, even though the day was a very long one, and it was then that matches were made for the next weekend. Golf was a very sociable game then, or was it only that we were all rather younger and keener and pleasanter people?

That is a difficult question, but I have a very soft spot in my heart for those old train journeys in dear departed second-class carriages with such nice cheap tickets. Certainly I used to put on—metaphorically—a mournful black tie on the Monday morning when I thought that there were five or even five and a half days to be spent in an odious office before the journey and wagonette and the *sauve qui peut* rush for the tee came round again. Not even the two defeated ones of my story can ever have felt more thoroughly depressed. I do hope none of them will have to exhibit those dreadful symbols next Monday.

Mixed Foursomes

Country Life
1921

I have just been engaged in an affair at once daring and delicate. I have screwed up my courage to make a proposal to a lady—to be my partner in a mixed foursome tournament. I am glad to say that she did not keep me in suspense "according," as Mr. Collins said in *Pride and Prejudice*, "to the usual practice of elegant females," and I now have an admirable partner to pull me along in what should be a most entertaining competition. This tournament is to take place at Worplesdon on October 24, 25 and 26, and ought to be delightfully novel and interesting. Really good mixed doubles at golf are rare. We have seen the best ladies engaged in pitched battles against good men, but, on the whole, it is better fun to watch them playing against each other, because in the Stoke Poges fights they have sometime seemed rather crushed by mere brute force. In a mixed foursome they will not suffer in that respect, and their extreme accuracy ought to make them most valuable allies. I shall be surprised if some of the couples do not play rounds very nearly, if not quite, as good as the arrogant male partner could play all by himself.

Let us now pass from the rarified atmosphere of tournaments to the ordinary average mixed foursome, such as may be seen at the present moment on many seaside courses. It is a delightful amusement for those who play in it; not quite so delightful sometimes for those who play behind it. It would generally, I think, be better fun for all parties if it were played on the terms that the ladies drove from their own tees. I have occasionally fancied, when following in the wake of such a foursome on a "holiday" course, that it would be better if the gentlemen also adopted this modest policy; but that is another story. If the ladies decide heroically to drive from the men's tees they are sometimes confronted with carries such that their best shots must be bunkered, and that is no fun for anybody. If they drive from their own, then it should be an admirable game and one that always seems to me a fine test of the male golfer's skill and nerve. He must do everything he reasonably can to gain length, or else at the end of two shots there will be just a little bit of distance left over and the alliance will not reach the green in the orthodox number of strokes. At the same time he must not take big risks in the way of big bunkers because, once in a bunker, it is "the usual practice of elegant females" to stay there. The really good lady player is very good out of bunkers; there is, for instance, no greater artist in sand than Miss Grant Suttie, and Miss Leitch is likewise magnificent out of any abominably bad place. But there is, in this respect, a great gulf fixed between the very good and the ordinary; the average lady player never seems quite to have grasped the principle that the way to get out of a bunker is to clench the teeth and hit venomously and blasphemously hard; or perhaps it is that she has not the strength to act on it. At any rate, it is much the best policy not to give her the chance of doing so, and she has every right to complain of a partner who does not obey the cardinal rule of foursome golf and "keep the ball in play."

Again, the man has always to look ahead and consider whether he is leaving the lady to make too dangerous and desperate a frontal attack upon the green. Many a man is comparatively brave when he has a bunker in front of him and will make a good enough shot; what frightens him and makes him go crooked is a narrow way between flanking hazards. With the average lady player it is, I think, rather the other way. She is courageous and trustworthy when it is a question of steering between Scylla and Charybdis; but when there is a chasm between her and the flags her partner must await the result with nervously averted eyes. Because she is not, as a rule, very strong in the hands and wrists, she is not very good at getting the ball into the air, and moderately bad lie makes it proportionately much more difficult for her. The man must therefore do some maneuvering for position and remember that in a mixed foursome the longest way round is often the shortest way home.

The lady's nerve, too, is tested, and that in a particularly trying way. She knows, or she ought to know (her partner, if he is a reasonably gallant man, cannot tell her so) that whether she hits a little longer or shorter, whether she takes her brassie through the green or her driving iron, does not so very greatly matter. What is required of her is a high standard of blamelessness in small things—and steady putting. Now, we all know that the shot wherein nothing is wanted but that we should keep out of trouble, is just the one with which we go most crooked; also that when we particularly want to putt well we putt most ill. That being so, the poor lady's lot is not so very easy or happy a one. Of course, as I said before, all these rather unchivalrous remarks apply only to the common or garden foursome. At Worplesdon all I shall try to do is to hit the mildest little "shotties" down the course and my partner will do all the rest.

The Dissembling Golfer

Country Life
1922

I have lately been reading Mr. Sidney Fry's book on billiards, with very great interest if with no hope of improving my own game, which is, indeed, played but once a year and is wholly a matter of chance. In his chapter of reminiscences there is a story of how, by way of a small joke, he was once introduced to a fellow guest as Mr. "Roast" instead of Mr. Fry, and under that title played him two matches, one at billiards and the other at golf. At billiards he managed to dissemble and make a close match of it by playing left-handed, with occasional, and for the most part, undetected, recourse to his right hand in case of emergency. At golf he masqueraded as a twelve handicap player, his opponent being fourteen, and here he was a less polished actor or else his energy gave out, for he won too easily, by 6 and 5.

The story set me thinking how very difficult it is to dissemble at golf. It is not, of course, a thing to be done seriously; but most of us have tried to do it at one time or another, either in a "rag" game or out of some momentary feeling of pity towards a completely crushed opponent, and we have generally made but a poor job of it. I have once seen it extraordinarily well done by somebody else in a foursome that was intended by two of the parties to come, by hook or by crook, to the last hole. My friend, whom I will call G., a very fine golfer, and I were the two tigers of the party; the two rabbits play golf only once a year. They both played for all they were worth, and for a while the match was closely fought. But my poor rabbit, who was not very well, fell away: he missed the ball twice at one hole, both times with his putter, and we became several holes down. Then G. rose to wonderful heights. Playing the one off three he drove the ball into inaccessible spots, with a most lifelike show of vexation. Once he was stymied, but the balls were but three inches apart, and a tactless caddie pointed out that the obstructing ball might be removed. "Ah, my boy," said G., "you aren't up to date. The rule has been changed"; and he forthwith knocked our ball into the hole in the most natural way in the world. Even so we were still one down with two to play: G. had a short putt on the seventeenth green to win the match, and our ball was on the other side of the hole. I waited breathlessly to see how his genius would find a way out. He did it by playing as brilliant a shot as ever I saw, just missing the hole, just touching our ball and cannoning off it at just such an angle as to leave his own rabbit a dead and hopeless stymie. And so the match was halved, and I really do not think that our two rabbits had any serious suspicions until the very end.

On a subsequent occasion I had to attempt something of the same sort myself, and then I realized to the full what a great man G. was. True, I missed a putt or two—anybody can do that—but it would not have availed if my fellow-tiger had not holed some very good ones, and that is a thing that very few people can do exactly when they want. As to my efforts in the long game, they were a miserable failure. I remember at one short-hole tee walking up to the ball with a fine assumption of reckless, devil-me-care swagger such as I hoped would produce a devastating top, and behold! the ball soared away beautifully, had a lucky kick into the bargain, and finished dead at the hole side. No, it is not an easy business to carry through with any artistic verisimilitude. The next time I essay it, I must remember the advice of one of the canniest and most cunning golfers of my acquaintance. This is, never to leave it to the green, where the fierce light of your opponent's eye beats right upon you, nor in any case to try deliberately to miss a shot, because you will probably hit it by mistake. The game is, he declares, to take the wrong club through the green. Then you may play a perfectly respectable shot that will escape notice. If you under-club yourself, the ball, though well enough struck, will quite naturally fall into the bunker short of the green; if you over-club, it will plunge into the deep heather beyond it. Your judgement may be impugned, but not your *bona fides*.

There is, if I remember rightly, in one of Harry Vardon's books a story of how, on his first visit to America, he and some brother professionals visited on an off-day a little rustic course. For several holes they amused themselves by pretending to be beginners and asking their caddies to instruct them; then, growing weary of missing the ball, they began to play their natural game. The caddies, feeling themselves insulted, thereupon threw down their clubs and marched off the course in a body. I recollect also to have heard a somewhat similar story, possibly apocryphal, of one of the visits of Vardon and Ray to America. They went to a small course, where they were not known by sight, and took out the local professional. He, however, had the laugh on his side, for when they revealed their identity he remained wholly unimpressed, declared that he had never heard the names of either Ray or Vardon and stuck to it stoutly to the end.

At any rate, I believe it is quite true that, in the summer of 1921, a very good American amateur, Mr. "Reggie" Lewis, was dressed up to personate a distinguished British lady golfer then in the country. He played several holes, quite unsuspected, and much admired alike for his personal charms and his golf, before he suddenly cast off his disguise, to the consternation of the gallery. That, however, is a height of dissembling to which few of us can aspire.

The Pampered Golfer

Country Life
1923

This article is not, as might perhaps be imagined from its title, an outcry against the luxury of the age and a plea for a luncheon of sandwiches and carrying one's own clubs. It is directed rather against those golfers who want the game made too easy for themselves by the elimination of all chances of what they deem undeserved disaster.

I have lately been playing on a course towards which I feel a devotion of many years, and I was pained to find in force at one hole there a local rule which seems to me an infamous one. At this hole there stretches across the course at a distance of something over 200 yards from the tee a deep and watery ditch. It cannot be carried unless by someone with the driving powers of Abe Mitchell, but when the ground is hard and there is a strong following wind the well-hit ball of an ordinary mortal may possibly reach it. The green can comfortably be attained in the second shot from a position short of the ditch, and one would imagine therefore that there was no great hardship in taking, on rare occasions, a spoon from the tee. The local pundits, however, have thought otherwise. They have staked off a portion of the ditch, which lies in the direct line to the hole, and have enacted that if the player drives into the ditch from the tee at any point between these two white posts he can lift without penalty. On the other hand, if he goes in with his second or any subsequent shot, he can only lift under penalty of a stroke.

On mature consideration I take this to be the worst local rule in the world. It is complicated, it is artificial, and it shows an entire misconception of the game of golf, which should be, in Mr. John Low's words, "a contest of risks." To make such a rule as this is in effect to lay down this principle, that the man who, without using his intelligence, hits the ball down the middle of the course off the middle of his club is in no circumstances whatever to suffer any inconvenience. And a very poor principle it is. I quite admit that, if I do happen to hit a straight and reasonably long drive and then get into trouble, I may complain bitterly at the moment of my bad luck. It is a human weakness to do so. I also admit that constantly to be compelled to play short from the tee would make a dull game of it. But, after all, to hit a good, straight drive is not a very wonderful achievement—one ought to do it quite often—and just once in a while to have to use one's head and restrain one's energies is not a very great hardship. It is surely a hundred times preferable to this artificial and pampering rule which makes it a case of "Heads I win and tails I can't lose." A distinguished professional once said to me that he liked St. Andrews better than any other course because (only he expressed it rather more strongly) "you might play a very good shot there and get into a very bad place." That is surely a more manful point of view than that which is indicated by those two wretched little white posts.

I had only just ceased from fulminating against the two posts when, oddly enough, I heard from a golfer of my acquaintance, expressing much the same views *à propos* of another and more famous course. There, so he told me, the authorities had had put before them by a scratch player a long and solemn proposal for a number of alterations to be made to the fairway at various holes. The object of them was that, whatever the wind, a flat lie and a good stance should invariably reward a good drive and that the scratch player should thus be able to reach the green with his second, whereas he might not be able to do it from an uphill lie. The answer given was, I believe, something to this effect: that if the proposed alterations were made it would be only fair to make others to suit those with longer handicaps and shorter driving powers, and that it would be altogether too colossal a task to flatten out the course from 120 yards to 300 yards from the tee. It was not added, but it might well have been, that to do so would be entirely to ruin one of the most charming golf courses in the world.

There is one point in the answer given to that scratch player which is particularly worthy of notice, namely that if hummocks are to be flattened to suit the long driver they must also be flattened for the short. Those of us who are still capable of hitting the ball a reasonable distance have, I think, a very imperfect sympathy with shorter drivers. Yet we have in point of hummocks a very easy time of it.

I realized this fully only when playing at St. Andrews with one who, having been in his day a great golfer, is now something too stiff to hit the ball far from the tee. Time and again his ball finished in a most difficult lie among humps and hollows while mine—through no merit of mine, but through the advantage of some twenty years—lay clear on even ground. He bore it like a Trojan, but he often lost nearly a whole stroke from the tee, and I have seen much the same thing happen at Sandwich and at other places. It is right that the longer of two players should have an advantage, but one does not like to see it made more overwhelming than need be.

We are all of us too apt to desire a course to suit our own game. I am disposed to think that my own tee shot, when I hit it, should be regarded as a standard of what is decently respectable, and that the smooth country and the bunkers should be placed accordingly. If people are so old and puny that they cannot hit so far as I do, or so young and strong that they can hit as far as Mr. Tolley or Mr. Wethered—well, they must take their chance. Only the other day, on a certain course, I came to what used to be a bunker and was now converted into a grassy hollow. I inquired the reason of the change. "Oh," was the rather bitter answer, "I suppose So-and-so (a prominent member of the Green Committee) drove into it one day. He always has bunkers filled up when he gets into them."

Clearly we all have to think a little more about other people's shots and a little less about our own if our opinions as to the courses on which we play are to be worth listening to. And we shall do this best by bearing in mind the principle which is so gravely transgressed by those two miserable white posts of mine. The whole game of golf does not consist in hitting the ball straight in the direction of the hole without any regard to the lie of the land, and a shot so hit is not necessarily a good shot.

Moreover, nobody, whatever the shot he has played, has an absolute and indefeasible right to a perfect lie and a perfect stance. "I quite appreciate," says my correspondent, "that it would be hard for a professional to lose the Championship from having a worse lie at the –th hole (a hole of many hummocks) from no fault of his own, but I have not heard complaints from pros, only from amateurs." If that be so, then the more shame to us amateurs who play the game for fun and have nothing to lose, save our tempers, through a bad lie or a bad stance. But I hope that we are not—most of us—quite so foolish as he thinks. Of course, we grouse at the moment, but we do not as a rule write to the Committee about it and we do not really like white posts.

Providence and Politeness

Out of the Rough
1932

A and *B* were coupled together the other day in a team match played by foursomes. Said *A* to *B* before they started: "You mustn't mind my being very short. I'm getting old and I can't hit hard—but I shall be all right when I get on the greens." He is as truthful a man as he is a modest one; he is, as a rule, a capital putter, and was really justified in what he said. Yet can anyone, who has experienced the singular malignancy of the golfing fates, have the least doubt what occurred? Of course he cannot. The tragedy is so inevitable as hardly to be worth setting down; on this particular day poor *A* had a series of putts of four and five feet on icy, slippery greens, and the ball would *not* go into the hole.

It is rash to say—whether to your partner or to anyone else—"Well, anyhow, I'm driving well—that won't let me down," or alternatively: "I can't get very far, but I can keep the ball in play." It would be much wiser to keep to yourself the fact that you feel thoroughly confident with your iron clubs. Yet in both these cases the fates may forgive you. Whatever you do, you must never say that you can putt, for then you will not be forgiven. There is nobody in the world who is a good enough putter to be able to prophesy that on this particular day he will putt well. He may do so on every other day in the year, but this will be the one day on which something goes wrong. There are a few fortunate mortals who never drive badly, but there is no such thing as an entirely trustworthy putter, nor would there be if the hole were made as big as a soup plate. *Nemo omnibus horis sapit*, which means that everybody misses the short ones sometimes. Most of us have learned our lesson and go out of our way to avoid tempting Providence. When we meet another match and ask the players how they are getting on, the man who is down will answer candidly enough, sometimes, indeed, ostentatiously magnifying the extent of the disaster; but the man who is leading will be tongue-tied and embarrassed. He will take refuge in generalities, such as that he is not doing so badly so far, or that he is a little up at present; if he is tactlessly pressed to give details he will make mysterious signs with his fingers, twisting himself into such a position that his adversary cannot see what he is doing. He does this partly from politeness, in that he does not want to appear to be chortling at his enemy's expense, but this is but a superficial motive compared with that deeply implanted fear of the Nemesis that waits for boasters; he is far more afraid of the evil chance than he is of bad manners.

Some while ago two small boys were playing a match in a juvenile competition. Near the turn one of them held a cheering lead of three. At that moment enters to him a small sister, who calls to him: "How are you getting on, George?" The leader, scarlet with embarrassment and looking at his opponent out of the corner of his eye, mutters that he is "all right." "Yes, but how's the match?" calls the sister, more shrilly; and again he answers, more uncomfortable than ever: "I'm all right." "How many up are you?" this time screams the relentless young lady, and then she proclaims to an invisible somebody in the background: "Hurrah! George is three up! Three up! He's going to win." Poor George did win in the end, but he suffered terribly in doing so, and probably told his sister very forcibly afterwards that these things were not done.

It is arguable that at golf we take too much pains to try to conceal our feelings (we do not do it very well, nevertheless), and that it would be better to be as simple and natural as was that young lady. An entirely inexperienced spectator sometimes feels inclined to shout with joy when the enemy misses a putt or goes into a bunker, but the indignant faces that look round at him from among his neighbors freeze the cheer upon his lips. I do not wish it to be otherwise, for golf is sufficiently agonizing and exasperating without that added horror. I am only reflecting how differently we behave when we are watching golf as compared with some other game. When somebody shoots at an open goal and misses, no chivalry prevents a fierce roar of joy and relief going up to Heaven; neither does it when our man ought to have been run out by yards and has been saved by a glorious muddle on the part of the fielder or the wicket-keeper. These two instances are comparable to that of a man missing a short putt, and yet we yell in the one case and stand in solemn and hypocritical silence in the other. It is, I suppose, largely because in golf the player's tragedy is entirely of his own making; his adversary has had nothing whatever to do with it; whereas in cricket we may say that we do not cheer because the enemy batsman has missed the ball, but because our own heroic bowler has hit the wicket. Also, in golf the spectators are so near to the player that there would be something particularly brutal in their cheering his misfortunes while standing right over him. We cannot, in moments of tension, help gloating, but there is something indecent in the notion of letting him see us.

This delicacy of deportment on the part of golfers leads to an odd difference in the scenes that follow the end of a big match. When a player has a putt for the match and holes it there goes up a splendid and spontaneous shout which does the heart good to hear; but when he has a putt to save the match and misses it, things can never be the same. There comes a perceptible pause, then someone begins to clap, and finally the clapping comes in scattered and irregular volleys; but the first fine rapture of community cheering is unattainable. If the putt missed is painfully short, it is impossible to make any great demonstration, no matter how fervently we have been wishing it missed. Even in a scoring competition the nature of the stroke with which the victor ends his labors makes all the difference. There is no more exciting moment than that in which the winner of the Open Championship makes his way through the crowd round the last green, flag bearers and stewards forcing a passage for him, to consummate his triumph; but we shout much more loudly if the last stroke is actually a good one. When Hagen came to the seventy-second hole at Muirfield in 1929 he was, humanly speaking, certain to win; we were all ready to cheer him with our whole souls, for he had played magnificently. He put his second in a bunker and then played a typically beautiful shot out to within four five feet of the pin. Now we were all a-tiptoe, and if he had holed that putt, as he nearly always would, what a yell there would have been! But he missed it, gave a little smile and shake of his head, and then tapped the ball in from two inches. Of course, we all cheered, but the supreme moment had passed without being seized and could not be recaptured. Sometimes, too, it happens on these occasions that the winner has to hole his putt first and then his obscure and neglected partner has to putt. That is bad stage management on the part of fate, and robs the scene of a perceptible part of its thrill.

A good many years ago I saw what seemed then, and still seems to me, a curious scene in the Ladies' Championship. There was a really splendid match between two most illustrious ladies. One of them was dormy one, and after each had played three shots their balls lay almost equidistant—some four feet—from the hole. The one who was dormy putted first and holed. That was the match; I uttered an excited squeak which was just going to turn into a shout when fierce female eyes glowered at me on all sides and I subsided, crushed. There was not a sound and nobody moved a muscle until the loser had also holed her four-foot putt in order to say that she was one down and not two down. Honesty as to short putts is certainly a virtue, but this was carrying it to a pitch of which I had never dreamed. However, I am not a heroic lady, but only a weak, erring man who likes to say he is as few holes down as he decently can.

Card and Pencil Golf

American Golfer
1927

A few days ago, in company with some of my fellow members of a golfing society, I went down to the seaside for a weekend. We were to play in a medal round and there were several very agreeable prizes for us to win if we could turn in a low enough score. The course on which we were to play is one of the best and pleasantest in the country, the weather promised to be perfect, we were all of us in good spirits, and having dined well—some of us beyond our means—retired to be full of delightful anticipations.

What a change there was in us next morning—the weather had fulfilled all our hopes, the greens looked velvety, but we were a hangdog crew—

Like the leaves of the forest when
Autumn hath blown
That host on the morrow lay
Withered and strown.

As we drive from our hotel to the course we looked with dreary eyes on the sunshiny sea and the white cliffs beyond. Then said one heaving a deep sigh: "What fun this would be if we were just going to play a friendly game." "Yes," said another, "Fancy coming all this way to this lovely course to play with a confounded card and pencil!" And all the rest of us cried in chorus: "Why on earth do we do it?"

It is a question which I have often asked myself before and to which I have still to find any adequate reply. I have never yet set out on a medal round without feeling sick and miserable; I have never yet completed one without having felt during some part of it exceedingly cross; I have never yet heard of the postponement of a competition in which I was going to take part without a desire to offer a votive table or the appropriate saint. Nor do I believe these sentiments to be in the least peculiar to myself. But the fact remains that if there had been no medal round and no prizes, if we had been bidden to assemble merely to play jovial and friendly matches amongst ourselves, we should none of us have come. The desire to acquire silver objects or to see our names in the newspapers must be deeply rooted in the human breast.

For my part I believe that the perfectly successful meeting can only be attained by guile. The prizes should be duly advertised, entrance fees paid, a time-sheet fixed, perhaps even scoring cards issued, and then at the very last moment the officials should announce that the competitions will not take place. With what a spontaneous outburst of joy and relief would those cards be torn into the smallest pieces! With what holiday faces would the players go out to their four-ball matches! I suppose everybody has had dreams of paying some day his periodical visit to the dentist, and after being duly pinioned and gagged and swung into mid-air, of receiving the intelligence that there was positively nothing to be done this time. Some of us have now come to a time when that vision has lost its poignancy; the dentist has done his worst—or his best—for us, and there are some things that can never happen again. But we can still imagine the ecstasy of that reprieve. It would have been heavenly, but not more so than would be the sudden remission of a sentence of card and pencil servitude.

III

Faults, Fixes, and the Tools of the Trade

“A Little Too Much Massy”

American Golfer
1921

A little while ago I had what I had never had before in all my life, and I wish I had had it many years earlier—a formal lesson in golf from an illustrious teacher. Even so I had not meant to have it. I had been to see the great man about something else, and then, since there was half an hour to spare, I plucked up my courage and asked him to give me a lesson.

I was afraid—I blush to confess to such vanity—that I should by some unlucky chance, and inspired by his presence, hit the ball quite respectably well, and that he would thereupon declare that there was nothing the matter. These are words that fall like music on the ear when a periodical exploration is made by the family dentist, but this time, being conscious of a complexity of lethal diseases, I should have found them disappointing.

However, I had a coat that was too tight and a club I disliked, so that I was not without hope, and indeed, I need have had no fear for my first shots were as feeble, as crooked, and as bad in every conceivable way as I could possibly have wished. Each one illustrated a new and separate disease.

For a while my teacher only stood over me in brooding and contemplative silence. Then he took me by the shoulders and heaved me into an attitude that may have looked classical, but felt extremely uncomfortable. Then he gave up my feet as a bad job, and attacked a limb that I myself knew to be old and hardened in crime—namely, the right elbow. Having found out the criminal, he gave it no peace. Whenever, as is its beastly habit, it insisted on brandishing itself in the air, he remarked, "A little too much Massy again that time, Sir." This was certainly unjust to the great Frenchman, who had won the Open at Hoylake in 1907, but it had a most illuminating and beneficial effect.

I do not know whether I was the more impressed by the astuteness of his comments, or by his kind and fatherly manner of nursing me back to a temporary convalescence. When a shot went wrong, and I exclaimed, almost in tears, "There, that wretched slice again," he would pat me—metaphorically—on the head and remark that the club had been swung properly, but that I had looked up just too soon.

Or he would say that it was not really a slice, but that I was "standing that way," and would demonstrate this comforting theory by putting his own feet into my footprints. Or, again, when I said in despair, "Oh! but I've often tried that and all that happens is etc.," he just let me talk, and then invented some beautiful explanation that should hearten me to try the particular experiment again. He was so soothing and so ingenious, and yet stuck so tenaciously to the main issue, discarding all minor points, that in about a quarter of an hour he had me lashing and slashing at the ball with confidence, and sending it, moreover, a very tolerable distance.

There have been relapses since, alas! I cannot, fortunately for him, for he would find me a sad bore, go and live on his doorstep, under his fatherly eye. But he gave me at least some exquisite moments, and I am still moderately full of faith.

What a hard life that great man must lead. I cannot doubt, as I said, that he found me a bore, but he only suffered me for half an hour, and he has to do the same sort of thing sometimes for several hours a day. Moreover, I cannot help thinking that some of his pupils are more tedious even than I was, for I did hit the ball at last, and some of them, whatever they may do in the next world, will never hit it in this. They are older than I am, their figures are more prohibitively convex. He tees up a row of balls for them, and they topple them along the ground. He picks up the balls, and tees them again, and they topple them once more, and he will go on teeing them with perfect suavity, and they will go on toppling them with perfect futility till the end of time. What a life!

And yet he remains philosophic and even serene. Surely there is lost in him the finest schoolmaster that ever lived.

Go to the Best Doctor

American Golfer
1928

I am quite sure that most of us do not go often enough to a golfing doctor. I am equally sure that when we do go we ought to go to the best. What we in fact do is to say to anyone who happens to be playing with us, "I say, just tell me what I am doing wrong." He tells us the first thing that comes into his head; we do not really believe in him but give his cure just one half-hearted trial, and our last state is worse than our first.

Such at least is apt to be my own slipshod habit in respect to medical advice. The other day, however, being in a more lamentable state of play than usual, and being lucky enough to be playing with one who is at once a great golfer and a great golfing doctor, I seized my golden opportunity. I begged him to tell me how I might be saved and promised him unreasoning and implicit obedience. After my first bad shot, which was not long in coming, he whispered one brief counsel in my ear, and behold I was instantly as a creature transfigured, doing threes and fours and then went twelve holes in goodness knows what.

Now what I want to know is exactly how much credit of these twelve holes—and some other quite respectable rounds that I have played since—will go to my doctor on the day of judgment. He is an extraordinarily acute observer and I am sure that his diagnosis of my malady was the correct one. But shall I not get a little of the credit too because I had so much faith? If I had not believed in him completely I suppose his words would have had but little effect. As it was, my faith was so great that had he advised me to play standing on my head I believe I should have made some show of hitting the ball.

That is why I say we should always go to the best doctor we can find. Not only is his prescription likely to be the best, but still more important we shall believe that it is. As a very famous professional said to me the other day, "It does not take much to bring confidence back to the game. Just hit two or three shots and off you go." The converse, alas! is also true, that it does not take much to take confidence away, but that is only a gloomy parenthesis. My point is that a golfing doctor who can give one confidence enough to hit just those two or three shots, may be worth untold gold.

My doctor, on this occasion, was an illustrious amateur, but I recollect another on which I besought a many times professional champion, almost with tears in my eyes, to tell me how to drive, and in about five minutes the trick was done. A lesser man might perhaps have told me the same thing, but I doubt if he would have had the same effect. I might have wanted to argue with him or to say disparagingly, "Oh yes, but I've tried that before and it's no good to me"; and then, of course, it would have been no good.

There is another thing I want to know about my latest cure. When I parted from my doctor with heartfelt thanks he said, "You'll be all right as long as you remember." Now I want to know whether he meant that literally or whether he only meant generally to cheer me. I think the latter, because though I have in fact been more or less "all right," it has been rather by forgetting than by remembering. What happened to me was what has happened to thousands of golfers. I remembered all too well. I, so to speak, doubled and trebled the dose of my medicine until it began to poison me. Luckily I found it out in time and figuratively put the medicine away on a shelf for a while. But the good it had done me still survived because that blessed confidence remained.

Whatever else one does I am certain of one thing: that when one is sick in a golfing sense one should not apply for advice to another sick man. Mutual doctoring is of no use at all. I remember some years ago going out to play some holes with a friend. He said he could not hit the ball, so we agreed to go out and help each other. A more dismal failure could not be imagined. The hopelessness of the situation was apparent from the moment our first two tee shots were struck. Both might be termed reasonably good ones in the sense that both were of a fair length and both ended on the fairway. "Well," I said to my friend, "that was a good one of yours anyway." "That cursed hook again," he growled in reply. "If I could hook a ball like that," I snarled angrily, "I should never grumble anymore." "Why dash it all," he positively yelled, "that's the very thing I wanted you to cure." And so we went on. That which I called my loathsome slice he called a nice little drift to the right which kept the ball safely in play, and the hook which I envied him so bitterly made him foam at the mouth with rage.

It was just the same with the rest of the game. I was playing my pitches pretty well and putting contemptibly; his iron play was absurd but he was holing everything. Each of us told the other that if we would only go up to the ball and hit it boldly all would be well. I must add that we were still friends at the end of the round but medically we had certainly done each other no good.

In books, ladies, when in private, are alleged always to talk about each other's maladies and to enjoy it immensely. I do not know if this is true but it certainly is not true of men and golfing maladies. The fact is that when we are slicing ourselves we are utterly selfish; we do not care a row of pins about other folk's slices, not even those of our dearest friends. When we are in robust golfing health, however, when a slice seems impossible and the easiest thing in the world is to crack the ball down the middle, then we are not without sympathy for the less fortunate and are prepared really to try to discover what is the matter with them. I do not say that on that account we shall be good doctors because we are willing ones. On the contrary, I think that those golfers with the real gift of healing are very rare, which is all the more reason for seeking out the best when there is healing to be done.

A Musical Cure

The Times
1935

"If music be the food of golf, play on." So spoke Orsino in the play, or if it was not exactly that it was something very like it.

Doubtless he was alluding to the necessity for rhythm, that indefinable and elusive something the presence of which we recognize in the swings of the great, while we are too painfully aware of its absence in our own. It comes and goes and, as we get older and stiffer, it is apt to go forever, but if by chance we have a fair day we are conscious that it has come faintly fluttering back, and for a moment we can "almost hear the beating of its wings." There is a traditional prescription for its recapture, which consists in swinging the club to a waltz tune. I tried it long since, as I must have tried almost everything once, but had forgotten all about it till I came across it again in the work of a highly distinguished American teacher, Mr. Seymour Dunn. So away I went to a secret valley, a very muddy one in the season of rain, where no human eye could see my contortions nor human ear hearken to my carolings, and " 'gad, there I was," as Jos Sedley once observed, "singing away like—a robin."

There are presumably many waltz tunes, but I could only think of two. The first was that eminently languorous one, title to me known, from "The Merry Widow"; the second, if it may be named with respect, was the tune of the hymn called "Happy birds that sing and fly," which at least sufficiently resembles a waltz. Between these two I was forced to alternate. I am no musician any more than I am a dancer, and prefer, if I sing at all, to have my notes drowned by the running waters of my morning bath or still better by the rattle and roar of a railway train, supposing that I have a carriage to myself. I fancy my singing, though here I may be flattering myself, to be not unlike that of Bertie Wooster when he daily gave vent to "Sonny Boy." For golfing purposes, however, that is rather an advantage than otherwise. Singers of this type, that is to say having naturally bad taste, no voice, and an imperfect ear, are given to a slow and sentimental sweetness long drawn out, and this lends itself admirably to the drowsy swing which we ought to cultivate.

I remember in the early stages of the War being at Aldershot when Sir Walford Davies (he was only Dr. then) kindly came down to teach the new army how to sing and form regimental choirs. He told his pupils not to sing "in the sloppy, Bank Holiday style," and a general and sheepish grin showed that the shot had gone home. Then he made them sing the Old Hundredth, which they did so lugubriously as to evoke the protest, "Now you know you wouldn't sing 'How's your lady friend' like that." Next, "The Old Folks at Home" was greeted with the friendly sarcasm, "Oh, come, sloppier than that!" Finally they were drilled into singing with a briskness and crispness that a little while before would have seemed incredible.

Sir Walford was clearly in the right, if it be not impertinent to say so; but I feel like Bob Acres when he refused to follow Sir Lucius's dueling precepts, and said firmly, "By my valor, I will stand edgeways." Music is one thing and golf is another, and for the purposes of this golfing cure I doubt if it be possible to sing too sloppily. Let the patient get all the intolerable pathos he can out of "One little hut among de bushes," "When will I hear de bees a-humming," and all the other words of that heartbreaking and beloved song. He can scarcely have too many tears in his voice, hardly be too maudlin, so long as nobody can hear him. If he tries to be too brisk he may soon be snatching and snapping at the ball as badly as ever.

A waltz tune is, no doubt, the best, but I am disposed, though diffidently, to think that almost any tune will do good, so long as we sing or whistle it with sufficient languor. It is not necessary to go on with "The Merry Widow" till it drives us mad. One important thing is not to take a deep breath at the top of the swing and come down on the ball with too violent a burst of melody. Another is not to stop as we reach the ball but to finish, of course in a chaste and classical attitude, with the music still flowing evenly from our lips. I ought to add that Mr. Dunn prescribes the waltz tune primarily for acquiring a rhythmic swing with no ball there. When there is a ball and we are inclined to press and jerk at it, he suggests a different musical remedy—namely, to "whistle a continuous, low, even note all the way through the swing." He may be right; he probably is, but this whistling of one note is by comparison a dreary and for some of us a difficult business. Do let us have our tune and get a little fun out of the treatment!

It may be observed that with singular modesty I have said nothing of the effect of this cure upon the particular patient in question. Well, hope does not spring as it did, and to hit the ball nowadays, if he ever does hit it, appears rather an ironical circumstance. Yet I will say this, that now and again he did seem to attain to some vestige of a pause at the top of the swing and actually did follow through. Moreover, and this is always a cheerful sign, the remedy was reasonably effective on the second day, whereas most remedies only last for one. The weather and the valley being now alike unspeakable he is wondering whether a musical treatment indoors would be good for putting. There might be a measure of compensation in putting at the drawing room table-legs when the household insists on listening to Bach on the wireless. But these musical people are so fussy; they say "Hush," and besides, I doubt if Bach is quite the man for the job.

To Underclub or Overclub

American Golfer
1932

Which is the worse—to overclub or underclub? Superficially the question seems a foolish one, for there is no doubt which of the two faults is usually spoken of as the more criminal. Someone describing a match will say that the player underclubbed himself "scandalously" or "ridiculously" or "idiotically." The man who took too big a club is spoken of with compassion, as if he had had bad luck or a villainous caddie who misdirected him.

Perhaps the reason is that the player who underclubs himself is always suspected of vanity. We accuse him of taking too small a club in order to show how far he can hit with it; the man who takes a brassie (2 wood), when an iron would have got him there, we regard as a pleasant modest creature whose only fault is that he does not know his own strength. Generally speaking, no doubt we are right in condemning the underclubber. Habitually to take the smaller club must lead to being short, and shortness is the commonest, the most all-pervading of golfing sins.

Therefore, we ought to train ourselves into a habit of taking the bigger club. But my goodness! It does need training; it is always a difficult thing to do and sometimes it is almost impossibly difficult. If we are in some doubt as to whether we can quite get up with a particular club, we are likely to hit too hard and may make a bad shot; but if we think we shall go too far, we do not hit out at the ball, and then we are absolutely certain to make a dreadfully bad shot. I suppose that most golfers would agree that, when we are nervous, the difficulty is to hit freely, and we cannot possibly hit freely if we are obsessed with the notion that we are going too far. We wince fatally at the moment of striking. A consciously spared shot by a nervous player is more likely to reach an unreachable bunker than any other shot in the world.

This subject was put into my head by rereading the other day an article by Mr. R. E. Howard. He was writing of Mr. Bob Gardner's being beaten in our Amateur championship at Deal in 1922, largely owing to a fatally chipped mashie shot at the thirteenth hole. Mr. Gardner said he had been in two minds as to the club and then "turning to Mr. Francis Ouimet he said 'I thought of a piece of advice I once heard you give: when in doubt underclub yourself and hit with all you are worth.' And I hit so hard that my head went up and forward just too soon."

I am inclined to think that this catastrophe was the exception to Mr. Ouimet's rule. At any rate there is a good deal to be said for that rule. With the shorter club, you may very possibly top and you may hook, but you will lash out. With the longer club, if you think it is too long, you may top or hook or slice (perhaps the likeliest of all), and it is a hundred to one you won't follow through.

I know this doctrine is contrary to that which the great men preach in their books, and they are in a sense quite right. Underclubbing is a dangerous doctrine for golfing babes and sucklings. I do believe, however, that the great men sometimes deliberately disobey their own written word when it comes to the crucial point. I remember years ago Mr. Laidlay, one of the really great amateurs of a past epoch, telling me that, if at a crisis he doubted between a brassie and a cleek (2 iron), he always took the cleek even though he thought he could not get quite up, just because having to hit out with it made him feel confident. Confident! That no doubt is the point. Anything that will make us feel even moderately confident at a crisis is worth doing, however unorthodox. Yet apparently it is not the right thing to say. Mr. Laidlay never wrote a book, but if he had, I suppose he would not have said it.

There are, I imagine, even among the greatest players, those who are constitutionally underclubbers and those who are the reverse. I remember I used to regard Hagen as an underclubber. In the first championship he won at Sandwich, he astonished everybody by taking iron clubs from what seemed an almost absurd range. Sometimes he did not hit very good iron shots, but at any rate he won the championship. He won another at Sandwich a few years later and then a subtle change seemed to have come over him; he apparently was not nearly so fond of hitting his soul out and much fonder of a brassie through the green. Edward Ray I should regard as something of a champion underclubber in that he loves a lofted iron club whenever he has any pretext for using it, and the more lofted the better. The shots he used to play with his niblick (8 iron) were staggering in their impertinence. Such a heave as he used to give! Such a divot as he used to cut out! Such a height as the ball used to go! But it finished on the green.

On the other hand I should be inclined to call Harry Vardon an overclubber, but then his swing is so wonderfully smooth and rhythmic that it is—or was—almost impossible to detect him making an extra effort. Moreover, he was so astonishingly good through the green with wood, and could pick up the ball with such utter ease with that upright swing of his, that he never had the least temptation to force an iron club beyond its limits. And yet he was very long with irons at his zenith and had a driving mashie (1 iron) that he could hit as far as anybody else's brassie. Another whom I should with due humility rank among the overclubbers would be our present British Open champion, Tommy Armour. Perhaps it is his old Scottish training in the days when the half shot was considered the hallmark of the fine golfer, and there were not so many nicely graded varieties of irons. At any rate, I should judge Armour to prefer to play a shot well within himself with the longer club rather than go all out with the shorter one.

And now to which class does the immortal Bobby belong? I really do not know and I can only assume that he is the perfect golfer that belongs to neither. One thing is certain, namely, that he is, like Harry Vardon, an abnormally good judge of distance, and, I suppose, if a man can judge distance well enough, he is never in doubt between two clubs. If he is in doubt, he never seems to be and there never was a golfer who so entirely dispensed with a caddie's advice. What a blissful state!

The Terrible Choice

Country Life
1957

I read with regret the other day of the death of an old golfing acquaintance whom I had not seen for many years. His name suddenly and vividly recalled to my mind a match we had once played together. It was hardly a match because we did not know which of us was up or down; we went out to cure each other's diseases. He was complaining of hooking his drives and I bemoaning a mild but temporarily incorrigible slice from the tee. Surely we should be able to help each other, but the round was not a success, for each of us, far from pitying the other's weakness, was bitterly envious of it; understanding was hopelessly imperfect.

He began with a fine long drive, as I should have called it, with a nice little turn to the left which just took it into some very innocent rough. "There is goes again!" he exclaimed, and was furious when I said that, if that was all, he had no need to be sorry for himself; I wished I had only half his complaint. Then I hit my drive, on the fairway to be sure, but having a paltry, slicy air. When I broke into loud lamentations he declared that I ought to be thankful and that a slice was far less calamitous than a hook. We returned to the clubhouse after eleven holes, our attempts at mutual doctoring have failed miserably.

Thinking over that round again I recalled W. S. Gilbert's famous lines, in the Sentry's song, declaring that every boy and every girl was born "either a little Liberal or else a little Conservative." I wondered whether we were all born hookers or slicers, and if so which was the more fortunate lot. Once upon a time I should have said that slicing was infinitely the worse of the two. I don't know that I was born either, and as a boy, if I may say so, I was rather a good driver, but in the middle of my first year at Cambridge I was suddenly stricken with an appalling attack of slicing. Perhaps no very good medical advice was at hand; at least, no one could cure me and for several years I was subject to periodical attacks. I remember one bout in a gale of wind at Westward Ho!, but even now the memory of my ball being swept into inaccessible rushes is too painful. In any case, my personal history is not interesting; enough then that in time I overcame the disease, but never, I think, quite overcame the fear of it, so that I lacked something of confidence in hitting ever afterwards.

Then it certainly seemed to me that to be a hooker was a blessing, and to be a slicer was a curse, and I am inclined to think that in those days of the gutty this was more or less true. The gutty was so light and could be such a helpless plaything for wind that blew on one's back; liability was utterly unlimited. The man who could hold the ball up into that wind seemed the most enviable of all mortals. To be sure, the hooker could also suffer from the opposite wind, but I decline to believe that his sufferings were so great. And then, of course, there was the question of length. Harold Hilton, who could do almost anything with the ball, deliberately cultivated a turn to the left to gain in distance of run. Moreover, there was something manly about a hook, even if it was occasionally disastrous, and a gentle feebleness about a slice. I was ashamed of mine.

Today things have considerably changed and I am by no means sure that the slicer is not the more to be envied. When I say "slicer," I ought to define my terms and say one whose ball is inclined to turn if anything to the right, so that he can hold the ball up into a right-hand wind. I suppose the class that swings "from inside out" is preeminently one of hookers. Such a master of the art as Henry Cotton no doubt "rides the whirlwind and directs the storm," but I have seen others of the inside-out school who lack his mastery, so finding great difficulty in approaching the green in a right-to-left wind. If American golfers have any weakness, as to which I am by no means certain, it is this. It is probably owing to the fact that they do not habitually play in such strong winds as we do. Even the great Bobby Jones, I think, preferred to play his shot to the green in a right-hand wind with a curl from the right. Of course, he could do it with great skill, as he could everything, but he was a little lacking in the shot right up to the green in that wind's eye. Such, at least, is my possibly irreverent impression.

On the whole, I fancy that the hooker, when he errs, does go into deeper and more disastrous trouble than the slicer. I have quoted before, but it gives me pleasure to quote again, dear James Braid's joyously malignant remark as Densmore Shute hit a wild hook at Walton Heath: "He'll want all his dynamiters there." James himself, if ever he did make a crooked shot, inclined to hit it to the left, sometimes, though very rarely, into real dynamiter country. I remember a famous golfer, a contemporary of his, saying that, considering his great powers, Braid's record of five Championships and all the rest did not really do him justice, and this he attributed to that very occasional but expensive hook. What a wonderful compliment! I am not saying that he was right or wrong, but it is an interesting opinion of one well worth listening to.

For a hooker to be able to turn himself into a member of the other school for a particular occasion is a splendor of skill that very, very few could accomplish. When Harold Hilton came up to Prestwick for the Amateur Championship of 1911 he found the ground dry and burned and fast as lightning. He had been habitually turning his drives from right to left for some years then and he found his tee shots just ending in the left-hand rough, whereas Cecil Hutchison, his opponent in the international match, whose ball turned a little the other way, was safe on the fairway. He instantly set to work to recapture his old method of driving with a slight turn to the right. Length mattered little on that iron-hard ground, but straightness was all-important. He had not much time in which to make the reform, but he did it and he won that championship. He won another championship two years later, having reverted to the drive with his ever-artistic turn of hook.

When on the subject of reforming hookers, I must not forget perhaps the greatest of them all, Ben Hogan. He used to have a very occasional hook and he thought that it had cost him very dearly. No doubt he was right in the highly competitive company he frequented, when a single stroke might make all the difference. Then, as he has told us, an inspiration came to him in the watches of the night and he could hardly wait before dashing to the practice tee to try the remedy. It was a great success, but what it was he told nobody for a long time. When he did disclose this "secret" it proved perhaps a little disappointing to those expecting some world-shaking revelation, since it consisted, if I remember rightly, only in a slightly increased opening of the face of the club.

Of course, such gross words as "hook" and "slice" ought really not to be used with regard to great men. I should rather have employed "draw" and "fade." "Draw" was the word that Hilton, I think, always used to describe his so beautifully controlled method of driving, when he was beginning to find he wanted a little more length. But for ordinary people I think that the old, cruder words are best. As I have said before, nobody knows what a slice could be unless he played with a gutty ball and a wooden shaft. The modern ball bores through the wind and the steel shaft does not leave the head behind as the wooden one used to do. I believe fading is today the art to be cultivated, but I cannot secretly help wishing I had been born a hooker. It is such a fine, virile vice. By the way, didn't J. H. once ask: "What's the matter with the middle of the course?" There is something to be said for that, too.

The Knot in the Handkerchief

The Times
1929

Our Ryder Cup team, after a hard course of tournaments, have now vanished into a mysterious and exciting seclusion. I gather that they are at Harrogate. Whether they are drinking waters with "a wery strong flavour o' warm flat irons" I do not know, though there would seem to be something vaguely appropriate in it if they were. Whatever their precise form of training. I feel tolerably sure that they are not, occult from the public eye, practicing with handkerchiefs tied into knots.

It is perhaps too late in the day to suggest it to them; yet a gentleman of my acquaintance has found in this apparently simple device the twin secrets of driving and happiness. He had played golf of a kind for years before he was suddenly smitten with a desire for indoor self-improvement. Fluffy woolen balls and India-rubber balls brought him no relief; then he tied the knot in his handkerchief, shut himself up with a library of textbooks, and emerged after a time a creature changed and radiant.

I went to see him in his office the other day, that he might show me how it was done. It was a solemn moment when he took from a drawer a large plain white handkerchief. He rolled it up until it looked like a very long attenuated sausage. Swiftly and surely he tied a knot in it, and yet another knot, and now it resembled—more or less—a golf ball with two airplane wings attached. He repeated the process with another handkerchief, and our supply of ammunition was complete. Then he hesitated a moment. However, it was past one o'clock, there was no one about, and even a senior partner can do what he likes with his own luncheon hour. He picked up a driver from the corner, and stealthily we crept out on to the landing. Not a mouse stirred behind the wainscot; all was well; he put one handkerchief on the ground to act as a tee, the airplane wings pointing in the direction of the imaginary hole. Finally, with the air of a priest taking the sacrificial knife, he grasped his driver. I retired to the safety of the staircase to look on.

At this supreme juncture there came a most untimely interruption. Steps were heard on the staircase—the steps of Miss Somebody returning to work after all too short a lunch. "Come along, Miss Somebody," said my friend blandly, as if he were doing the most ordinary thing in the world, and with an embarrassed smile she plunged through the nearest glass door. Silence reigned once more, but only for an instant. Bang! There came a noise like a pistol shot. He had swung his driver round his head and the handkerchief had hurled itself against the wall. "There!" he called proudly, and I, like Mr. Wemmick's aged parent, when the cannon went off, exclaimed: "He's fired! I heerd him!" But I had missed something of the point. The striker's exulting gaze was directed not at the handkerchief against the wall, but at the other one upon the ground. There it had remained, immovable and untouched, even as the face of the trusting spectator's watch from which Kirkwood drives his ball. The achievement was complete.

After that we went to lunch. I carried away with me one of the handkerchiefs tied by the master hand, and shall no more dare untie it than I dare unroll my umbrella when an artist has rolled it for me. I have, however, ventured to hit it, because before writing this plain and unvarnished tale I thought I ought to have a little trial on my own account. I admit, however, that I feel cramped and frightened in the drawing room and so began by taking it on to the lawn. It whizzed away satisfactorily enough, but I could not make quite the same splendid bang with it as its creator had done. It may have been my puny hitting, or it may be that the real reverberating sound can only be obtained within four walls.

I may seem to have written lightly, almost frivolously, of this adventure, but in fact the knot in the handkerchief is, I believe, a capital device. One thing is certain, that it is much better to practice swinging at something than at nothing. When we swing merely at the empty air we may look like all the photographs of all the champions, and get our knees and elbows into exactly the right places, but there is absent one intensely important element—namely that of timing. With nothing to aim at, we are much more likely—and Heaven knows we are likely enough when there is a real ball—to hit too soon. "Wait for it" is one of the eternal imperatives of golf; we cannot wait for nothing, but we can wait for a handkerchief.

I cross-examined my friend rather sternly about hooking and slicing, since it seemed to me that he might be acquiring bad habits in one of these two directions without knowing it. He made some admissions but came back to the solid, satisfying fact that he had found out how to drive a golf ball after being unable to do so for almost unnumbered years. I only wish I had half his complaint. Crash! Bang! That was the genuine note. I have left that blessed handkerchief in the hall, and somebody else has had a shot at it. It sounds—it really does sound—as if he had broken something.

Cures and Cathedrals

American Golfer
1929

I have received a letter from an American friend of mine, a very good golfer, whom I hope soon to see again in the flesh. He has lately landed here with his family, and they are engaged in touring England in a motorcar. There appears to be some difference of opinion between them as to their respective amusements; so they have come to a compromise. For every eighteen holes of golf played at least one cathedral must be visited, an agreement which, as he says, "preserves a delicate balance between the culture of the mind and of the body."

I do not know precisely how fond my correspondent is of cathedrals, but, presuming a temperate and reasonable affection for them, it seems to me that he has got all the worst of this bargain. A day's golf—yes, that might be fair enough, but to set a mere eighteen holes against a whole cathedral is iniquitous.

Just consider the two enterprises in light of their after-effects. A round of golf leaves a man comparatively fresh and unjaded, while a cathedral is more prostrating even than a picture gallery and makes of him a wreck, with aching legs and watering eyes.

I fancy my poor friend, after a whole day at Chester, dashing over to Hoylake, which he has never seen before, to be untimely ripped from it just when he is beginning to appreciate its flat and curious beauties. Or, again, here is a harder case—Canterbury and Sandwich! He plays a single round of St. George's and is not granted so much as to see the two other great courses which are next door to it. It is obvious that he has allowed himself to be scandalously over-reached.

I am writing to him to suggest a countermove. Let him go to Canterbury and have in the most outwardly docile manner. Let him not only do the Cathedral thoroughly but also the ruins of St. Augustine's Monastery and St. Martin's Church; let him even throw out hints that Fordwich, with its delicious little town hall, should on no account be missed when they are so near to it. He may even add with an air of transparent innocence that it possesses a ducking stool for scolding wives. At the end of the day his family will be reduced to pulp. They will say, as did Mr. Micawber after a visit to Canterbury, that their ashes "will be found commingled in the cemetery attached to a venerable pile for which the spot has acquired a reputation, shall I say, from China to Peru."

At this moment he must unmask his bitterness, declaring that the bargain has not been kept. They have had much more than their pound of flesh. He must demand, at least, one round of Deal and one of Prince's in exchange for all that additional sightseeing, and they will be far too much exhausted to resist him. If he takes a firm stand, he may even get Rye and Littlestone thrown in and be lot off Rochester altogether.

It will be seen that in a general way my sympathies are entirely with my friend. And yet at this particular moment I would personally rather see a cathedral than a golf course. Nor, I am convinced, am I alone in holding these sentiments. There was about last weekend's match at Sunningdale, in which various eminent persons were taking part, an air of lassitude. One of the most eminent persons even told me that the sight of a golf club filled him with horror and loathing. I was, to be sure, his partner, which may have had something to do with it.

Yet when it comes to quitting there are difficulties. When we arrive at this pass, the probability is that we have been playing badly, and that makes it for some of us harder, and not easier, to stop. We go on wondering what we were doing wrong; we are not satisfied with the knowledge that we were doing everything wrong because we were too tired of golf to do anything right. It is almost worthwhile to try just one more round in order that we may leave off in a more tranquil and reasonable frame of mind; but this may lead to an eternity of vain attempts.

If we can, like Mr. Bob Sawyer and Mr. Ben Allen, "try a little abstinence," we shall have a joyful day to which to look forward. We may hardly have realized that we are convalescent when suddenly the desire to play golf again, the conviction that it is really quite a pleasant game, will burst upon us. We shall enjoy it as frantically as we do the whiting and milk-pudding—not in themselves an exciting diet—which are given us after another sort of illness.

By the time my American friend has finished his tour and come to London, his discipline somewhat relaxed, I hope I may have arrived at that happy state and be ready to play with him. So now give me a dim, restful, twilighty cathedral, or, failing that, a small chapel in a small corner of England.

Nine Inches

Playing the Like
1934

There has come to me lately a letter from a friend who is playing golf in a sunny foreign clime. It is the kind of letter which, however reticent and considerate its expressions, seems at this bitter season of the year to be in the nature of "rubbing it in."

Yet this particular letter had its compensations. It began by describing the horrors of a stormy voyage, and that was one up to me, even though the writer did add that within two hours of landing, as I hope, rather limp and miserable, he had done a hole in two. Next he briefly expatiated on the glories of the sunshine, while I ground my teeth, and that made us all even. Then he went on to say that owing to previous vagaries of the climate the course, which I take to be a new one, was hardly at its best; the greens he described as "a huge joke," and, he added with formidable underlining, "You are not dead at nine inches."

That ought to have made me one up again, since the joke of that sort of green is apt to pall, but being an honest man I must admit that, as I finished the letter, I was a little jealous of him. Still, nine inches! It is rather consoling, as I shiver over a fire, to think of those tiny putts. I wish I knew exactly what effect they are having on him. The cheerful possibility is that they will have so entirely shattered him that when next we play together—on good greens—he will still be missing them. The depressing possibility is that such iron discipline will have given him nerves of iron; that all generosity will have been crushed out of him in a hard school, so that he will expect me to hole all the nine-inch putts. In my mind's eye I can see him standing with that air of ostentatious detachment which gives no hope.

Nine inches is not much. Nevertheless I would distinctly prefer to be given a putt of those trifling dimensions than have to hole it. It would be very good for me, good for all of us, if we always had to hole them, for who can say what precise number of inches constitutes "dead"?

"Halved hole," says the foe; but "No," I say, "No";
"Putt it out, mine enemie!
You're dead but not buried." He's shaky and flurried!
Oh! a terrible miss makes he.

There is always the chance that it is we who may make the terrible miss, and even if we do not, the continual settling down to an ignominious putt takes something out of us. Nine inches ought not to be so prostrating, but what about ten inches or eleven or twelve—down hill and down wind—on a fast green with a perceptible borrow?

At what range does a ball cease to be merely "dead" and become "stone dead"? It is a delicate question. There is a certain distance as to which we grumble to ourselves. "The beast has laid it dead"; but we should never dream of giving him the putt. We may recall dear Joe Gargery when Pip asked him if Miss Havisham was dead. "Why, you see, old chap," said Joe, "I wouldn't go so far as to say that, for that's a deal to say; but she ain't———" "Living, Joe?" "That's nigher where it is," said Joe; "she ain't living." So it is with putts. There are so many that we would not go so far as to call missable and yet it would be a deal to say that they were dead.

The obvious moral is that there should be no giving of putts, and the highest authorities have recommended that we should not give them to each other, but human nature is, and always will be, too strong. To make a law against the practice is even more hopeless than to make a law against a bowler bowling at a particular spot, and having a particular number of fielders in particular positions. No law, human or divine, can prevent a man from picking up his ball when he has had enough. There is always this resort of golfing suicide, whether cold and calculated or in a fit of temporary insanity, accompanied by the breaking of the putter across the knee. No one can rob us of that last dread indulgence.

We give putts primarily in the expectation of reciprocal favors, but there is also, I hope, another motive less sordid. Admittedly we are always grateful for small mercies, and it is an unspeakable relief in a hard-fought match to see the enemy miss a small putt; but, unless we are in a very vindictive mood, we would much rather win or halve the hole in some other way. We need never be ashamed of our joy, though we have to dissemble it, when his ball goes plump into a bunker, but there is a certain inevitable feeling of shame when he misses a ridiculous little putt. It is something of the same kind of impersonal shame that we experience as onlookers when a fieldsman gets a catch right into his hands and then lets the ball slither down his trembling legs, or a football player with a place-kick straight in front of goal lifts his head and produces a half-topped slice. We may not restrain a gasp of relief or even a yell of delight if we are partisans and our side has profited, but at the same time we are humiliated. A great game seems momentarily to have been brought into contempt. As for seeing a man miss short putts all the way round, we might almost as well go to see him hanged. We turn away with a shudder. It is horrible.

These feelings may possibly do some credit to our hearts, but they do none to our heads, and we ought, of course, to repress them. We ought, though this is asking a great deal, to be glad that our adversary shows no maudlin liberality. There is, too, this more strictly practical point that, once the ball is safely in the hole, it is far more satisfactory to have begun the match by holing a hard putt than by being given one of a foot. It is a great thing to get the ball actually into the hole as early as possible in the round, for the unavoidable moment becomes far worse from being put off. Besides, to look on the brighter side of an odious business, there is some sensual satisfaction in the tapping or popping of the ball into the hole at short range. Tapping and popping; yes, surely there is a pleasant onomatopoeic quality about the words. It suggests the ring of the ball against the tin, and when we are really very near indeed to the hole we do hit the ball against the back of the tin with delightful freedom and boldness.

I am working myself up into the right frame of mind. Let my friend come back quickly from his bloated baskings. He shall not find me quail at nine inches, and at eighteen inches I shall be ready to make a fair exchange.

The Rebirth of a Golfer

Out of the Rough
1932

There are few pleasanter stories and few which make one more bitterly envious than Hans Andersen's story of the Tinder Box. It will be remembered that the soldier had only to rub this box (which, I regret to say, he had stolen from an old witch) and three dogs instantly appeared before him, one with eyes as big as saucers, a second with eyes as big as mill wheels and a third whose eyes were positively of the size of towers. These dogs brought him money—copper, silver or gold—whenever he wanted it; they brought him the beautiful princess in her sleep, and they finally saved him from being executed when he richly deserved it, and frightened the King into giving him the princess as a bride.

They were, in short, the most invaluable animals, and they always set me thinking about the benevolent magician who will some day appear and grant me everything I wish. There is one wish which would, I believe, make us all happy, if we could have it granted. It is a very modest one, being no more than that we shall be allowed to begin all over again the learning of some pleasant art. There is bicycling, for instance, which today appears merely a tedious method of getting about when there is no car. Yet can anybody deny that there was a romantic thrill in his earliest wobbles on that despised instrument? I can remember wonderfully clearly my first beginnings, a blazing hot day in September on the lawn at home, an angelic and perspiring parent who held me and the bicycle, while we made curious zigzags across the grass. And then the sensation of going unaided, and the first ride on the open highway! The Huntingdon road at Cambridge is not celebrated for its beauty; it is flat, straight and rather ugly; but when I think of that first bicycle—Somebody's *Grand Modèle de Luxe*—the road seems to me, in retrospect, to have been fringed by fairy trees and jeweled flowers.

I began golf so long ago and at such an immature age that I can recall nothing about it, but it must have been delicious, and I wish it could happen all over again. If one had the strength of mind to do it, I believe it would be well worthwhile to start again as a one-handed player and pant for the day when one was given a twenty-four handicap. Or, perhaps, left-handed would be better, because then one could laboriously transpose all the rules one had learned and hold tight with the right hand and loose with the left, and so on. No doubt there would be disappointments in store, but one would be getting slowly better instead of getting rather quickly worse, and there are few sensations more enchanting than the consciousness of improvement.

I have just had a letter from a golfer who began again left-handed, and his experiences are rather interesting. He did not do it deliberately from a spirit of adventure, but because, owing to a rheumatic left shoulder, he could play no longer in the ordinary way. So, after twenty years of right-handed playing he became a humble novice, bought fresh clubs and stood on the other side.

"And do you know," he says, "it was great fun." I am sure it must have been, and I envy him the luxury of his feelings in that new blossoming. "I was a little better, of course," he adds, "than when I started playing right-handed, because I knew the importance of a steady head, firm stance, and so on." That seems rather surprising. I will not be so cynical as to say that these pieces of knowledge do more harm than good, but I should not have expected them to counterbalance the strangeness and topsy-turvey-dom of being on the wrong side of the ball. Many years ago I amused myself by cultivating a left-handed iron, and though I did attain to hitting a teed ball with a modest accuracy, I never felt anything but horribly clumsy, a duffer with no touch and no eye, who never would be anything but a duffer.

My correspondent was less humble, for he came to the conclusion that, whereas his lowest handicap in his unregenerate days had been eight or nine, left-handed he was going to be "a real tiger." Well, he wasn't; that is, in brief, the sad end of the story. He soon found that he was "committing the old mistakes in a very much accentuated form." He played matches against "old, old men and middle-aged ladies," and I rather gather that these despised persons would sometimes have beaten him, if it had not been for one circumstance; his shoulder was not so ill but that he retained the power of playing quite short strokes right-handed. Thus he could sometimes, when apparently *in extremis*, lay a pitch dead and dash the cup of victory from the old ladies' lips. The end of the story is not really sad, because in the last paragraph of his letter he tells me that his shoulder was suddenly cured, so that he could play right-handed once more. Moreover, he plays a little better for the discipline which he has undergone. Perhaps he carries one left-handed club in his bag and, when his ball lies apparently unplayable under a wall, he plays a brilliant shot with it and gives his enemy a shock just as he used to do to the old ladies.

To be able to play equally well from either side of the ball would be a wonderful thing. I am not thinking of that occasional ball wedged under a fence; I have just conceived the luminous idea that to this happy ambidextrous golfer the fear of slicing would be dead. If the wind blew hard on his back when he stood to the ball right-handed, he would just stand the other way and take a left-handed club and the slicy wind would become a hooky one: a friend and helper instead of a tyrannical foe. The prevailing wind at St. Andrews, in my experience at any rate, blows from left to right on the way out, and one is often so exhausted with fighting the slice and keeping out of the whins, that one has no energy left to revel in the hook on the inward half. To the ambidextrous golfer the round would be one long delicious orgy of hooking. With what freedom would he lash at his ball! What a splendid, virile, fearless creature he would be! When I get my tinderbox, here is another gift for me to wish for. Meanwhile, if I could find it, I would go out and practice with that old left-handed iron of mine; but, alas! I know it has been ruthlessly swept away to a jumble sale long since.

Aces of Clubs

Country Life
1928

A golfing friend of mine announced quite suddenly at luncheon the other day that he had lost many matches because his opponent possessed better clubs than he did; indeed, he was convinced that nearly all his defeats were attributable to this cause. The others of us believed this to be merely a sally of sparkling exaggeration, but he added, with marks of the most serious concern on his face, that, try as he would, he never, never could buy a good or even a decent club.

This seemed curious, as he is, in other walks of life, as I should judge, something of a connoisseur who would choose with deliberation, discretion and success. It is, however, an undeniable fact that comparatively few people have an eye for a club. I know that I have not got it, for, though I can now and again acquire a club which I like myself, nobody else ever likes it—a state of things reassuring as regards theft, but otherwise humiliating. In order to console our friend we all, there and then, declared ourselves to be wholly incompetent in the choosing of clubs. Especially did we say that which is quite true, that in a big shop away from the links the mind grows hopelessly dizzy with looking at clubs, and the wrists lost all sensation with waggling them; the mere fact of soling a club not on turf, which is its natural element, but upon wood or linoleum, seems to have some subtly disastrous effect, so that we are capable of buying a club either far flatter or far more upright than is our normal pattern. One shrewd person declared that he never bought a club unless he were allowed to take it for a trial round in his bag on sale or return. Various other pieces of good advice were proffered, but the best was the last. "After all," said somebody, "So-and-so's way is really the only one. When he sees a good club in another man's bag, he just puts it in his own." "Yes," added a still more defamatory somebody else, "and changes the grip in case it should be identified."

I am not, personally, afraid of So-and-so. Nobody (touching wood and in a good hour be it spoken) steals my clubs, just as I truly believe myself not to have stolen anyone else's, but I have known what it is to lose a favorite iron, and it is for the moment, and sometimes for a long while, a sad blow. I doubt whether it is a blow that befalls people as often as it once did, not because there is a higher level of honesty in the clubhouse, but because there are not so many long-treasured irons as there were. Indeed, I have just been reading somewhere in an American magazine an article saying that the favorite (spelled, of course, without its "u") club is disappearing. If this be so, it is due to those elaborate series of matched and numbered irons with which everybody plays today. There are five or six of them in a set, all bearing so strong a family resemblance to one another that it seems hardly possible for the owner to conceive a wild passion for any particular one of them. Not long ago I was watching a golf match, and there was among my fellow-watchers one who should, but for a recent and, as I trust, temporary lapse of form, have been playing in it. To console himself and regain hope he had bought a beautifully matched set, and as he watched he dandled one of them—number three or four or five. He did so with an air of genuine affection, and I sincerely hope it will serve him well, but it can never be quite what a unique and favorite iron once was; it has too many sisters that will do almost as well.

The favorite club of an older generation was, as a rule, a servant of all work. It had one main function, of course, but it also had several subsidiary ones, and it was often called on to perform one of these at an extreme crisis. It was, let us say, what was once called a driving iron and would today be called a "No. 2." It chiefly drove, but it had on occasions pitched, especially against a wind, it constantly ran up and, once or twice, when the putter had gone obstinately on strike, it had come nobly to the rescue and had scuffled two or three putts of most crucial length into the hole. Probably, it had also taken part in some one-club matches which had put money into its owner's pocket. So it was an old and trusted friend "well tried through many a varying year," and its owner, conscious that orthodoxy demanded some other club for a particular stroke, had yet often said, "No, hang it, give me the old one. I feel safer with that."

As time goes on there will be fewer and fewer such clubs as that, except in the corners of lockers or, perhaps, suspended honorably upon the wall. For the sake of pure skill it is, probably, a good thing that there should be fewer. It is difficult not to work a favorite club a little too hard; we take it because we know we can make some sort of a respectable stroke with it, and thus put off and off the hour of learning to play the shot with the right club. A favorite driving mashie may be bad for its owner's brassie play, a pitching mashie may render atrophied his half-iron shot, and so on. Moreover, a favorite is often a club of such strong and peculiar character that it is impossible to get any others like it; it makes all the other irons in the bag feel a little strange and uncomfortable. I have never possessed matched quadruplets or quintuplets, but the advertisements tell me that, if I did, I should not be able to tell one from the other with my eyes shut. I should swing them all in just one way and play the same old shot, sometimes with one and sometimes with the other, forever and ever. If I were some years younger and could learn to do it, what a much better iron player I might be; but, ye gods! how dull!

As it is, my set of irons, though I am not conscious that they quarrel very violently among themselves, certainly do not bear any close or obvious relationship to one another; I cannot think that they are even the most distant of cousins. My so-called driving iron, bought for somebody else and then—well, not stolen, but gradually reabsorbed into my bag—is a perfectly straightforward, ordinary iron, but while other people would have a "No. 3" of the same type, I have a "jigger," with a shallow face and a bulging back view, of an entirely different pattern. Then after that comes a mashie without a heel, built according to the prescription of Mr. G. F. Smith. The mashie-niblick also has a kink in its neck, so, I suppose, these two may be considered related. Generally speaking, however, they must be admitted to be a job lot. It is, of course, open to anyone to infer that I should play better if they were not.

P.S.—On rereading this article I find I have told a lie, and, like George Washington, I can't. I did once steal a golf club, but it was only from the Red Cross, and we all stole things in wartime, and I did want it so very badly. I still have it now, and for ten whole years I have been meaning to play just one stroke with it again, and have postponed the attempt. It was so great a favorite once that I dare not risk the disillusionment.

Black or Silver

Out of the Rough
1932

The other day both my caddie and my irons reappeared after luncheon looking rather pale. On inquiry it appeared that the caddie had been trying to clean the irons, which had remained uncleaned since I visited America in 1922. No wonder the poor fellow looked wan; he had, by a prodigious display of energy, just got through the outer crust of dirt when a fellow caddie had told him of my singular habits and bidden him desist. I felt thoroughly ashamed, the more especially as my play in the morning had justified his probable belief that his master had not used those irons for several years.

Once upon a time, to use unpolished clubs would have been unthinkable and, indeed, even now, after nine years of it, it sometimes gives me a shameful and slovenly feeling, as if I were to come down to breakfast unshaven. At the same time it is now recognized as a perfectly respectable thing, and hardly even eccentric, for the most illustrious persons do it. The first golfer of eminence whom I recollect playing with black clubs was Mr. Herbert Fowler. He was regarded for some years as an erratic genius and no one imitated him. Then—and I hope I am not defaming anyone—came Mr. Robert Harris and then several of the Americans, among them Mr. Bobby Jones, who, if he did not have his irons wholly black, at least forbade his caddie to clean the centers of them. After that the habit became for a while positively fashionable.

No doubt these distinguished persons had excellent reasons for their eccentricity. The statement is attributed to Young Tommy Morris that amateurs allow their eyes to be lured from the ball by the glitter of a polished head; that may have been one of the reasons, and there is much to be said for it. For myself I can assign no such easily defensible reason for my habit. It arose partly by chance, partly from pure laziness. When I was in America I found that the caddies considered it beneath the dignity of a freeborn citizen to perform any such menial task. Therefore I paid the professional some fraction of a dollar to perform it, but I always had to leave that particular course before he had done so, and this offended my economical soul. Furthermore, on what may be called my home course I often dispense with a caddie, and I do not want the bother of cleaning my very muddy clubs after the round. Yet another reason is a decided popularity with the caddie, if I do have one, since he gets the orthodox tip and has less work to earn it. These are not, I admit, very good reasons, but there is one that is, namely, that clubs uncleaned will never wear out. If I live or play till ninety, I shall still be using, if I have a mind to it, the rather disreputable and ill-matched set of irons with which I now play my indifferent shots. The weight of a favorite iron can be slowly but surely altered in the course of years by cleaning, so that its owner wakes up suddenly one morning to find that he cannot "feel the head" because that head has grown "tinny" and emaciated.

I read somewhere the other day a remark of Duncan's that caddies must be watched with the eyes of a lynx when they clean clubs. They start, he said, with a new piece of sandpaper, on the heel of the iron and expend there the chief part of their elbow-grease, with the result that the heel becomes rapidly lightened and the balance of the club spoiled. I cannot say that I had noticed that subtle point for myself, but I am sure he is right, and about the more general altering of the weight there can be no doubt at all. Mr. Laidlay's famous putting cleek grew so thin with the years that at last he took to an ordinary aluminum putter. He than endeavored to make us believe that this was the easier club to play with, but it was, I believe, only an artifice to cover up a tragedy. At the present moment I have taken once more to putting—it is, in my case, but a courtesy title—with a dear old cleek which I bought at Sandwich on the occasion of my first University match in 1895. It is still, in my eyes, a delicious club, but it has had to have some additional metal soldered to its back. If I had begun by keeping it unpolished, it might still be the original club which I bought from Ramsay Hunter and with which I used once to be able to putt almost well.

There are various other advantages of the non-cleaning policy that may be tentatively suggested. For instance, no one is likely to steal a club that appears superficially so grubby and unappetizing. For that matter, I have—touching wood—never found anyone who wanted to steal my clubs or even to borrow them. Again, there is the rather disgraceful hope of picking up a stray half-crown or two by being a "flat-catcher." An unsuspecting stranger might well think that nobody could possibly hit the ball with so seedy an armory of irons. Nevertheless, the owner of black clubs does now and then feel an almost passionate longing to have them cleaned, much as, I presume, the owner of a beard sometimes feels his fingers itch to shave it off, simply for the sake of novelty. Nor is this desire so foolish and capricious as it may appear, because novelty can improve our golf by giving us a new interest in the game. It is so easy for our minds as well as our bodies to get stale and bored.

I am sure I have quoted before the case of Mr. Guy Ellis, who, when in his brief and conquering prime, declared that he played three rounds of St. Andrews a day and used a different set of clubs for each round "because then it was impossible to get stale." I can cite other celebrated personages. When Sir Harold Gillies took to his monstrously high tee he played monstrously well for a while and could advance all sorts of reasons why the tee made it easier to swing the club. The reasons were doubtless unimpeachable, but it is my belief that they had mighty little to do with the matter, and that he played so well simply because his interest in the game was titillated. At the present moment he seems to have retired from the fray, but if he only discovers something else to amuse him, he will soon be beating everybody's head off again. May he discover that something quickly! Then there is Leo Diegel, who has an engagingly fantastic outlook on the game. He has a habit of suddenly having the head or the shaft of a wooden club painted another color, or otherwise disguised in some such way, in order that the club, while unchanged in essentials, may seem to its owner to be a new one. Major Thorburn is another player who occurs to me. The leather grips of his wooden clubs come much farther down the shaft than is usual. This does not mean that he holds the clubs low down on the grip. His motive is, I believe, simply this: that the long grip makes the club look shorter, and he feels as if the shorter club would be easier to control.

Some people may think these antics of the great merely nonsensical, but, if they think so, they should suspect themselves of being too stolid and unimaginative. There is such a great deal of fun, and some profit as well, to be got out of the game which we called, when we were very young, "pretending." The trouble is that as we grow older we lose some of the power of playing it. A child can enjoy the game, even if it has to coach the grown-up in his part—thus: "Now I'll hide under the table, and then you say, 'I wonder where that naughty, tiresome little girl can have go to'." When the poor, stupid grown-up has said his first sentence like a parrot, he is taught his next one, and so the game goes on in installments. When we are old we cannot rise to such heights of pretending; but still, if we are not too self-conscious, we never wholly lose the knack of it and can recapture more of it by deliberate effort. So, if anybody sees me playing with beautifully burnished irons, he need not think that I have succeeded to a large estate and bought some new ones; I shall only be pretending that I have acquired a wonderful new numbered set from America and that I am going to hit the ball with the crisp click of a shutting knife forevermore.

Alien Clubs

Country Life
1952

I began my last week's article with a reference to Addington, and, behold, on the very night it was written came the burning of the clubhouse there! Everybody must feel sympathy with golfers thus bereft of their home, and in particular with those whose clubs had been left there and so were consumed. To lose a whole bag of clubs will always be tragic, and today it must be worse than ever on the purely economic grounds that they cost so much to replace. Long, happy years ago one could buy a club or two out of income whenever one had the mind; today a new set must amount to a capital expenditure. But it is, of course, the loss of cherished and trusty allies that is the really harrowing part of it. But yesterday they were things of beauty; the sheen of them "was like stars on the sea"; today they are no more than blackened and twisted bits of metal. Those that were the oldest friends possibly came from the days before the invasion of steel shafts—a putter, perhaps, or a faithful little "Sammy" or a "Benny"; each of them had its individual pedigree and history; it had come from a famous man's shop, or, perhaps, at a great price from the champion's own playing set—the gap left by such a friend as that no other club can quite fill.

Such old favorites are now, however, growing rare; they are to be found as pensioned veterans in cupboards rather than on active service in bags. So let us hope that not many of them are lost. Clubs that are bought and sold in sets, though of admirable workmanship and better than were their predecessors, cannot wind themselves round the heart in quite the same way. No one of them is unique, and however excellent each is yet only one of a class. To replace them will doubless cost much pure gold, but another set almost as like the last one as one pea is to another will surely be found. This is, I think, particularly true of irons. Even before this mass-produced age it was always much easier to use another man's irons than his driver or brassie, and still today there is more individual feeling and character about wooden clubs; they will always be the harder for which to find substitutes.

Sad as it is to lose old clubs, it is pleasantly exciting to obtain fresh ones, and, assuming him providently insured or wallowing in riches, I can almost find myself envying the man who must begin golfing life all over again with a brand new set. What fun he will have and how he will waggle those glittering baubles till he scarcely knows whether he is on his head or his heels! One piece of advice I venture to give him, namely that he should do his waggling on the turf and not merely on the floor of a shop. There is something about a shop, and particularly a great store, which will make "his judgment go out a wisitin," to use Mr. Weller's expressive words, and he may find that he can scarcely recognize on the morrow the club that has enchanted him today.

Let me reinforce this advice by that of someone much better worth listening to, Harold Hilton. After saying that artificial light invests a club with some spurious glamour, he goes on, "I have learnt my lesson, and nowadays I never buy a club except in daylight, and moreover I try to avoid buying a club within the precincts of a domicile or a clubhouse, as clubs have a habit of appearing at their very best when reposing for inspection on a carpet or even on oilcloth. If I were in the business I should certainly cover the floor of my showroom with a thick, heavy carpet. The carpet might cost money, but I should possibly get rid of many ugly ducklings thereby."

Though it is on the whole a sad thing to lose clubs, it is surely remarkable how many people do lose them—and yet perhaps it is not so remarkable considering how ladies leave diamond tiaras and diplomats the most secret papers in taxis. At any rate the strange thing does occur and that often. I happened the other day on something I had written about sixteen years ago, on coming across an advertisement from a Railway Lost Property Depot. There were offered for sale at prices between a guinea (£1.05) and twenty-five shillings (£1.25) apiece "forty sets of modern golf clubs"; and to make the offer more inviting they were "all guaranteed." What they were guaranteed to do I have no evidence, but if it was to make all the purchasers' shots successful, then it was an example of the dashing quality of private enterprise; I fancy a nationalized railway would be more cautious.

What puzzled me then and puzzles me now is not so much why the owners lost them—anybody can leave things behind in a railway carriage—as why they did not take the trouble to get them back. Some of them may have been so disgusted with their play that day that they resolved to give up the game, and so deliberately left their clubs as people sometimes leave unwanted babies on the rack. Perchance they left them in the cloakroom, meaning to reclaim them, and then something happened that changed the whole course of their lives so that they never came back. Did they elope? Were they suddenly moved to empty the till and decamp? They can scarcely have forgotten them, and yet there were those forty sets that had waited and waited for their faithless owners. I have sometimes seen and even been tempted by bundles of old clubs exposed outside a pawnbroker's shop. The reason why they have never been reclaimed is all too plain, but that railway treasure trove remains something of a mystery.

Incidentally, since everything to do with golf has now grown so dear, might not some of this lost legion of clubs be cheaply let out to those who want to play and round and have no clubs or, at any rate, none with them? A friend told me the other day that at municipal courses in Scotland the visitor often hires clubs. In particular he told me of a friend of his who had done so, appropriately enough, at Aberdeen, and paid an extremely small sum for the loan of some half-dozen clubs. It may be that this is a perfectly well-known custom on public courses and that I am simply ignorant and behind the times. At any rate it sounds a good plan and one might find in that job lot the magic wand for which one had been searching for years.

A borrowed club will sometimes do wonders, and then the borrower insinuates as clearly as he can, without actual mendicancy, that he would like to keep it, and the lender must either harden his heart or give way with the best grace he can muster. Douglas Rolland had a habit of arriving without any clubs for an exhibition match and borrowing a few with which he performed prodigies; but the really historic example of borrowed clubs is Walter Tavis's victory in our Amateur Championship in 1904. He had been putting very badly and almost at the last moment he borrowed from a compatriot the Schenectady putter which thereupon became famous. He also used a spoon that Ben Sayers insisted on lending him, and, if it was not so conspicuously deadly as the putter, it yet did great deeds. I can still remember as vividly as possible two shots that Travis played in the final with that spoon, one up to the second hole against the wind and another at the twelfth. They were played with a masterly control that remains unforgettable.

I, too, borrowed a spoon once, and for a little while did great things with it. This was in Macedonia. The spoon belonged to a hospital nurse and was lent to me through a third party. She was at once a generous and a hard-hearted lady; generous for trusting me with so rare a club, in a land where they were hard to come by; hard-hearted on demanding its return when I had grown so fond of it. Unfortunately I had written rather scornfully about the golf course at her hospital and those who played on it. Suppose she was justified, but I have never quite forgiven nor forgotten. It was a really exquisite spoon.

The Ball That Cannot Be Sliced

American Golfer
1925

Every individual hair of my head stood on end when I read, a day or two ago, an article in our English *Golf Illustrated.* It declared that an "unnamed man of science in the midlands had discovered a golf ball which, owing to a particular and nicely adjusted marking, would spin neither to the right nor to the left and, however cut, flew straight in the direction in which it was hit." The death-ray, I thought, was nothing to this. Here was the end of golf and so, in effect, of the world. The statement that the experiment was a "wholly scientific" one did not console me. Some one man who had been chronically afflicted by a slice or a hook would take to the ball and everyone else would have to follow suit in self-defense and the game would be ruined.

Then I read on a little further and found some comfort, for it was said that in addition to its other qualities the ball refused to soar; "its tendency was earthwards." If that be so, golf may yet be saved. The ball will only be a good ball at a hole where the fairway is very narrow, the ground very hard and full of running and there are no cross hazards. An effective spoke can be put in its wheel, if such a metaphor be permissible, by the building of good old-fashioned ramparts across the course. Yes, I think that ought to do it, that is indeed if the scientific gentleman in the midlands and his ball really exist, and I and other serious-minded golfers are not the victims of a hoax.

The nearest approach to this ball, with which we are threatened, was the old "Eclipse" which used to be made years ago by a firm in Edinburgh. I am an old enough golfer to remember it. It used to be called the "putty" as opposed to the ordinary "gutty." It was an ugly-looking fellow of a yellowish color which had but little bounce in it and went off the club, as somebody said, "like a thief in the night," with no cheerful ring. I remember very well when I was at school at Eton going to a photographer's shop in town—why a photographer should sell golf balls I do not know—and buying one golf ball with my last shilling. I could not understand why all my shots seemed to be half topped: I could not get that ball into the air and it was some little time before I realized that it was an Eclipse.

The ball had its triumphs. Mr. Horace Hutchinson played with it and won his first two Amateur Championships with it. In his "Fifty Years of Golf" he tells us something about it. "It was," he says, "indestructible. Then it was a wonderful ball for keeping its line on the putting green—far the best putting ball that ever has come into being during the half century of golf that I have known. But the quality, which perhaps was its highest virtue, was that it did not go off the line nearly as much as the gutty when pulled or sliced . . . Of course it was possible to pull or slice the putty, if you played badly enough, though it did not take the act nearly as freely as the gutty . . . It was a fine ball against the wind—it kept so low and straight. On hard ground it would make up in its run for its loss of carry. But . . . it was an impossible ball to stop on the green off a lofted shot—it would not take a cut when one purposely tried to stop it."

I seem to recollect that it was not a popular ball, in that even those who played with it did not get much joy out of it and sometimes felt even a little ashamed of it. And of course the professionals, who were ball makers, did not like it. Mr. Hutchinson quotes Old Tom Morris as saying with a twinkle whenever an Eclipse did find trouble, "Eh, the potties—I thoeht the potties never gaed aff the line." At any rate it was been dead, buried and forgotten for many years now but apropos of this menace from the midlands, Mr. Hutchinson's account of it makes interesting reading.

Golf would certainly be a funny game if this unsliceable, unhookable ball came in. It would save the Green Committee a great deal of money since only the narrowest strip of fairway would be necessary; all lateral hazards would be at a discount and the game would consist in direct frontal attacks upon complicated systems of trenches across the course. If the Committee built anything in the shape of a small mountain there would be an outcry against the gross unfairness of a bunker more than ten feet high.

These are however, I hope, the idlest speculations, for after all we do play golf for fun and the greatest fun in golf is to hit the ball into the sky. It is better to have lofted and sliced than never to have lofted at all, and nothing could make amends, if we were never to see again the white ball "sailing with supreme dominion through the azure fields of air."

The Winds of Heaven

Country Life
1934

I was playing the other day with a perfectly good golfer. We were coming to the Long Hole In, and he had hit a perfectly good drive, well out of the reach of all the Beardies. He had, unless I am mistaken, visions of carrying Hell with a superb second, when—quite suddenly and unexpectedly–he missed the globe. There was a mighty swing, the club whistled through the air, and the ball remained *in statu quo*. Was it a practice swing, or had the incredible thing really happened? The rest of us hardly knew what to do, whether to laugh or, pityingly, to avert the eye. After he had had another shot and topped the ball some distance, one of us asked him politely whether he had played three, and he blushingly admitted the impeachment. It was a remarkable feat; and let nobody think he was a beginner. On the contrary, he has a handicap of six or so, which could very soon be reduced. Moreover, did he not—

confound him!—win the match for his side at the crucial moment by doing two admirable and consecutive fours at the Corner of the Dyke and the Road hole?

He missed the globe in the fullest and most glorious sense of the words, since he struck nothing but the winds of heaven. I am never sure whether we are entitled to say that we have performed that feat when our club strikes the ground before passing over the ball. It all depends on what the coiner of the phrase meant by the term "globe." Was he alluding to the round earth, or did he use the word as a synonym for ball, in the same way that the sporting reporter used to talk of "planting the leather between the uprights"? Personally, I prefer the first alternative, but I am afraid I must be wrong.

In search of an authoritative pronouncement I looked up the glossary at the end of the *Badminton* volume, and there found: "Missing the globe. To fail to strike the ball either by swinging right over the top of it, or by hitting the ground behind." If that be right, then I am wrong, but I shall always stick to my view that the only genuine and dramatic air shot is one in which the club meets nothing but air. A highly distinguished friend of mine, who has played for his county, was known for some while among the Deal caddies as "the blighter that hit the air shot," but I maintain he had not fully earned the title. I saw the stroke—in the Halford Hewitt Cup; his ball lay on an up-slope of one of the hills at the fifth hole, and it remained there in precisely the same place after he had done, but his club struck the ground. Similarly, I should like to be able to say that I once missed the globe on the first teeing ground and then won a scratch medal. In the *Badminton* sense it would be true. We played for the scratch medal at Cambridge on frozen snow, and I may charitably assume that I slipped on that first tee. At any rate, the ball did not move, but my driver head was covered with snow. I cannot claim the real distinction. I did not "swing right over the top" of the ball. To do so is, in fact, for a golfer of any experience, a comparatively rare achievement.

That it should be so always seems to me one of the standing wonders of golf. The ball is so very small, and the clubhead is not very large. It is surely remarkable that they make contact so regularly. At lawn tennis we—I mean players of my humble class—are perfectly familiar with the sensation of having a hole in the middle of the racket, and at cricket the most eminent constantly miss the ball. Prosaic and laborious persons will no doubt explain to me that in these cases the ball is moving and that in golf it is stationary. Still, the thing remains to me a minor source of astonishment, and one day, towards the end of last month, at St. Andrews, at eight o'clock in the morning, when the rain was coming down mercilessly and I had not had my breakfast, it seemed a positive miracle. I cannot help thinking, however, that the ball was not a globe at all. It reminded me, even in the moment of agony, of Mr. Mantalini's words: "The Countesses had no outlines at all, and the dowager's was a demd outline." This ball had the demdest, vaguest, fuzziest outline and anybody might have missed it.

So far I have been talking of missing the globe with a full swing, but it attains, perhaps, the quintessence of poignancy as a spectacle when it is done in a short shot. There was an old friend of mine, now dead, who was prone to do it quite close to the hole. He was afflicted with a quick, nervous jerk, afflicted so badly that he came to eschew playing matches and preferred solitary practice. Even then he was not immune, and I have more than once seen him pass high over the ball with his mashie, cast a hasty look round to discover if there was any other eye upon him but his Maker's, and then pick the ball up casually and walk on.

Most of us have at some time or other jabbed our putters into the ground and left the ball motionless; but to pass clean over the ball on the green is rare. I saw it happen once in the case of an agitated young subaltern, who had just joined his regiment and had to play in a foursome with a major. On the very last green, under the clubhouse windows, with everything depending on the hole, he left the ball severely alone; he must have missed it by a good six inches. Taking everything into consideration, I think that was the finest and most flawless example of the air shot that I ever saw. To be sure, it was not long ago that I played behind a man who made four consecutive air shots through the green; but he must have been a beginner, and beginners are not eligible for championships in this business of globe-missing; their advantages are too great. Neither can we consider the feats of Members of Parliament opening a new local course in their constituency, nor of Mayors who attempt a stroke in their robes and chains. In point of fact, I only once saw a Mayor open a course, and then it was a putting course. He holed a good long putt of several yards, and I can only say, as Jasper Petulengro did of the Bow Street runner, "I am of opinion, brother, that Mayor must have been a regular fine fellow."

The Ladies

Rubs of the Green
1936

Every afternoon, as I sat down to try to write an account of the mixed foursomes at Worplesdon, I meant no merely to describe the day's play but also to indulge in some reflections of a general character.

They would doubtless have been both profound and original had I ever had time to think of them or space to write them down; but there were always so many facts clamoring to be related, so many sparkling three's and calamitous eight's, so much "allonging and marshonging" to the nineteenth hole, just when one had settled down in a peaceful corner. The reporter had so much to tell that the philosopher never had a chance. I have had time now and, even so, the generalities are not nearly so numerous or so exciting as I had hoped. In fact, there is only one thing that I really want to say. It can be summed up in the words of Mr. Turveydrop, "Woman, lovely woman, what a sex you are!"

He said those words, we are told, "with a very disagreeable gallantry" and I trust that my reasons are free from that objection. I think I like watching women better than men because their golf is more interesting, and it is more interesting because of their wooden-club play; this is more accurate than that of the men, and there is more of it. It may be that nothing can give quite so exquisite a thrill as the difficult iron shot perfectly executed, but day in and day out, that which excites the wildest hopes and the deadliest fears beforehand, the greatest relief and enthusiasm when it has been well played, is the brassy shot. And how well these modern ladies do play their brassies! Time was—I speak now as an unchivalrous adversary—when one might hope for a fluff or a top unless the lie were perfect. Today, were I playing, the best I should hope for would be a shot so good that it found a bunker believed to be out of reach.

And then there were the wooden-club shots played at the short holes. These, too, were admirable in their accuracy and often put the man and his iron to shame. One of the great gathering places at Worplesdon is the terrace in front of the clubhouse overlooking the fourth green. It is there that all but the insanely conscientious await the players, getting a hazy view of the happenings at the first three lowland holes and avoiding a climb. If ever at this fourth hole one saw a ball behind a tree or in the heather there was a lady with a brave smile and a mashie-niblick about to play it. If there was a ball on the green there was a complacent man with a putter. There have always been two schools of thought at Worplesdon as to the holes at which the men should drive, and once it was an argument in favor of their driving at the evens that the fourth and the sixteenth were too long for the ladies; it was inhuman to demand such shots from a poor, weak woman. Today the ladies bang the ball up on to those greens with their spoons as if it was the easiest thing in the world, and they keep on banging them straight.

Admittedly—and this is a reflection to console the senile—a certain spurious reputation for straightness can be gained by extreme shortness. Many a ball that reposes blamelessly a few yards from the edge of the rough would have gone into it had it been harder hit; but this argument really will not do as regards the modern lady's driving, for she hits the ball very truly and accurately and she is far from short. Now and again she is cruelly out-driven by the opposing man, but, generally speaking, she keeps within hail of him and sometimes she gets in front of him. "Do you generally outdrive Mr. So-and-So like this?" a young lady was asked jocosely in regard to a famous adversary. "I don't know" was the answer. "I've never played with him before."

I have made my compliments to the ladies with the utmost sincerity. At the same time I spy an opening for a little mild propaganda. I wish that the long-driving young gentlemen could and would see that golf would be for them a far better game, more amusing, and more testing, if they had to play it as the ladies do and play brassy shots up to the flag instead of heaving up ball and divot with a number something. Golf as played today by the best ladies is golf at its best; the holes are of the right length for them, and they have to play them as Providence or the architect intended; they cannot destroy the proper geography of a hole. To my mind it was more interesting and more exhilarating to watch the ladies at Worplesdon than to see the professionals crushing the fine two-shot holes at Muirfield (what a bitter mockery to call them so!) with their Juggernaut strides.

It is very easy to talk and very difficult to do anything. A course that should make the best modern men play brassy shots to the green would leave the ladies with little to hope for but dull five's while some of us would never get up at all. We read that for the next Open Championship Hoylake is to be over 7,000 yards long; such stretching of the course may be necessary, but it is not in the least cheering to hear of; it opens up no real way out of the difficulty. Perhaps there is no way, but, if there is, it lies in doing something to the ball and not to the course. Meanwhile let us be thankful to the ladies for giving us a glimpse of what golf ought to be.

IV

The Players, Ridiculous and *Sublime*

The Happy Golfer

American Golfer
1927

Go out and watch a match in which Mr. Jones or Mr. Tolley is playing, and listen to the remarks among the crowd. You will hear a middle-aged golfer with a handicap verging on double figures, who can play many shots ill and none especially well, say something like this: "Ah! If I could only drive the ball like these young fellows, I could do the rest of it well enough."

And what he means, though he dare not quite say so, is that he could do it a great deal better than they can. It is a delusion, of course, since he forgets that one of these young heroes can pitch like an angel, and that the other can putt like a fiend; but still it is a pleasant delusion and does nobody any harm.

I have lately been falling into this sin of covetousness while playing with a friend of mine. He is not a champion. Far from it indeed, for I can give him strokes, and yet he fills me alternately with envy and rage. First comes envy. If I had the golfing gifts that nature has lavished on him, how would I not use them! Then comes rage, because he wastes them so criminally and then envy again, because he remains perfectly happy whether he hits the ball or whether he misses it, and never inquires into the cause of either occurrence.

Let me describe the game of this exasperating prodigal. He has, first of all, the nameless and priceless gift of making the club move fast. His driver hums like a hornet through the air. He can hit shots that the gods might envy. Sometimes they are long and low, sometimes long and high, and sometimes, alas! they are so short and so low as to bury themselves at his very feet. It is in keeping with the rest of his perverse genius that when he is driving against a hurricane, which reduced his adversaries to utter impotence, he will hit a succession of Braid-like "screamers," and, when there is a gentle wind behind him, such as would encourage the veriest foozler, he tops outrageously and persistently.

Then as to his iron play. He has the easy and commanding stance of an Open Champion about the play a "push-shot." There are the hands a little in front, just as the books tell us they ought to be; the feet would fit into exactly their right place on one of those mats marked out in white squares on which the truly great are photographed: purely by the light of nature he looks like a picture of one of the Old Masters. You would swear that the club would come flashing down, time after time, with mechanical accuracy; away would fly the ball—a masterful divot with it—low at first and then rising to fall biting its way into the turf. And do these things happen? Well, occasionally they do, and are a joy to witness.

In fact, as he comes nearer to the hole, he is so prone to the common fluff that among his intimates that particular shot is always named after him. I will call it colorlessly a "Smith," lest any susceptibilities be wounded.

It is no uncommon event for him to hit a magnificent drive to within a mashie (5 iron) shot of the green, and then play two or three short, sharp "Smiths" before he reaches it. When he does reach it, he will probably hole a very long putt, and so add one more to his irritating qualities by getting a half after all. The putting of such a player can be so easily imagined as hardly to need description. He always looks as if he were going to hole out: he always stands up and gives the ball a fine, free, fearless knock, except very occasionally when he plays a "Smith" with his putter, and his opponent's only comfort lies in the fact that sometimes the hole is in the wrong place.

History relates that once he did himself full justice with all clubs. He could pull or slice, hit low or high at will: he did not play so much as the ghost of a "Smith." And then, after those two wonderful hours, he relapsed placidly into his old condition, in which every round is "unrhythmic, patched, the even and the odd"; and, when he has dubbed once, he is quite likely to dub two, three, and four more times in quick succession. He does not know whence the inspiration came, nor why it went away again, and—confound the fellow!—he does not care.

Portrait of a High-Handicap Golfer

Golf Courses of the British Isles
1910

I should like at the outset briefly to explain who I am and why I am writing this chapter. I am known to every golfer—I play fairly regularly, generally on a Saturday afternoon, sometimes in the evening during the summer; I am genuinely keen on the game, and can honestly say that I devote a good deal of thought and attention to it; I enter for all the competitions at my club, but my name rarely appears on the list of those who have returned scores—my card is generally torn up about the fourteenth hole, frequently earlier. I believe that I come in for a good deal of abuse at the hands of the very low handicap man. "These chaps ought not to be allowed on the course," or "There should be a special time for starting these high-handicap men," or again, "My good sir, I've seen the man in front of me play his third, and he's not yet reached the bunker yet!" These and similar remarks are samples of what one has to bear.

One might perhaps gently remind the impatient expert that, after all, we high-handicap men do serve some useful purpose; they, too, were once even as we are now, and, moreover, without us the spoils of the fortnightly "sweep" would be distinctly lessened; now and again, also, one of us suddenly "comes on his game," and, if it be in a knockout competition, spreads havoc and devastation among the players with handicaps of under six.

I am sometimes inclined to think that the high-handicap players gets quite as much, if not more, enjoyment from his golf than does the man who receives only a small number of strokes from scratch. We are not so much depressed when we miss our drive, because it happens to us so much more frequently, and the joy we experience when we execute a perfect shot (and this *does* sometimes happen) is all the keener because of its comparative rarity. Furthermore, our anguish, when we are "right off our game," can be nothing in comparison with that of the skilled golfer who is in a similar condition (and I understand that this happens to even the greatest—have we not heard of Vardon failing at two-foot putts and Massy missing the ball altogether?).

I have been privileged to read Mr. Darwin's account of the famous courses of the British Isles, and it has been suggested that the thought might occur to high-handicap players like myself that, reading of these fours and threes which figure so frequently, one may be tempted to despair and say, "This is all very fine for the plus man, but what sort of a game could I play on such a course? My low, raking shot will not land me home on to the green; it will, I know, inevitably take me into a bunker—in how many strokes may I reasonably expect to accomplish the hole?"

I propose, therefore, under the kindly veil of anonymity, to describe the course on which I habitually play, from my point of view; the scratch man may skip this chapter or glance at it with amused scorn; it may possibly be of interest to my high-handicap fellows, who will, at any rate, sympathize with my appreciation of dangers and terrors unsuspected by the more expert player.

The course, is, like so many links in the neighborhood of London, essentially a summer course; in the winter it is little better than a mud heap; we have a local rule which allows us (from October to March) to lift and drop without penalty if the ball is buried—and in the ordinary friendly match the wiser players agree to tee their balls through the green rather than laboriously hack them out of the villainous lies, where they are almost inevitably to be found during the winter months.

But in summer it can hold its own with most inland courses; the situation is delightful, the views extensive, and one can scarcely believe that one is not far from the four-mile radius.

The course is crowded on a fine Saturday afternoon, and it is necessary to put down a ball and give our names to a starter. We note that the man who put down a ball just after us whispers to his opponent: we also know quite well what he is saying, though we cannot hear him. "It will be all right, they are sure to lose a ball at the first two or three holes"—to which the other replies under his breath, "No such luck, they don't hit far enough to lose a ball!"

Our first drive is of the type described by Mr. Darwin as "exhilarating"—that is, we stand on a height and drive down a hill. The plus men take their cleeks (when the wind is behind them), and wait until the party in front is off the green; we do not take a cleek, but we wait, from pride of heart rather than fear of manslaughter, until the starter says, "All right now, sir!"

After our stroke we say, "It's brutal driving off before a gallery!" After his, he replies, "Yes, it always puts me off."

There are several other holes of an "exhilarating" character—the eighth, fourteenth and fifteenth. At the first-named there is splendid opportunity of driving out of bounds; at the fourteenth we should strongly advise the player to avoid the wire-netting about twenty yards in front of the tee to the left; the stance for the second shot leaves a good deal to be desired. A really fine slice at the fifteenth will take us comfortably on the green—but it is the fourteenth green, and, choose we never so wisely the spot on which to drop our ball, there still remains a hedge to negotiate; it is not an easy green to approach—if you elect to play short of the green and run on, your ball stops dead; while if you play a nice, firm shot onto the green, it invariably abandons all idea of being a pitch at all, and suddenly converts itself into the magnificent running approach and careers gaily right across the green towards the ninth flag.

The third is our short hole; a good, honest thump with a mashie lands us in the hedge on the left of the green, whence recovery is somewhat difficult, while the ordinary foozle meets with an even worse fate in a hedge just in front; in the ditch beyond the first hedge is a large heap of cut grass. There is ample opportunity here for skillful niblick work, which compels the admiration of the two or three couples behind us, who have meanwhile collected on the tee.

The ninth is a shortish hole, for which one is popularly supposed to take an iron club. As this course of action always results in our having to play a long second out of the rough, we usually take a wooden club and slice into the tennis courts or the field beyond. With our third we may reach a cross-bunker, and a well-executed niblick shot takes us into a ditch on the other side. We wend our way once more behind the bunker (fortunately, we cannot hear the remarks of the couple behind us), and with a skimming, half-topped mashie shot reach the edge of the green. Three firm putts should see us down, winning the hole from our adversary, who misses a "very short one."

The sixteenth is the long hole; it has, I believe, been done in four; it has also been done in fourteen—I can vouch for the latter figure. There is nothing very terrible about the drive; one may certainly go unpleasantly near a tree and a hedge, but only a very long driver, slicing his best, can hope to reach them; it is true, a bad pull lands us in a ditch which runs parallel to the fairway, but the usual topped ball merely comes to rest in very moderately rough grass. Our second shot needs some "placing," for the path which runs through the bunker is perilously narrow—we shall probably do better to play short deliberately (in which case I always find that I can hit so much farther than I had supposed); little by little, we make our way up the slope to the ditch in front of the fourteenth tee, and from there you may take any number of strokes to the green, according as you avoid the very long grass.

Perhaps the best hole on the course is the thirteenth. A sliced drive disturbs the equanimity of players coming to the seventeenth green, but a long second takes us out of danger of sudden death, and lands us comfortably in a cross-bunker. If, in addition to our crime of topping, we have added that of slicing, we have brought ourselves well up against some very awkward trees, and, in extricating ourselves from these, anything may happen. If we escape double figures here, we may consider that we are at the top of our form.

It is of no use to hope that your drive will jump the bunker at the fifth: I have tried the long, low, raking shot here many times, but the bunker is too high and too far away to be run through successfully; it is much better to slice unblushingly into comparative safety. Our second shot needs to be spared—my "spared" shots usually travel about ten yards—but a "low, scuffling" shot runs obligingly down the slope, and may (or may not) stop on the green. Another way, as Mrs. Glasse says, is to play violently to the left, strike the bank and run down towards the hole—it is necessary, however, to carry out the second part of the program, or we may be in serious trouble in the rough.

At the end of our round we return to the clubhouse, flushed with healthy exercise, with a full and particular knowledge of the bunkers of the course, but with the proud consciousness that we have not been passed, and that we have faithfully replaced every divot.

Francis

Out of the Rough
1932

The other day I had paid me a very pleasant honor; I was asked by Mr. Francis Ouimet to write some words of introduction to a book of his. This put it into my head to try to set down something about one of the best golfers, in every sense of the term, that ever came out of America. Certainly, no more popular one has ever come here.

I have perhaps some small claim to do so because it so happened that I was one of the very first English golfers who had the chance of "discovering" Mr. Ouimet. In 1913 I went to America for *The Times* and was taken straight to Garden City, where the American Amateur Championship was just going to be played. On the night after my arrival, I was one of a party taken by Mr. Cornelius O'Sullivan to that glorified Earls Court of the world, Coney Island. Among his guests was a young golfer, just emerged from the schoolboy, in which he felt an interest because he came from New England. I was told that his name was Francis Ouimet (everybody called and does call him Francis with a short a) and that he was Champion of Massachusetts—a fact which did not impress me as much as it ought; in those days, despite Mr. Travis, whose memory had begun to fade, we did not realize how good American amateurs were. He did impress me however as a most engaging person, and he went down the switchback and took part in the other delights with a boyish and unsophisticated zest.

A day or so later he nearly headed the field in the qualifying rounds and then gave Mr. Jerome Travers, the reigning champion, a terrific fight in one of the best matches I ever saw. Clearly, to be Champion of Massachusetts was to be a very good golfer, but even so, if I had been told that three weeks later he would beat our own Ray and Vardon and set the whole world ablaze, I should have laughed the prophecy to scorn.

Still, that is what he did in the memorable triple tie at the Country Club at Brookline, and I must check a tendency to tell that now ancient story yet once more. It is difficult for me to refrain, because the mere mention of it brings back the whole scene and fills my ears with the sounds of it—the endless dripping of the rain and the triumphant yells that greeted Francis's progress. It was one of the most momentous of all rounds, because, in a sense, it founded the American Golfing Empire; but purely on its own merits it was a terrific exhibition. Francis was not then so good a player as he became afterwards, neither was he as good as his two adversaries, but on that day he was inspired and incomparable, and outplayed them till they cracked under the strain.

Watching that fight was in some ways rather like watching Mr. Travis at Sandwich. We had begun by not being at all frightened of Mr. Travis and then gradually, as he got further and further through, a deadly terror had seized us by the throat. Similarly I, a lonely Briton, had set out with that tie not very much perturbed about Francis Ouimet. He had done incredibly glorious things, and whatever happened, the moral victory was his, but he had had a night to sleep—or lie awake—on the ordeal before him, and surely he could not be going to beat both Vardon and Ray. And then slowly and relentlessly it was borne in on me that he was matching them stroke for stroke, that he was not going to crack, that it was going to be a horribly close-run thing, and finally that my men were going to be beaten. There was this difference, however, between the battle of Sandwich and the battle of Brookline. At Sandwich one had continued to pray passionately to the very end that Mr. Travis should be beaten. At Brookline there came a moment when one felt that it would be an outrage if this young American hero did not win. As I watched him making ready to play his second shot to the home hole, I realized that all my heart was now with him. If by some horrid miracle he had put his ball into the watery, muddy bunker in front of the green, no American patriot could have been more distressed than I should have been.

The perfect calmness and cheerfulness with which Francis played through that championship were astonishing. I think I have seen him since when I have suspected him of being inwardly nervous. Perhaps that is because he now knows more about it. At Brookline he never for a moment looked nervous. Sometimes men play brilliantly at a crisis, but play as if they were in a trance and might wake up suddenly and ask what was happening. This was not Francis's case. He was perfectly conscious and master of himself. When at the fifteenth hole in the afternoon, some imbecile came up and talked to him about his (the imbecile's) driving, he was answered with a civility that would have been wonderful in far less trying circumstances. In short, his whole manner was entirely normal, just as it had been the night before, when he had had to finish with three holes in ten strokes to tie. So it was the day after the championship, when we lunched in company at the Country Club. As far as golf was concerned, much the biggest thing that ever could happen to him had happened and never could again, and yet no human being could have told from his demeanor that anything had happened at all.

Francis Ouimet affords as good an illustration as anyone can want of the American golfing temperament, which is, by the way, often misunderstood by English golfers. He is, or at any rate used to be, intensely keen; he can work at the game like a slave and fight like a hero, but he has the national genius for "letting up" between battles, and there is no more cheerful and amusing person in all the championship field. "Francis was solemn as a judge; he always is in a match," says Bobby Jones, in describing one of their championship battles, and I suppose that is true, but his solemnity is entirely without self-consciousness or fierceness, whereas when we try to be very solemn on a big occasion we often look as if we were trying to be fierce and sad into the bargain. I know nothing which is such an education to watch in point of good golfing manners as a hard fight between two American golfers. As they have taught themselves the best style, so they seem to me to have taught themselves the best temperament.

In the twinkling of an eye they can turn from the serious to the lighthearted, and that is what we cannot do so well. I think it must be at their colleges that they learn the habit of what we should call community singing, and they seem to keep ever afterwards a pleasant habit of bursting suddenly into song. I feel as if I had heard an American side headed by Francis Ouimet and Robert Gardner breaking out in this manner on the very road to a Walker Cup match. This is worth mentioning because Britons too often imagine American golfers as gloomy fanatics who neither drink nor smoke nor do anything companionable, who practice for hours and never speak; whose one gloomy thought is of victory. There never was a more monstrous notion, but then, we are apt to take into our heads, monstrous notions about other people. I grow furious and weary with the people who say that, of course, the American golfers are so good because they never do anything else whereas *we* are all-round game players. In vain I point out to them that Mr. Gardner held the pole jumping record of the world and won the doubles rackets championship of America, and that Mr. Sweetser was a very fine quarter-miler. In vain do I carry the war into their country by asking the names of all those players on the British side who have distinguished themselves at anything but golf. They give no answer, but I know they go away and say the same complacent, stupid and untruthful thing to the next person they meet . . .

The Man from Titusville

Out of the Rough
1932

" 'All right,' said the Cat; and this time it vanished quite slowly, beginning with the end of the tail, and ending with the grin which remained some time after the rest of it had gone."

When I read my *Alice in Wonderland* and come to that sentence about the Cheshire Cat, I think of Gene Sarazen. His grin is so very much an integral part of him, and even when he has dashed away after winning our Championship to win that of his own country, he leaves an agreeable appearance in the air, resembling a grin, to remind us of him.

It is by no means an unchanging grin, as was that of the Cat. It grows perceptibly broader as he holes a long putt at a crucial moment, seeming then to spread entirely across his pleasant olive face. It contracts into something of a wry smile when the putts just decline to drop and he has perhaps hard work to keep smiling at all. It is, however, impossible to think of him without it, because it is the outward and visible sign of the very charming and at the same time very strong and resolute personality that is Sarazen.

I first met that grin in a hotel in New York in the autumn of 1922. Its owner had leaped into sudden fame earlier in the year by winning the Open championship at Skokie, a Chicago course. He then came from a course called Titusville. Nobody here had ever heard either of it or of him and even in his own country I do not think his fame was as yet very great. He soon proceeded to show that his win was no fluke, for he won the Professional championship of his country and beat Hagen in a set match over 72 holes, a thing that at that time no other golfer in the world was likely to do.

It was with the glory of his championship still upon him that he first came over here, in 1923, to play for our Open championship at Troon. His golf at once made a great impression on all who saw him. Arnaud Massy is capable of enthusiastic outbursts of hero-worship, and I remember his declaring that the championship was over before it had begun, since nothing could prevent Sarazen from winning by strokes and strokes. And then, by some astonishing accident, he failed to qualify. He had a bad first round, but played up gallantly in the second and was believed to have saved his bacon. I remember it well because after dispatching my telegram saying that he had qualified, I had departed far from Troon. Next morning I was horror-stricken to hear that someone had come in at the last moment and ousted him. Fortunately, there was a trusty person in London who had altered my message or furious editors would have had my head on a charger.

When we saw him after an interval of nine years at Prince's playing the sort of golf that seemed incapable of going wrong, it was almost impossible to believe in that earlier failure; but in the first place he was then nine years younger, and decidedly more "temperamental," and in the second, allowance must always be made for the strangeness of a strange land. When Bobby Jones first played in our championship he tore up his card and drove his ball out to sea; when Hagen first played he finished in something like the fifteenth place. It is hard work to play a game in the other fellow's country, and it seems that a probationary visit is needed before even the greatest can give of their best. However it happened, Sarazen accepted his downfall very well and declared that he would come again if he had to swim across. He had to come again several times, but the long lane had a glorious turning at last.

Even in his own country Sarazen's golf suffered for a while a period of partial eclipse. I fancy that having at first played the game almost entirely by the light of nature he took to thinking about it. That is a thing that has almost got to happen to any good young golfer at some time and occasionally the young golfer is never so good again afterwards; the "first fine careless rapture" of hitting, the splendid confidence are never satisfactorily replaced. If on the other hand he gets safely through this inevitable distemper he is a better golfer than ever he was, for he has knowledge to fall back on in evil days. Sarazen, I believe, tried experiments. He tried for instance the fashionable overlapping grip instead of the interlocking one that had come to him almost instinctively in his caddie days. I think in the end he did make some slight change for I remember his asking me when we met again if I saw anything different; I had to confess that I did not and asked humbly to be told. At any rate the period of thoughtful sickness was safely passed and there emerged a Sarazen who, though he did not win another Open championship till this year, was yet a better golfer than before. He was always there or thereabouts, and I imagine that during the last few years no professional has equaled his record of earnings in the big tournaments for big prize money.

Today he is obviously a thoughtful person with plenty of decided and rather original notions as to the playing of the game. I remember for example his telling me that when he taught Mrs. Sarazen to play golf he insisted on her learning with heavy clubs. I am afraid to say how heavy they were; they sounded to me almost cruelly so, but they had the right effect in making the pupil swing the club and let it do the work. It is probably on this principle that he himself is apt to practice swinging not with one club but with two or even three (it is a baseball player's trick) so that he looks like a lictor with a whole bundle of rods; but then he is as strong as a little bull and could doubtless swing a bundle of battle axes.

Not only has he thought much about method but he is using his head all the time and plays the game strategically. At Prince's he several times took a spoon off the tee, so that he could reach the best place from which to play the second shot, without any fear of going just too far. It was particularly noticeable how he always took this spoon for his tee shot to the 15th. There was here no danger of the rough in going too far, but the pitch to that small plateau, cocked up amid all manner of perils, is perceptibly easier if it is not too short and so the ball can be hit the harder. How wise in him it was to take his iron for the second at the 17th in the last round, when he was growing rather shaky and knew it. In the other rounds he had been hitting the most glorious seconds right home with wood, but this time his ball lay a little more to the right, the danger of the bunker was a little greater and his confidence was a little on the wane; so he took his iron and played safely for a five. It is not everyone who would have had so much self-control at that moment, for the strokes had been slipping away, he knew all about Havers's 68 and, in short, things were not too comfortable.

That grin of his is the mark of a sunny and delightful nature, but not of an altogether placid one. He has had, unless I am much mistaken, to overcome something in his Latin blood that used to surge up untimely. Like Bobby Jones, he can boil inside and sometimes on rare occasions he used to boil over. When he was second to Hagen in the Open championship at Sandwich in 1928 he might have won or at least have tied but for one little ebullition. It was at the Suez Canal hole; his ball lay in the rough off the tee and his admirable caddie wanted him, I feel pretty sure, to take an iron. He took wood, missed the shot badly and then advanced on the ball again with the same club without giving himself time to think. Just for that moment he lost himself and that disastrous hole may well have lost him the championship. He would not have done that at Carnoustie last year when he fought on with a fine stoicism in the face of adverse fate. Twice in he course of the three days the wind changed between morning and afternoon, and each time it changed in favor of Armour and against Sarazen. That, to be sure, is one of those things that are "all about the game" but it made a great difference. Sarazen's only comment was that in order to win "you must have the breaks"—an undeniable truth but one hard to enunciate calmly in times of disappointment.

At Prince's he had no "breaks" as far as the play or the weather were concerned. Indeed, in one respect he seemed rather unlucky, for he constantly hit the hole with his putts and the ball did not drop; but this misfortune is perhaps inherent in his method; he goes boldly for the back of the tin and will have no truck with timorous trickling in at the side door. One bit of luck he did have in that he was drawn to start early on the last day, and so he could, just as in his original triumph at Skokie, set up a mark for his wretched pursuers to shoot at. He left Havers with a 68 to tie, and that was a task that seemed hopeless. I should have written "was" instead of "seemed" had it not been for Sarazen's own achievement in the American championship a fortnight later. Then he was left with a 69 to tie. He did a 66 and won by three strokes. If anybody likes to say that this was, in the circumstances, the greatest round of golf ever played, I do not see how anybody else can quarrel with him.

Finally in our Open champion we salute not merely one of the finest hitters of a golf ball that ever lived but also one worthy of the name of a good golfer, than which no man can look forward to a better epitaph. We may apply to him Hazlitt's famous words about Cavanagh the fives player, and I shall write them down yet again just for the pleasure of doing so. "He had no affectation, no trifling. He did not throw away the game to show off an attitude, or try an experiment. He was a fine, sensible, manly player, who did what he could." Of that last round at Fresh Meadow at any rate we may add Hazlitt's final sentence—"but that was more than anyone else could even affect to do."

Ghastly, Horrible, but True

The Times
1929

Miss Joyce Wethered beat Miss Glenna Collett in the final of the Ladies' championship at St. Andrews by three holes up and one to play. Many epithets will be used to describe the fluctuations of the match and the quality of the play. I feel unequal to the effort and will let stark figures without adjectives speak. Miss Collett went out in 34 and was five up. She came home in 41 and was pulled down to two at luncheon. She went out in 42, lost six holes out of nine and was four down at the turn in the afternoon. She did the next eight holes in 36, including a seven, got one hole back and lost by three and one.

It was a great match, greatly played, and the statement that Miss Wethered played her game and yet was taken to the 35th hole is the highest compliment that could be paid to Miss Collett. Both played magnificently, and that before so big a crowd, well behaved, impartial, and amenable to the refining influence of women with the flag, but yet so big and so eager as to make the players' task a hard and exhausting one. I can only echo the words of a famous St. Andrews golfer who stood by me in the crowd and murmured over and over again in dazed admiration: "Wonderful how they can do it!" It was wonderful, and America can be every bit as proud of the lady champion who has come here and lost as she is of her various male champions who have come here and won.

As to Miss Wethered, if she prefers now once more to retire into private golf she can do so with the knowledge that she has given as complete proof of surpassing greatness as any game player of either sex that ever lived.

It was gray, still, perfect golfing weather when the first round began. Miss Collett had the honor and outdrove Miss Wethered by a few yards. Incidentally there was very little in it in the point of length but what there was, perhaps five or six yards on the average, was in Miss Wethered's favor since, leaving out of account two short holes, Miss Collett played the odd ten times more than Miss Wethered in this first round.

A rather loose, wide approach by Miss Wethered followed by three putts gave Miss Collett the first hole. It was at the second, however, that things began to look a little ugly. Miss Collett was wide on the right with her second and ran her third several yards past the hole. Miss Wethered had a perfect second and seemed sure of her four but putted six feet short. The fates did not forgive her. Miss Collett banged in her curly putt, the ball running right round the tin before dropping. Miss Wethered missed and in place of all square England was two down. Miss Wethered revived our spirits with a lovely three at the 3rd, the third successive three she has had at this hole, and the 4th was halved in four. Then, just as we felt that all was well and would soon be better still, epoch-making events began to happen in an almost incredible manner.

Both were on the green in three at the Long hole; Miss Wethered putted first and overran the hole, Miss Collett holed a four- or five-yard putt for a four, and was two up again. The Heathery hole was halved, Miss Wethered only saving herself by the skin of her teeth, and next came the blackest half-hour of all. Miss Collett was caught in the nasty little pot bunker behind the High hole green; Miss Wethered was perfectly safe just off the green and ran up the odd to within four feet. That was tolerably cheerful but Miss Collett ploughed her ball splendidly out of the sand and holed another four-yarder. Miss Wethered who palpably had not got the touch of her putter missed in the like and that was three down.

Worse and still worse were to come. Miss Collett was only just on the 8th green with her tee shot but she holed a twenty-five-yard putt for two. It was black magic, ghastly, horrible, but true. Miss Wethered made a noble attempt for a half and her ball stopped just the fraction of a millimeter short of the hole. At the 9th Miss Wethered was bunkered from the tee, played a lovely pitch out, had a four in her grasp and then putted dreadfully short and took six. Miss Collett made no mistake; that was 34 out and five up.

Never have I heard so grim a silence fall on a crowd since Mr. Walter Travis was holing long putts against Mr. Edward Blackwell at Sandwich in 1904. At the 10th a hole seemed sure to come back, for Miss Wethered played a great approach shot and from her putt the ball disappeared into the hole. Out it came again, however, through some malign influence, and Miss Collett got her four and a half. The 11th was halved in three; Miss Collett was still five up and had holed eleven holes in 41 shots without a single five. It was overwhelming golf worthy of any male champion. She seemed certain to be six up at the 12th where Miss Wethered was again terribly short and Miss Collett had only to hole from a yard to win, but she dragged the ball across the hole and missed. There came a sigh of relief from the crowd. Every man, woman and child felt that now was the time. The crisis was past and Miss Wethered was going to recover.

The change did not come at once, however, for Miss Wethered again putted very, very short at the Hole o' the Cross and had to hole a supremely gallant putt of four yards to save her neck. Then at last, at the Long hole, came a real gleam of sunshine. With one just over the green and one just short, it was Miss Wethered who got nearest in four, Miss Wethered who got her five. Down to four. At the 16th Miss Wethered was a little inside all the way. She had a five-foot putt to win and she put it in. Down to three. The Road hole was halved in five but at the last hole Miss Wethered again had the best of the putting. Going out Miss Collett had looked as though she could miss nothing; now she was human once more. She played the odd from five feet and missed; Miss Wethered had her four-footer for the hole and everybody felt it was an intensely crucial putt. Two down in four meant better than three down. In it went and again there was a great sigh of relief, "It's all right; she's got her now." Such was the general verdict and some even added as the ball rang against the tin: "That's the match."

The afternoon round began with a greatly increased crowd and an almost overwhelming feeling of confidence in our own champion. Sure enough, everything went swimmingly. Miss Wethered was at her very best. Miss Collett never cracked or looked like cracking, but she was putting iron shots a little farther from the hole than in the morning, and she had become an ordinary, uninspired mortal on the greens. So the fours turned to fives and fives were no good here. Miss Wethered began by holing a six-yard putt for a win in three. The 2nd was halved in five and Miss Wethered had the inside turn all the way to the 3rd and squared. The same thing happened at the 4th and she was one up. Miss Collett came back at her bravely and holed a fine putt at the Long hole for her four after Miss Wethered had reached the green with two giant shots. The tide was however setting too strongly in Miss Wethered's favor and for a while Miss Collett could not fight it. She was bunkered with rather hooked tee shots at the Heathery and High holes and she took three putts at the 8th. Miss Wethered played all three holes perfectly and won them all, and then rubbed it in by laying her approach dead at the 9th for a three. Four up at the turn and all seemed over.

Little did we imagine we were yet to suffer tortures. Now was the time of Miss Collett's supremely courageous counter-attack. A fine pitch and a three-yard putt won her the 9th in three; she played a beauty to the 11th and Miss Wethered hooked into the Hill bunker. She won the hole in three to four and that was down to two. She saved herself with a good putt at the 12th but cut her second at the Hole o' the Cross and lost it. The counter-attack seemed to be definitely stopped. Three up with five to play was surely good enough. But no, the most agonizing time was to come. Both players after all this magnificent golf went suddenly and simultaneously mad for just one hole. They got into bunkers, they bolted for the hole and ran past; they laid stymies, they missed short putts, Miss Wethered missed the shortest and lost in eight against seven. The next moment both were sane again and playing as skillfully as ever. Miss Collett played the 15th perfectly; she lay stone dead in three. Miss Wethered pushed her drive, went a little short with her approach, and a little strong with her run-up. She lay five or six yards away and down to one stared her in the face. Then, heaven be praised, she hit that putt slap bang into the middle of the hole. It was hard on Miss Collett but it was a putt that deserved to win a championship and it settled this one. Miss Collett stuck to it splendidly but she had no more chances. The 16th was beautifully halved and that was dormy two. Each hit two admirable wooden club shots to the Road hole; each was a little too canny with the approach. It was about impossible to see what happened and every stroke seemed to take an eternity since the crowd had to be compressed and chaperoned before a shot could be played. At last a ball rolled up on the green and stayed ten feet short. Somebody tall enough to see said it was Miss Collett's. Another rolled up and lay eighteen inches from the hole. A mighty shout left no doubt that it was Miss Wethered's. Miss Collett tried for a three and missed, and a great match was over.

The Immortal Bobby

Golf Between Two Wars
1944

Still sticking to the amateurs I come now with faltering pen to the greatest of them all. As far as the United States are concerned the Bobby Jones era began, I suppose, in 1916 when at the age of 14½ he reached the third round of the American National Championship at Merion and went down after a hard match before an ex-champion, Robert Gardner. From this time onward till he retired full of honors if not of years, he was a great figure in American golf. For us, however, his era began somewhat later, since he came here first in 1922 and did not show us his full powers till 1926 when he had reached the immense age of 24. He then won our Open Championship for the first time and perhaps this is the best place to set out his record in the barest and briefest outline. In his own country he won the Open Championship four times (he also tied for it twice and lost the playoff) and the Amateur

Championship five times. Here he won one Amateur and three Open Championships. In 1930 he established what has been picturesquely called "the impregnable quadrilateral" by winning the Open and Amateur Championships of both countries in a single summer. He played against Britain in six International matches, five of them for the Walker Cup; he won his single every time, sometimes by immense margins, and he won his foursome five times and lost once by a single hole.

Bobby's first appearance here was in the International Match preceding the Amateur Championship at Hoylake in 1921. He won both his single and his foursome handsomely and impressed everybody, as he could not fail to do. Then came anticlimax. His career in the Amateur Championship was short and rather checkered. He began well enough against a good Scottish player, Mr. Manford, and there followed that rather farcical encounter with Mr. Hamlet of Wrexham. Whatever he might be at Wrexham it is pardonable to say that Mr. Hamlet was not of the stature to face Hoylake, even though it was made less formidably long than usual by the hard ground. Yet with the match all square going to the Royal, which is the seventeenth, it really seemed as if he were going to beat Bobby, which, as Euclid might remark, would have been absurd. This was not due to any great golf of his but to a sort of general futility and paralysis on the greens on Bobby's part. However, the crisis passed, Bobby scrambled through with a score nearer ninety than eighty and proceeded to play devastatingly well in his next match against Mr. Robert Harris. He had got his bad round over, he was going to win—and then he relapsed again and was beaten by many holes by Mr. Allan Graham. There was a chance of redeeming himself in the Open at St. Andrews but all went ill: he felt a puzzled hatred for the links which he came afterwards to love and at the eleventh hole in the third round he picked up his ball. Legend declares that he relieved his feelings by teeing it up and driving it far out into the Eden. If he did it was a gesture deserving of sympathy, and if he did not I am very sure he wanted to.

In 1921, at the age of 19, Bobby was already a magnificent golfer, as great a hitter of the ball though not as great a player of matches of medal rounds as he ever was. Several years before Mr. Walter Travis had said he could never improve his strokes, and that was true enough; there was, humanly speaking, no room for improvement; it was simply a matter of stringing them together more successfully. There could be no more fascinating player to watch not only for the free and rhythmic character of his swing but for the swiftness with which he played. He had as brief a preliminary address as Duncan himself, but there was nothing hurried or slapdash about it and the swing itself, if not positively slow, had a certain drowsy beauty which gave the feeling of slowness. There was nothing that could conceivably be called a weak spot. The utmost that could be said—and this may be a purely personal impression—was that he did not seem quite so supremely happy with a mashie-niblick as when playing approaches with longer irons.

People liked Bobby at once, and that not only for his natural pleasantness of manner; they discerned in him a very human quality; he was no cold machine but took his game very much to heart as did humbler people. In his almost infantile days he had been inclined to throw his clubs about. This we were told since the American press had once emphasized it rather unkindly; otherwise we should never have guessed it, for he had already tamed his naturally fiery temperament into betraying no outward signs. Those indeed who knew him well professed to know the symptoms which showed the flames leaping up within. I remember once watching him at an Open Championship, it may have been at St. Anne's, in company with that fine American golfer, the late Mr. J. G. Anderson; Bobby missed a shortish putt and "Now, he's mad," said my companion. I could detect nothing, but doubtless Mr. Anderson knew his man and Bobby did hate missing a shot. Perhaps that was why he missed so few, for in the end that highly strung nervous temperament, if it had never been his master, became his invaluable servant. In his most youthful and tempestuous days he had never been angry with his opponent and not often, I think, with Fate, but he had been furiously angry with himself. He set himself an almost impossibly high standard; he thought it an act of incredible folly if not a positive crime to make a stroke that was not exactly as it ought to be made and as he knew he could make it. If he ever derogated from that standard he may even in his most mature days have been "mad" in the recesses of his heart, but he became outwardly a man of ice, with the very best of golfing manners.

How much other people have suffered over their golf we do not always know; the light of fame has not beaten on them so fiercely and they have not possessed such a friend and *vates sacer* combined as Bobby had in Mr. O. B. Keeler. Of Bobby we do know that he suffered greatly. How he could scarcely eat anything till the day's play was over; how on occasion he felt that he could not even button his shirt collar for fear of the direst consequences; how he could lose a stone in weight during a championship; how he was capable of breaking down to the point of tears not from any distress but from pure emotional over-strain—these things are now well known and may be found in Mr. Keeler's admirable and Boswellian pages. No doubt his capacity for an emotional outlet was at that time a relief and a help to him, but there must be a limit. I was in his company soon after he had finished his fourth round when he won the last of his three Open Championships here in 1930, and seeing him nearly past speech I thought that the time had come for him to call a halt and that this game could not much longer be worth such an agonizing candle. He had great courage and great ambition, and these not only pulled him through but probably made him a more successful player than he would have been had he been gifted with a more placid temperament. There is much to be said for the stolid, phlegmatic player, but the great golfers have never had what I once heard Jack White call a dead nerve. It is worth remembering that James Braid, most rock-like and apparently impassive of men, has said that he "liked to be a wee bit nervous" before a big game. The steady-going and unimaginative will often beat the more eager champion and they will get very near the top, but there, I think, they will stop. The prose laborer must yield to the poet and Bobby as a golfer had a strain of poetry in him. He stands forever as the greatest encourager of the highly strung player who is bent on conquering himself.

In 1926 we saw Bobby on his second visit. Four years had passed since he had been here before and he had now, as the Americans called it, "broken through"; the lean years were over. In 1923 he had won the American Open after a tie with Cruikshank, thus emulating Mr. Hilton here in winning the Open before the Amateur. In the following year he had put this to rights by winning the Amateur with triumphant ease and had been runner-up in the Open. In 1925 he had won the Amateur again and had tied in the Open, to lose rather surprisingly after a protracted playoff with Willie Macfarlane. He was in the plenitude of his powers and who should stand before him? And yet there was a moment when it seemed as if his second visit, like his first, would end in disappointment. All went swimmingly in the Amateur Championship at Muirfield till he reached the fifth round and then out he went and that with a resounding crash, for he was well and truly beaten by Mr. Andrew Jamieson who was then hardly known outside Scotland. I believe that Bobby woke with a stiff neck that morning though he was most anxious to conceal it. Certainly he seemed to lack something of his usual ease, but Jamieson, a very neat, unobtrusive, efficient golfer, did play uncommonly well, well enough to beat anybody if anybody gave him, as Bobby did, the very slightest opening. What was more, having got away with a lead he never grew frightened of it but played with victorious confidence. I saw only odd holes of the match but I remember one vividly. This was the short thirteenth called "The Postage Stamp," though whether it or the hole at Troon has the prior right to the title I do not know. The hole, as it then was, had a long narrow green with a drop to perdition on the right, and on the left a high rough bank. Jamieson, with victory firmly in his grasp, if he could keep steady, had the honor and he made a slip; he hooked his tee shot and the ball lighted on the top of the left-hand bank. Would it stay there? It hovered for a moment and then, audibly encouraged by the crowd, began to topple downward by stages, almost coming to rest and then moving on again till at last it ended its rather nefarious career on the green. That was the final blow and Jamieson, having had his little bit of luck, went on to win calmly and easily by 4 and 3.

Mrs. Gamp has remarked how little we know "what lays before us." If Bobby had won that championship he has said that he would have sailed straight for home after the Walker Cup match. As it was he decided to give himself another chance in the Open at St. Anne's. So, after duly doing his deadly stuff at St. Andrews in the Walker Cup—he beat Cyril Tolley by 12 and 11—he went to Sunningdale for the qualifying rounds of the Open and proceeded to play there what was by common consent as nearly flawless a round as ever had been played. He went round in 66 and he may be said to have holed only one putt worthy of mention, one of eight yards or so for a three on the fifth. Otherwise if he missed nothing short—and there were one or two putts missed to be called shortish—he holed nothing that could conceivably be called long. He simply went on and on with exact perfection. There was indeed one slip, an iron shot pushed out into a bunker at the short thirteenth, but it cost the player nothing since he chipped the ball out dead. It probably brought relief to him as it did to the spectators, who had been feeling that they must scream if perfection endured much longer. It was Mr. Keeler, I think, who once wrote, "They wound up the mechanical man of golf yesterday and set him clicking round the East Lake course." All great golfers at their best are more or less mechanical, for they do the same thing over and over again, but I doubt if any of them save perhaps one has given quite such an impression of well-oiled, impeccable machinery as Bobby did from tee to green. The notions of beauty and machinery do not go well together; the word "clicking" may suggest something done "by numbers" and so far it is inappropriate; but Mr. Keeler's was nevertheless an apt and memorable phrase. Harry Vardon and Bobby Jones combined exquisiteness of art with utterly relentless precision in a way not quite given to any other golfers.

Few joys in this world are unalloyed, and though Bobby was naturally and humanly pleased with that 66 he was a trifle worried because he had "reached the peak" rather too soon before going to St. Anne's. His second round of 68, with, if I remember, one innocuous misunderstanding with a tree, did nothing to reassure him on this point and he was so far right that, though he won at St. Anne's, his play there was not quite of the same unrippled smoothness as at Sunningdale. The game was by contrast "aye fechtin' " against him and he had to work hard for his scores. That was as exciting a championship as any between wars, save only for this, that from the very start it seemed that no Briton was likely to win it. Mitchell ended fifth but he only accomplished so much by two very fine rounds on the last day; as far as winning was concerned he had put himself out of court by beginning with two 78's. So to the narrowly patriotic this championship was merely a brilliant, alien exhibition context.

The invaders went off with a bang: Hagen had a 68 and the powerful, broad-backed, rough-hewn Mehlhorn, said to have graduated as hod-carrier to the champion bricklayer of America, had a 70. Then come M'Leod, an expatriated Scot, and Al Watrous with 71 and then Bobby in the position he liked, lying well up but not prematurely leading, with a 72. It was a good round but he had to fight for it, since at each one of the last four holes he made some sort of a slip and had, in Mr. Laidlay's phrase, to "trust to a pitch and a putt" to get his four. In the second round Hagen had a compensating and disastrous 77 and at the end of it Mehlhorn with 70 and 74 and Bobby with two 72's led the field. Watrous, 71 and 75, was two shots behind them.

On the last day Bobby and Watrous were drawn together, and as it turned out this chance involved just such a strain on them and just such a terrific duel for first place as Vardon and Taylor had endured at Prestwick ten years earlier. Watrous was a very good player who has left no very distinct image on my mind; he had no tremendous power, but he had all the American virtue of smoothness and rhythm and he was a very fine putter, bang on his putting. Bobby was two strokes ahead when they set out and he had a 73 in a good fresh wind, but Watrous playing perfectly had a 69 and so—again this brought back memories of Vardon and Taylor—turned the deficit of two into a lead of two. Hagen took 74 and Mehlhorn began to fade. So the battle was to be fought out between these two and they were fully conscious of it as they went back to their hotel together, lunched together and even lay down to rest in the same room—a pleasant picture of friendly rivalry.

When it was all over and Mr. Topping, who had been in charge of this couple, gave away the prizes he declared that Bobby had made but one remark to him in the course of the last round: "My golf is terrible." In fact, it was terribly good except in one important respect: he was taking too many putts. By his own account he took 39 of them and what he gained on Watrous in length he certainly threw away on the greens. The short ninth which had consistently bothered him beat him again and he was still two down with five to play; in what was in effect a match the language of match play may be used. Then at last the strokes came back one at a time and the pair were all square with three to play. At the seventeenth came Bobby's historic second, which I must presently describe yet again, but before that on the sixteenth came an incident of which a friend has lately reminded me; it gives force to the ruthless doctrine that someone ought to murder a photographer *pour encourager les autres*. Watrous had played his second to the green and Bobby had got halfway up with some pitching club when a fiend with a camera stepped out and tried to snap him. Bobby stopped and began again, and again the photographer tried. This time he was metaphorically lynched; he was shooed out of the way, and Bobby, by a considerable display of control, pitched safely to the green and the hole was halved in four.

Now for the seventeenth, a hole a little over 400 yards in length. The course of the hole bends to the left and the line is well out to the right, in order to get a clear view of the hole and avoid the sandhills guarding the left-hand side of the green. Nor is that the only reason for keeping to the right, for on the left of the fairway is a wilderness of sandy, scrubby country dotted here and there with bunkers. Bobby with the honor, drew his tee shot, not badly but badly enough to be obviously in some form of trouble; Watrous went straight and playing the odd reached the green; he was some way from the hole but he was on the green and that looked good enough. Bobby's ball lay in a shallow bunker and it lay clean, but he was 170 yards or more from the flag and between him and it were the sandhills. He took what I think he called his mashie-iron (it now reposes a sacred relic in the St. Anne's Club) and hit the ball perfectly clean, playing it somewhat out into the wind so that it came in to finish on the green and nearer the hole than his opponent. Admittedly the ball lay as clean as clean could be and this was the kind of shot that he might very well have played in a practice game, but in the circumstances, when a teaspoonful too much sand might have meant irretrievable ruin, it was a staggering shot, and it staggered poor Al Watrous. He took three putts, Bobby got down in two and everybody felt that that shot had settled it. Watrous was bunkered at the home hole, Bobby nearly bunkered but not quite; he got a four against a five and finished in 74 against 78, 291 against 293.

There still remained Hagen and George Von Elm, both of whom were rumored to be doing well. Hagen arrived on the last tee wanting a four for 74 and a two to tie. He could doubtless have tied for second place with Watrous but Hagen was never interested in second prizes. After a fine drive, he walked some way forward and then with a characteristic gesture had the flag taken out. His ball very nearly pitched into the role and ran on into the bunker behind the green. *Aut Caesar*, etc. His effort had failed and he took four more to get down, so that Von Elm coming with a wet sheet and a 72 tied with him for third place. Let me add as a postscript that the Council of the Royal Lytham and St. Anne's Club have now decided to mark, as far as it can exactly be done, the spot at the seventeenth from which Bobby played his shot. This is a precedent that could not often be followed, but here the geographical conditions are favorable and if now and then someone has to lift a drop from behind the monument he will do so in a reverent rather than an exasperated spirit.

I have written at perhaps excessive length about the St. Anne's Championship both because it was Bobby's first and because it was so dramatic. When he came back next year to defend his title at St. Andrews, having in the meanwhile won the American Open at Scioto, he played unquestionably better; he enjoyed the greatest single triumph he ever had here, but there seems much less to say about it, for the reason that it was "his" championship, he was winning all the while. By this time St. Andrews had taken a thorough hold on him. He was amused by its problems; he knew whereabouts were its hidden bunkers and was not annoyed by them, as some people never cease to be, because they are hidden; he had devised some three different ways of playing the Long Hole In according to the wind; he had realized that for a player of his parts the Road Hole need hold no excessive terrors, unless he is overambitious. In short he had proved the truth of Mrs. Malaprop's saying that " 'Tis safest in matrimony to begin with a little aversion," for he was now thoroughly in love with the Old Course and played it as if he loved it.

Bobby's four rounds were 68, 72, 73 and 72 and he led from the start. I do not know that he played any better for his 68 than in any of the other three rounds; it was simply that everything came off for him, as for example a putt holed for three at the Hole o' Cross going out. It is by far the biggest green in the world and if this was not the longest putt ever holed it must have been very nearly so. Mr. Keeler's brow was a little knitted, for he was not sure how his man would like to be "in the lead" straight away instead of lying a stroke or two behind, but the general impression was that there would be no holding Bobby. After two rounds he only led Hodson by two strokes, but good player as Hodson was he could scarcely hope to give the leader two strokes; in fact the third round destroyed him as far as winning was concerned and those who were more likely to hold on were several shots further behind. At the end of the third round Bobby led Fred Robson, who had just done a splendid 69, by four shots and Aubrey Boomer by six, and it was for him to set the pace.

Only at the beginning of the last round was there a moment's doubt, for Bobby frittered away a couple of shots in the first four holes, and so with an orthodox five at the fifth his score was three over fours—a definitely vulnerable star. At that point I left him to look at other people, meaning to pick him up again at the thirteenth on the way home. Some bursts of clapping from the neighborhood of the "loop" suggested that he was doing well, but how well no one of us waiting on the big double green knew. The advanced guard of his crowd came towards us, in the van one who trotted briskly, as if big with news to impart. I have a well-grounded distrust of spectators' tales but this one looked a man of good counsel, sober and unimaginative; so I buttonholed him and asked his tidings. When he said that Bobby was now two under fours I thought he was only the usual liar, but what he said was true, for Bobby had done the holes from the sixth to the twelfth in 24 shots. After that the round was a triumphal procession. His second to the last hole was a little cautious and ended in the Valley of Sin. Thence he ran it up dead and as he scaled the bank the crowd stormed up after him and lined the edge of the green, barely restraining themselves. He holed his short one and the next instant there was no green visible, only a dark seething mass, in the midst of which was Bobby hoisted on fervent shoulders and holding his putter, "Calamity Jane," at arm's length over his head lest she be crushed to death. Calamity Jane had two pieces of whipping bound round her shaft where she had been broken, not we may trust in anger but by some mischance. When some years later the market was flooded with exact models of her, each of them duly bore two superfluous black bands. Did ever imitation pay sincerer flattery than that?

Only once more, in 1930, were we destined to see Bobby here in battle array, though he has returned once since his retirement and in playing a friendly round of the Old Course took the major part of St. Andrews round with him. It was at St. Andrews in 1930, the year of the "impregnable quadrilateral," that he realized almost his last unachieved ambition and won our Amateur Championship. He did not win it without his bad moments, for he had never concealed his dislike of eighteen-hole matches. In the American Championship the first two rounds, which were of eighteen holes only, had at least once brought him to grief and he had had, in the words of old Beldham the cricketer, "many an all but." Once safely through them and in the haven of thirty-six holes, where he felt that he had space to maneuver, he had crushed his men one after the other by murderous margins. Thus in our championship he could never feel really at ease until in the final and he had never yet reached the final. He set out on the enterprise strung up to a high pitch and no one who saw the beginning of his match against a good Nottinghamshire golfer, Mr. Roper, will forget it. On the first green he holed a long putt for a three, the ball going in with an almost suspicious rattle against the back of the tin. Bobby looked a little apologetic and made several little practice movements of his club. I remember Mr. Hilton whispering to me that he was trying to get the swing of his putter smooth; that first putt, successful as it was, had shown signs of tension. After a four at the second he holed another and shorter putt for a three at the Cartgate and then at the fourth hit a very long tee shot rather to the left into the Cottage bunker. Thence, a culminating atrocity, he holed out, a full shot of 150 yards or so, with some sort of iron, for a two.

After this astonishing display Bobby became comparatively quiescent and had to struggle as hard to get through as many less gifted players have done. Two of his most close-run things were against compatriots, Mr. Harrison Johnston and Mr. George Voigt. Mr. Johnston, after being several holes down, chased him to the last gasp and Mr. Voigt, if I may permit myself an "if," ought to have beaten him. Bobby was obviously struggling and when Mr. Voigt, very cool and steady and putting beautifully, stood two up with five to go, he looked like a winner. And then he committed what the onlooker, who has nothing to do but criticize, felt inclined to call a gratuitous folly. With the broad space of the Elysian Fields to drive into, he cut his tee shot over the wall and out of bounds. It was a heaven-sent reprieve; Bobby took it and fought his way home to win by a hole.

Yet even this paled before his battle with Cyril Tolley. Every man, woman and child in St. Andrews went out to watch it, and Mr. Gerard Fairley was quite right to set the scene of the murder in one of his stories on the afternoon of that match. There would have been ample opportunity to commit several murders and escape undetected through the lonely streets, though stained with the marks of crime. Never was there more perceptible the silence of expectation, that lull before the storm in which men speak instinctively in whispers, and Cyril gave it if possible a more thrilling emphasis, since he began with a full-blooded top from the first tee. It was ominous but it was no presage of disaster for he played finely afterwards and a dog-fight on a magnificent scale ensued, which delighted everyone save other poor wretches who were trying to play their own insignificant matches. Each man seeing the mighty flood approach him must needs crouch over his ball guarding it as best he might and pick himself up again when the torrent has swept over him. The most discussed shot in the match was Bobby's second to the Road Hole, as to which hundreds are prepared to take their oath that the ball would have been on the road if it had not hit a spectator and an equal number of witnesses are quite certain that it would not. I was there but was running for my life with my head well down at the moment and can offer no opinion. The hole was halved; so was the last and Bobby won at the nineteenth, where his adversary played a rather loose second and was punished by a stymie. Exactly how good the golf was I cannot now remember for there are occasions when that is of secondary importance. It was the devil of a match.

At last Bobby was in the final—against Mr. Wethered; his chance had come and he did not mean to waste it; he was on his favorite long trail of thirty-six holes. At the very first hole a shudder of surprise went through the crowd as he entirely missed his pitch and stayed short of the burn, but from there he chipped dead and got his four; nor did he ever exceed that figure till he put his second into the Road bunker at the seventeenth. I can see him very clearly now, as the stewards are moving away the crowd at the back of the green. He is gently smiling a protest to the effect that he does not mean to go on to the road. In fact his explosion shot gave him quite a good chance of a four but the putt did not drop; there was to be no fiveless round for him. His opponent fought manfully but without avail and Bobby won by 7 and 6.

Now for the last lap, the Open at Hoylake, which was won in the end as had been that at St. Anne's by sheer, hard fighting. As at St. Andrews Bobby jumped away with the lead with a 70 which was equaled by Macdonald Smith. He added a 72 while Mac Smith took 77 and his nearest pursuer was now Fred Robson with 143. The third round was sound enough, 74, but meanwhile another British hope had arisen. Compston, who had begun with 74 and 73, added to these a tremendous 68 and led Bobby by a stroke. Diegel was not far behind with a 71, giving him a total of 228; but Diegel, though having an astonishing game in him, has been in championships one of those unfortunates who can never quite do it. He has said bitterly himself that however hard the other fellows try to give it him he will not take it. This may be partly due to his highly artificial methods of putting, "contorted almost to anguish," as was written of a fine putter of a much older generation. Such styles are always apt to break down under strain, and apart from this Diegel was cursed with a temperament the most highly strung possible. Water Hagen, once sitting up cheerfully late before a final against Diegel, was told in a tone of mild reproach that his adversary had been in bed for hours. "Ah," said Hagen, "but he's not asleep." I have seen Diegel, as "crazy" as ever was Duncan, and as brilliant as anyone I ever did see, but somehow he did not quite seem the man to stop Bobby, and in any case it was with Compston that were all British hearts.

I went out to see him play the fist hole in the last round. His drive was perfect; his iron shot adequate, to the edge of the green, and he took three putts. One five meant nothing to be sure but there came other fives and the final 82 was heartbreaking. So out again in search of Bobby. All went if not perfectly according to plan at least reasonably well until he came to the eighth or Far Hole, which measures according to the books 527 yards, two shots and a pitch for Bobby in ordinary conditions with the ground fairly fast. The two shots were entirely satisfactory but the pitch was weak and the ball rolled back from the plateau; the next was nothing to boast of and at the last he missed a shortish putt; result, a horrid seven without touching a bunker. As Ben Sayers might have said, "It was no possible but it was a fact." The news of that seven quickly spread all over the links bringing consternation or encouragement. To Bobby himself it must have been a cruel blow but he pulled himself together and fought his way home, much, I imagine, in the frame of mind of a runner running himself blind, not seeing the tape but determined to get there. He was round in 75 and now we knew what had to be done. Compston was dead and buried; Diegel did a 75, good but not quite good enough for he had started two strokes behind. Those of us who were with him in one of the smaller rooms of the clubhouse united in assuring Bobby that all was well, as he wandered restlessly about holding a glass in two hands. And then there came a suggestion that all might not be well since Mac Smith was doing great things. To be sure he had to do a 69 to tie and that to an impartial judgment seemed very unlikely, but at such moments judgments can scarcely be impartial.

I remember very well going out to meet him. I could not go far for I had to broadcast and time was getting hideously short, but I *must* know. He holed out at the Dun taking to my jaundiced eye a very long time over it, and then we knew; two threes to tie. It was almost but not quite impossible. I saw him play the Royal—I was to broadcast from a house not far off—and his putt for three did not go in. Two to tie and that was surely impossible, but with an obstinate fidelity to duty I waited till his second had pitched on the home green and had palpably not holed out. Then I ran and ran and arrived just in time to announce in breathless tones to an expectant world that Bobby had won again.

I will not follow him home to America. He won the Open at Interlaken and the Amateur at Merion where he had played in his first championship at 14 and won his first Amateur Championship at 22. But as far as this country is concerned he departed in a blaze of glory from Hoylake.

He retired at the right time and could say with Charles Lamb, "I have worked task work and have the rest of the day to myself." After Tom Cribb had beaten Molineaux for the second time in the great battle of Thistleton Gap it was decided that he need never fight again but should bear the title of Champion to the end of his days. I think that most golfers in their hearts grant the same privilege to Bobby Jones.

That Small Colossus: Hogan at Carnoustie

Country Life
1953

As long as golfers talk championship golf, 1953 will be recalled as Hogan's year. Indeed, I think it would have been even if he had not won, so entirely did that small colossus bestride and dominate the tournament.

It was Hogan that sold the tickets in their thousands to the great joy of the authorities and filled the huge park with row upon serried row of shining cars; it was Hogan that produced what was, I think, the greatest crowd of spectators that I ever saw at a championship; and it was Hogan that every single one of them wanted to watch. Hardly anyone there had seen him play before since, when he was here in 1949, he was still too ill to play, and in less than no time anyone with any knowledge of golf came back overawed and abashed by the splendor of his game,

There were to begin with certain local patriots disposed to speak of him as "Your man Hogan," and to murmur that he might do all manner of things on American inland courses, but let him wait till he comes to play over the great Carnoustie course in a Carnoustie wind. Yet even those parochial critics were soon convinced, for they knew golf and were too honest not to admit that here was such a player as occurs only once in a generation or indeed once in a lifetime. As soon as the one Scottish hope, Eric Brown, had faded away, I think the whole of that vast crowd wanted Hogan to win. This is not to say that Dai Rees, the ultimate British hope, who had played most gallantly, would not have been a most popular winner. He certainly would, but the feeling that the best man ought to win—there was no earthly doubt who that was—overrode all other sentiments.

And what a wonderful win it was! He did what Bobby Jones, Hagen and Sarazen had all failed to do at the first attempt. He came here weighed down by his immense reputation, and for the first two rounds his putting was unworthy of him and he seemed to have got the slowness of the greens a little on his nerves so far as he has any nerves. Yet when he once began to take some of the chances which his magnificent iron play gave him, when the putts began to drop so that we said "Now he's off!", and when it was almost a case of in the one class Hogan and in the other class all the other golfers, it was a measure of his quality that having been hard pressed for three rounds, sharing the lead with one very fine player, and having all sorts of others hard on his very heels, he yet managed to win with something like ease.

It is an impossible task to give anything like an impression of the player to those who have not seen him, but one can perhaps pick out one or two points. Hogan stands decidedly upright with his weight rather forward on the left foot and the right foot drawn a little back. He holds his hands decidedly high, the right hand notably far over, and the right wrist almost arched. The swing is rhythmic and easy and not as long as I had expected from the photographs. The club at the top of the swing may, in fact, go a little past the horizontal, but, if so, the eye—or my eye—cannot detect it. The impressive part of the swing comes in what the books call the hitting area. Then the clubhead appears to travel with such irresistible speed that it goes right through the ball and far past it before it begins to come up again. He has, incidentally, a good deal of power in reserve, and when he really means to hit out, as he did with his two wooden clubs at the long 6th hole, his length is very great indeed. I suppose, however, it is his iron play—particularly his long-iron play—which is most striking. It is that which gives him so many chances of threes because he hits so appallingly straight. When we were all waiting behind the home green for his iron shot to the 72nd hole and Hogan, no doubt giving the out-of-bounds on the left a wisely wide berth, finished up eight or nine yards to the right of the pin, somebody remarked: "He's dreadfully crooked, isn't he?" It was a true word spoken in jest. Eight yards to the left or right of the pin was definitely crooked for Hogan.

His putting is, to me at least, the least attractive part of his game, as far as looks are concerned. He has the ball very far forward opposite, or almost in front of, his left foot, with his right foot back, and the whole attitude has something of stiffness. But if ever there was a case of handsome is as handsome does, this is it, for he hits the ball a wonderfully solid blow. The ball does not trickle away at the end of the putt; it goes right in, and when a putt is particularly crucial, he seems positively to will it into the hole.

Hogan is a compelling subject, and I have been running on about him like "a new barrow with the wheel greased." So I must do scanty justice to others. There is Locke, for instance, who lost the championship but lost it like a champion; his first round of 72 when the northwesterly wind was really blowing hard, was splendid, but he seemed to make just too many inaccurate iron shots. I think I have never seen Rees play better, and I think his temperament was in as good order as his golf. His finish of two threes in the second round swept us off our feet with a wave of enthusiasm. I suppose that on the whole he did not play the finishing holes as well as the others. As he came off the green at the end of his last round, having tied with the leaders, but knowing that Hogan would catch them, he exclaimed sadly: "The 15th and 16th again!"

Eric Brown's two 71s showed his quality. I think he is a little too easily disturbed and not quite philosophical enough to win through at the moment. The one who seems to have the perfect temperament is the young Australian, Peter Thomson. He has now been second twice and he is only twenty-three. As far as anyone can be sure to be a champion he is, and a most worthy and popular one he would be. The two South Americans, Cerda and de Vicenzo, raised golfing eyebrows. Either is just about good enough to win.

Finally, in a quadruple tie for second place was our now old friend Frank Stranahan. He not only played very, very well, but with tremendous courage. He provided one of the most dramatic moments of the tournament in the last round. He seemed out of the hunt so far as winning was concerned, when suddenly it was discovered that he was piling one three upon another and wanted a four at the home hole to be home in 33 and round in 70. The case was altered with a vengeance and when he holed his long putt for a three—he had holed a chip for a three at the very same hole in the morning—and got his 69, it looked as though anything might happen. "We have seen the putt which won the championship," said one very shrewd friend in an ecstasy of excitement. When we reckoned up what the others had to do, it had seemed very possible. "No, I think Hogan will just do it," I said, or I think I said, but I didn't think he would do it by four whole strokes. If there was one hole more than another that made that last round of Hogan's, it was his three at the 5th, where he holed his chip from a nasty rough place on the back of a bunker. No doubt it was a help, but he was in an unstoppable mood. Carnoustie certainly showed itself a fine, stern examination paper for champions. Only the best could get full marks there.

Hydes and Jekylls

The Times
1935

Every golfer has a dual nature, in every one of us a Jekyll and a Hyde are constantly contending. The Jekyll of the story was a fine, well-grown man, while Hyde was light and dwarfish. Of most golfers I am afraid that the converse is much more nearly true: Jekyll is small, sickly, puny; Hyde a lusty monster. Yet even the worst of us have our moments, not in which we are wholly virtuous, but in which the good for all too short a while conquers the evil. It is then that we display the temperate smoothness, the suavity and rhythm of a Jekyll, that all unseemly haste and passion are temporarily absent from our swing, that we stand up to the ball as though we feared to look no man in the face. And then there comes over us swiftly the dreadful change, and it is our own doing. Sometimes we have, like that unhappy doctor, "smarted in the fires of abstinence" too long, so that there catches us by the throat a sudden lust to hit the ball hard, as hard as ever we can. At others we "lick the chops of memory," contrasting with our present and insipid methods the gorgeous carefree driving of some unforgettable summer evening, when it did not seem to matter how we stood or how quickly we swung or even whether we looked at the ball.

Again it may happen that we do not fall through any active wickedness, but suffer only, as did Dr. Jekyll at the outset of his career, from "a certain impatient gaiety of disposition." We want some new and comparatively innocent experience; we grow tired, however modestly successful it may be, of our own style and think it would be amusing to imitate somebody else's or to try only for a stroke or two, insidious advice that we have read in a book. It matters not precisely how our fall is accomplished; we ourselves have precipitated it, and our devil, long caged, comes out roaring.

All too easily can we recognize the marks of change. The Hyde in us is unmistakable. Observe his tense muscles, his evil crouch, his furious address to the ball, his reckless loss of balance, his ape-like contortions. For a moment or two we find a hideous enjoyment in his antics, we leap at the ball with a misbegotten confidence, but too soon the spirit of hell awakes in us and we lash and slash till, on a sudden, tragedy and destruction overtake us. Then realizing our danger, even as Hyde did after battering Sir Dancers Carew to death, we fly back to Jekyll as our city of refuge, only to find that we are cut off from it, that we have not got the key.

It will be remembered that the magic draught failed at last; the reconversion from Hyde to Jekyll no longer took place. Its inventor believed that this was owing to some quality in one of the original ingredients which was absent from all the fresh supplies for which he ransacked the chemists' shops in London. Whether this was really so or whether the elixir had lost its potency from some subtler reason we cannot tell. It matters not which it was; our case is that of Dr. Jekyll. We can recall, in its minutest details as to hips or elbows, the remedy which has before transmuted us from a pressing, forcing demon to a leisurely, true-swinging Christian. We can swear that we have forgotten nothing; stance, grip, even waggle are precisely as they were in happier days; we go through all the motions as we did before—and nothing happens. There come none of the momentarily racking pains of change to end in an overpowering passion of relief; Hyde is still in full possession. Nor can we ever tell whether we have unconsciously varied the recipe or whether that particular potion has become stale and unprofitable.

I have been talking hitherto of the everyday run of sufferers. There are some golfers so great, dwelling so far above us on such cold, chaste heights that it is hardly possible to believe of any one of them that he contains even a germ of Hyde. They may have been, as was Dr. Jekyll, wild in their youth and, indeed, I have heard one of the most famous of golfers remark that he did not like to see a youngster too careful; but look at them now, stately, polished monuments of control! We cannot harbor even the breath of a suspicion. When we saw Harry Vardon swing the club (would that we could see him now!) we thought that here was not an impure Jekyll in which the good preponderated, but pure unsullied good, even as Hyde was pure evil. On the other hand, there are very, very great ones in whom the fiend lurks. Let me take as an example, with infinite respect, the sage of Walton Heath [James Braid]. Just once in a while, when he gives his club an additional waggle, when his knees crumple beneath him with the exuberance of the blow, when he hits a stupendous and magnificent hook into the heather, do we not catch a glimpse beneath that angelic exterior of the simian Hyde? And is there not, O my fellow sinners, just a grain of comfort in that?

V

A Golfer's Almanac

New Year's Eve Cheer

American Golfer
1933

There is an old friend of mine with whom I have often passed New Year's Day at his pleasant house on the hill overlooking a seaside links. We drink his fine old crusted vintages, tell fine old crusted stories, play a little mild golf by day and a little, if possible, milder bridge at night. He has just written to me asking me to come again and tells me that, when I arrive, I shall find him with a beard.

That seems to me typical of the new year spirit in golfers; they have got to do something new and exciting. If the beginning of the year came in summer, they would be busy prophesying what fresh heroes would wear the championship crowns. As it comes at a dead season of golf, they are entirely occupied with their own games and the wonderful changes they are going to make in them. Here is a gentlemen who up to the age of 76 or so has had a smoothly shaven chin. Now he has grown tired of it and wants a novelty; so it is a bearded chin that he will for the future, in obedience to Mr. Alex Morrison's advice, point at a spot just back of the ball.

How admirable is this youthful and adventurous spirit and yet it is one common amongst golfers. We may have come to a stage where we do not like birthdays or New Year's Day; we may pretend we are slipping slowly down the hill, and we may be quite sure that our contemporaries are doing so, but nothing can make us say die. We may not think that in the coming year we are going to be better than ever we were, but we are sure that we are going to be better than last year. That pleasantly fatuous belief never really leaves us, but it flames up more brightly than usual on the first of January, because that day is like the ninth hole in a round.

How often when we start playing very badly we say that we shall do better after the turn, and how often our words come true. We want just that definite turning point to set us on the right road and the New Year supplies us with it. On any ordinary summer day of the year if we go to bed slicers we do not expect to wake up driving with a slight, beautiful and controlled shaded draw; but as we take our bedroom candlestick with yawn on the night of December thirty-first, there seems nothing in the least improbable about such a miracle.

How grateful we golfers ought to be that our game will last us almost as long as we last ourselves, and that hope can still spring eternally in our ridiculous breasts. There comes a time of life when the sprinter realizes that, if he has not run one hundred yards in ten seconds, he never will; he is done once and for all. Similarly the golfer must sometimes know, though he does not admit it, that it is extraordinarily unlikely that he will ever drive any farther than he does now. But our game holds, forever, scope for improvement in one direction: we can never chip and putt so well but that we may not learn to do it better.

No other game contains so definite, so incontrovertible a reason for cheering up and cheering up at our time in life is an incalculable blessing.

Stripping for Action

Out of the Rough
1932

You cannot teach an old dog new tricks, but if the dog is going to have apoplexy unless he learns the trick you must at least from motives of common humanity try to teach him.

This observation is produced by the hot weather. Some time ago I played in a two-day match, and, together with one other old dog, I played, as is my custom, in a coat, while the other fourteen players engaged played more or less in their shirtsleeves. At the end of the two days I was so entirely prostrated that two alternatives presented themselves. Either to learn to play in shirtsleeves of give up midsummer golf.

It is not, if an egotistical explanation may be pardoned, that I have any violently Tory views about coatlessness. During two summers I played on the torrid marshes of the Vardar in khaki shirts which turned canary colored from the sunshine, but I never grew accustomed to a garb which seemed to increase, from its unnatural freedom, a natural slice. Safe at home again, I put on a nice, tight, gray flannel coat, and this was no mere gesture, such as the shaving off of a moustache, to show that adjutant-generals had ceased to trouble; it was a serious attempt to cure that slice, and it produced for a while a blessed tendency to hook. Since then I have flirted once or twice with jerseys and jerkins, but have always swung myself into such complicated knots that the coat had to be resumed. But now something must be done. What the Americans can learn to do, surely an Englishman can learn too. "Whereby," as Jack Bunsby remarked, "Why not? If so, what odds? Can any man say otherwise? No. Awast then!"

That the art of playing without a coat does require some learning there is surely no doubt. The delicious sense of freedom is full of perils and can produce terrific errors. Two venerable gentlemen of my acquaintance were watching the match that I mentioned, and, as the ball went flying into the rough, one of them remarked that when he used to take part in the match people did not play like that. The other, essentially more charitable, suggested that perhaps it was that the players were suffering from having suddenly taken their coats off. He received only an angry snort in reply, but he may have been right; it is tolerably certain, at any rate, that not for a long time have so many good golfers hit the ball so often and so far into such luxuriant hay.

On the other hand, this freedom may have its advantages, if only the player realizes its dangers. He is put on his guard against swinging too fast and too far; he is extremely conscious of the temptation to hurry, and by taking measures against it may even attain to a smoothness and rhythm of which he has hitherto only dreamed. If he is not so sinuous or so slim as he used to be, he will be surprised to find the clubhead coming once more within his range of vision at the top of the swing. That will gratify him as he remembers that Bobby Jones has said that Britons do not swing far enough, but he must not presume on his newfound joy, or he will spin round like an insane teetotum on the way down and "pivot" himself to glory and the grave. While not forgetting the words of the American sage, he should also recall those of a Scottish one:—"A good swing seems to the onlooker swift and flexible; but if the player feels supple he exhibits an awkward, stiff, straggling movement. The player ought to be, in his own hands, a stiff bow which he bends and shoots with."

With my head full of these and other wise maxims I went to a sequestered valley to practice. When I got there I took off my coat, but, if I may delicately allude to them, I retained my braces in order to begin by degrees. The solitude of the valley was not quite so complete as in my self-consciousness I could have wished. There were one or two assiduous ladies thumping their way round, card in hand, and the lines of an old cricket poem jingled themselves in my head.

Each nymph looks askance at her favourite swain,
And views him half-stripped with both pleasure and pain.

Luckily they were quite inappropriate, for I did not know the ladies and they showed no interest whatever in me. Still, it was pleasanter when they disappeared and I teed my ball on the brink of the great adventure. The first few shots gave me a sensation of having drunk some elixir of youth, but then I knew they would; so had the first strokes in the jerseys and jerkins, flattering only most horribly to deceive. I was trying to imitate the Americans, and clearly I must behave as they would, hitting hundred of balls and not stopping pusillanimously after a few respectable shots. Looking at it as if it belonged to somebody else, I thought there was really something almost heroic in that solitary figure tramping up and down the valley under a broiling sun. The ladies reappeared, having thumped several holes, and vanished again, and still the figure toiled on, nor were its efforts by any means unsuccessful. The litheness and grace of its follow-through positively compelled my admiration; the ball, with the sunburned ground to help it, went considerable distances and decently straight. Only after an hour and a half of solid slogging did the figure pick up its coat and climb very slowly out of the valley and up the hill. It looked decidedly limp but not unhappy.

Goodness only knows I am not puffed up; the battle is not won yet, for practice is one thing and a game quite another, and I shall be terribly frightened when first I face an enemy without my trusty coat. In any case, slicing must be presumed to be preferable to dying, though this is open to argument. The question of removing the braces is at the moment in abeyance. After all, William Lillywhite bowled in them and Fuller Pilch batted in them, and that ought to be enough for humbler folk.

Out-Of-Season Joys

Country Life
1931

On the night when the Open Championship ended at Carnoustie I crossed the Tay and made for St. Andrews, deeming it a crime to be so near and not have one day's golf there before returning south. Fortune was cruel, and it rained so hard that there was really nothing for it but to sit in the club and look drearily through the big window. Out of that window, usually so interesting a watchtower, there was very little to look at, for only two or three heroic ladies in mackintoshes drove off the first tee. Yet even so, though I raged at fate, there was something novel and exciting about the experience, because I realized that, often as I had been to St. Andrews, this was the first time I had been there in more or less of an off season, when the place belonged to itself and not to me, the golfing tripper. The novelty was emphasized as the day wore on, because at last, in despair, two companions and I went out, each with a club and two or three balls, and slashed about between the clubhouse and the burn, with nobody to object to us or get in our way.

My two companions, who lived at St. Andrews, took it as a matter of course, but to me there seemed something almost sacrilegious about it. Never before had I dreamed of such a thing. As a rule, when I want to practice at St. Andrews I am driven to the seashore, which, except for occasional lovers, dogs and motor-bicyclists, is not a bad place and agreeably flatters one's driving powers. Now here I was, practicing on a spot which had always seemed to me as impossible for that purpose as, let us say, Trafalgar Square. What a miserable southern tourist I was, a mere member of a holiday rabble! It occurred to me that I had once had much the same experience at another famous links—Prestwick. I have, as a rule, been to Prestwick at a time of championships, and so have only made an intolerably slow progress round a course all too full both of players and onlookers. Yet just once I did go there on an off day and, behold, we had the whole of that noble expanse to ourselves and played a five-ball match with nobody in front and nobody behind.

I could say much the same of other great Scottish courses, and the moral is that many of us English are very foolish in not trying more resolutely to go to Scotland when all the rest of the world is not going there, too. There are, of course, excellent reasons—such tiresome things as time and work and money—but, still, there is something wrong in a state of things that connects Scottish golf in the mind with a struggle for a time and a struggle for a caddie. And I hereby register a vow that some time before I die I am going north at a season when other southern golfers are sticking to their desks, and then I shall have the most delightful golf of all my life. At the present moment I know of a happy band who have made a plan to go to St. Andrews and play foursomes *after the medal is over*. They have suggested that I should go with them, but it sounds almost too good to be true: one of the dreams that will never be realized.

Nevertheless, it is very pleasant to indulge in hopeless day-dreams, and I amuse myself now and then with this one, wondering the while what it is that makes the thought of Scottish golf more exciting than that of any other kind. Sometimes I think it is the burns that make the difference. Water hazards are not, so far as I know, particularly good things in themselves. There are some on English courses that give no gratification. I get no thrill from my ball sailing over or plunging into the Suez Canal at Sandwich, nor the brook in front of the first hole at Deal. I love Westward Ho! and I have a profound respect for the home hole there, but I do not love the Stygian drain that guards that green. On my best beloved Woking I have often put my second shot in a streamlet before the sixth green and topped into it again from the eighth tee, but I have no pleasure in the recollection and I call it not a stream but a ditch—with an epithet. Yet the moment the Scottish border is crossed a burn seems to be endued with magical qualities and no properly constituted course is complete without one. Moreover, it really is a burn, and there is no affectation in so calling it. The late Mr. W. T. Linskill wrote of the Coldham Common that "its hazards are several burns," but no one else at Cambridge had the splendid and unselfconscious courage to use the term; "ditches" faintly described them.

To be sure they have much better burns in Scotland then we have in England. The Swilcan at St. Andrews may not be much to look at, and any impudent young Remus without a "crocky" knee can jump over it, but it has done a lot of damage in its time and turned the issue of famous battles. I always think that a tablet ought to be put up on its banks recording how three great men, Mr. Willie Greig, Mr. Laurence Auchterlonie, and Mr. John Ball, all went into it at the nineteenth hole against Mr. Leslie Balfour Melville when he won the Championship. Yet, if the best known, it is certainly not the greatest of burns. That honor should surely be given to the Barry burn at Carnoustie, which enjoys a justly enhanced celebrity since this year's Open Championship. No mere English brook could wind itself in so complex a manner and guard so many greens at once. Either the tenth hole, "South America," or the home hole would make the reputation of any ordinary burn, and this Barry burn makes both holes what they are and the seventeenth as well, where poor Jurado lost a championship in the "black and dowie waters." And then there is the Pow burn at Prestwick, which is the making of one of the greatest of all holes, the fourth, and also plays its part at the Cardinal and the Himalayas home. I have mentioned only three, but the list could be prolonged indefinitely. Lifting and dropping may be poor fun and poor golf, but a burn is a burn "for a' that," and in Scotland it is a noble and romantic hazard.

Then there is the matter of caddies. Some people like to hand themselves over body and soul to their caddies, but I am one of those vain and irritable creatures who do not like to be too sternly dragooned. By nature I prefer the silent English beast of burden to the imperious Scot. I have no evidence that the Scottish caddie can play better than I can the stroke on which he pours scorn; I am not convinced he knows more about the game and I do not relish his domineering manner. "By nature" I repeat; yet when I go to a Scottish links I should probably feel a little disappointed if my caddie did not order me about and openly despise me. There would be a feeling that I might as well have stayed at home and that I was not getting my money's worth. There would be something lacking in the glamor and the atmosphere without this discipline.

I have ventured to suggest two reasons why Scottish golf is more romantic than any other, but, of course, everybody can best think of his own reasons, impalpable and inexpressible things, woven out of all manner of pleasant memories. Let me end by quoting something about it written in the *Cornhill* some sixty-four years ago. "There is a comfortable little club at St. Andrews, which, like all the other institutions of the town, is subservient to golf. It stands at the end of the links, or downs, upon which the game is played, and from the windows, with a good opera glass, you can rake the first part of the course, and judge from the features and gestures of the players returning, whether they are losing or winning . . . The golfer, having finished a large and late breakfast, lights a cigar, and turns his steps towards the links and the club. Presently he is joined by another, and then another golfer, and about eleven o'clock little knots form in front of the club and in the parlor, and the process of matchmaking begins." That is a delightful picture, though not quite a true one of "the comfortable little club" in August and September nowadays, but when some day I take my dream holiday there, there it will be beautifully and exactly true.

The Golfless Holiday

Country Life
1942

Last week I took as my text a letter from one friend whom the course of his military duties had taken to the neighborhood of a pleasant links. Whereupon, aided by two 74s, he had been once more filled with enthusiasm for the game. This week I have had a letter from another which is clearly intended by Providence to supply me with a corollary. This friend—a very old one—is just about to take a well-earned holiday. He is clearly the bravest and most resolute of men. He may be the wisest as well, or he may be the most foolish. As to that I cannot make up my mind, and the reader must judge. He is going to the greatest of all links, and he is taking no golf clubs with him, but only a shooting-stick. "I intend," he writes, "to spend a week there in laughing at the golfing foibles of my friends," and he adds firmly: "I am sure I am right."

He does not attempt to propitiate me by any excuses, but he does give an explanation. He has not hit a single ball for a whole year; he has neither time nor inclination for intensive practice beforehand, and he does not feel "in the mood." If he took his bag of clubs with him—and it is a large one, for he was a great patron of the clubmakers—he would only bring it back again, "disillusioned and profoundly unhappy"; and so he is leaving it behind. I shall admit one thing, that he is a man of character. I, too, have been to that noble spot without my clubs and been very happy there, but then there was a championship that I had to watch. To go there for a holiday without clubs demands a captaincy of the soul to which I can make no pretensions. Am I not right in saying that it shows either great wisdom or great folly?

Not being in the mood for golf is a horribly common complaint in such times as these: I am suffering from it myself at the present moment, but shall I not be convalescent—touching wood—towards the end of September when the time comes for me to look up, quite superfluously, in *Bradshaw* the same dear old train? The appetite comes in eating, a proverb of which my old friend may find out the truth before his week is sped. Meanwhile, I like to picture him after a late and lazy breakfast strolling down to the clubhouse on his first morning. He will exchange cheerful, almost uproarious, greetings with those who appear to have been sitting in exactly the same chairs ever since he was last there. He will then ensconce himself behind the big window, drinking in great draughts of felicity as he contemplates the familiar scene. Ever and anon he will indulge in a biting quip or two as to the eccentricities of those driving off from the first teeing ground. Here, he will say to himself, is the perfectly restful holiday alike for body and mind, and he will be more than ever complacent about his resolution.

Presently there will appear on the tee four friends whom it would particularly amuse him to watch, and with an effort he will dislodge himself from his window seat and, shouldering his shooting-stick in a jaunty manner, will set out with them. If they make bad shots he will guffaw; if they make good ones he will cordially and unenviously admire; if they are kept back by those tiresome people in front he will be no whit impatient, but will repose placidly on the shooting-stick. He may even "remember with advantages" how once upon a time, when haply I was playing with him, we were delayed in an intolerable manner by the Bishop of Barchester and his three octogenarian companions and took three and half hours, full measure, to get round. In short, that first morning and even perhaps the whole first two days will be sheer bliss.

About the third day he may, as I calculate, become a little less sure that he was right. Exactly how the blow will fall I cannot say. No doubt he will borrow somebody's putter on one green or another, but this will hardly do it, for putting is so separate and self-contained a branch of golf that a little indulgence will not inspire a wild lust for a whole round. Rather I imagine that one of the four he is watching will insidiously put into his hand a most seductive iron, or perhaps a spoon, together with a couple of balls, and suggest that he have a smack or two on the New Course next door and then rejoin the party later on. That will be the crucial moment. If he hits a good smack he will long to play a round, and if he does not he may lack the fortitude required to leave off with a bad one. In either case he will feel bitterly sorry that he did not bring his own clubs with him. He will be like the man in the story who died and found himself on the most beautiful golf course with rows of shining clubs ready to his hand. He thought that some fortunate mistake had been made by the recording angel and that he must be in Heaven after all, when another damned soul enlightened him by saying: "There are no balls."

This mood of not being in the mood is a very sensitive and mutable thing; it does not take much to overset it. The man who thinks he has given up golf for a while is like to him who thinks he has given up smoking. The abstainer from tobacco is so sure that he has overcome the craving that, out of pure bravado and in order to prove he is right, he accepts a cigarette. It tastes like nothing in particular, and he is still more sure he is right, but somehow he takes another and then he is done for. So the golfing abstainer's first shot with the borrowed iron may not feel very good; it will probably be mistimed and jar his fingers, but the second or third ball will fly sweetly away and it will be all over with him.

A very little thing will bring back the lost mood. The other day a friend at a club told me casually that he had been having a day at Hoylake. That might have left me tranquil, even indifferent, but he described with a positively infernal eloquence how it had been blowing hard (don't I know that wind?), how he had just got past the corner of the field with his first tee shot and then, with the very best brassie shot he could hit into the teeth of the wind, had reached the edge of the green and obtained his four. I gathered that after this he was less successful, but I scarcely heard him, for I was lost in a selfish dream of Hoylake. I knew I could not get up at that first hole in two against the wind (I wonder, incidentally, whether the tee was at all forward), but I reckoned at what holes that same wind would help me. It would make the tee shot to the Telegraph comparatively simple; it would blow me kindly along at the Dun, and surely the cross-bunker at the home hole would not catch my second. Instantly I felt in the mood to take the next train to Liverpool and imagined with what a thrill I should look down on a sulphurous Widnes out of my carriage window.

I remember how, a good many years ago, I arrived at a familiar and hospitable house and, after the first greetings with half a dozen fellow guests, I exclaimed: "Well, whom do I have to play tomorrow?" The answer came in chorus: "Oh, we none of us play golf." It was too true, for every single one of them had something the matter with one limb or another. How sorry I then felt for them! Sorrier, perhaps, than I should now when I understand more of these inevitable afflictions. Nevertheless, if, all being well, I go there soon I shall take my bag, a light one with half a dozen clubs in it, and though I am sure, in my friend's words, to be disillusioned, I hope I shall not be too profoundly unhappy. Meanwhile, I unreservedly withdraw any malign remarks I may have made about him. I trust and believe that he will enjoy his holiday.

The Evening Round

The Times
1935

A correspondent has just written to me saying that the time has surely come for me to dilate upon golf after tea. He even goes so far as to say that I ought to do it every year, and here, being painfully conscious of my own bad habits, I thought at first that I detected a rather bitter irony. On rereading his letter I came to the conclusion that he meant kindly; the irony is to be found in the circumstance, which he did not know, that I am not allowed to play golf even before tea.

The supreme moment can only come once a year, and this year I have missed it. For certain people it always comes on the same day, the Saturday of a weekend at Worlington. Then when the serious business of the day is over we sally forth with one club apiece. No doubt other and happier people did so last Saturday, but I had gone home snuffling and sneezing to bed, and that particular moment cannot be recaptured till another whole year has passed. Even as I write some time after tea there is plenty of light in the garden, light for putting and pitching, light even for what I am pleased to call driving, but it may not be.

The case, it may be said, is not a very hard one; the time of the first green mist of the hedges, of the first cuckoo that is not a mischievous little boy, has not yet come; there are plenty of evenings ahead. Yet the maddening part of golf is that the only time we feel a real longing to play it is when we cannot do so. In the morning I was allowed out for a little walk in the fresh air. I was exceedingly well wrapped up, and felt like Uncle Joseph in the coat of marten's fur and the health boots prescribed by Sir Faraday Bond. All Nature seemed determined to emphasize my lamentable state. In a little wood a missel-thrush sang loudly and triumphantly, and if ever a thrush sang "Golf after tea," that was the identical bird.

Through the wood there runs a wide, grassy glade. It was all flecked with sunshine and had in it just a suspicion of a "dogleg" bend to the right, that kept calling and calling in my ears for a shot with a little drift in it. I plodded to the end of it—the prescribed limit of my walk—and turned; there was an equally fascinating bend to the left, and it positively shouted, "Now for a little hook!" Outside the wood lay a meadow, bathed in light, close-cropped and inviting, with not so much as a single intrusive cow in it. All the new styles that I had thought of as I lay in my bed came welling up simultaneously in my mind and I could not try a single one of them, because it would never do to get "overheated." I was assured that I should be able to do it another day, but I did not want to do it another day; I may never want to do it on any other day, but I did so dreadfully want to have just one shot then.

There is something magical about the first rounds of spring, so that we remember some of them long, long after we have played them, not on account of any petty personal triumphs or disasters, but from the pure joy of being alive, club in hand. There was one Easter half at school, when the sun was so hot and the ground so dry that I lay and basked on the grass between my shots. I can see the particular spot now, just after turning away from the river and the terrific short hole with the solitary willow behind the green. There was another round at Sandwich, a first round on that noble course before a first University match. There was no lying on the grass that time, but a rush straight from the station to the club-house, and a race round the course in a blue serge suit to beat the fading daylight. Yet the same kind of ecstatic glory hangs round the memories of both rounds; I know that in the first of them my driver had a brown head, and in the second a yellow one, or perhaps, since the occasion was so romantic, I should say, of palest gold.

By way of encouraging in myself this maudlin state of mind I have been looking in an ancient diary to see which day of the year, something over thirty years ago, saw the first evening round. As a rule it was year in and year out within a day or two of this very Saturday, March 9, but in one year it came much earlier. On one February 25 I find recorded a tremendous display of energy; first of all a 36-hole Single, won at the very last hole, and then "Played a 14-hole match afterwards which lost." Since no margin is given I think it may safely be stated that it was lost by a good many holes. What time of the morning we started and why we did it I cannot state; indeed if I did not know myself to have kept that diary with remarkable honesty I should not believe in the entry any more than I believe in those gentlemen who are incapable of deception and write to the newspapers to say that they have heard the cuckoo in February.

The time of third rounds is over and will not come back. It is pitch dark outside my window now, but the daylight will come back and perhaps, if it is very warm and sunshiny, I shall be let out, without that confounded muffler, for just one spring shot with my springy driver. I wonder which style I shall try.

Stormy Weather

Country Life
1961

Sitting at home listening to the rain pattering on the window and waiting for news from Birkdale, I recalled other championships put off or nearly put off owing to rain. And I must begin by sympathizing with the Royal Birkdale Club. There is no club, I think, more conscious of the honor of housing the Championship; no club of which the members more energetically combine to undertake all manner of necessary duties. The weather was very hard on them, and it was at least comforting that the conditions improved on the last day and the course emerged triumphant, as a fine test of golf.

I read that we have to go back to 1910 for an instance of the Championship being washed out as it was on the second day at Birkdale. Well, I can go back to the year 1910, at St. Andrews, and a memorable one it was. One is apt to remember small ways in which one was oneself affected, and that storm of rain prevented me from going to Dornoch. It upset my plans, and in fact I have never seen Dornoch, a sad gap in my education. Then I remember going out in a downpour to see Willie Park. I had met him but never seen him play, and now here he was playing the first hole. He successfully reached the green in two and took two putts with his wry-necked putter, which he made so famous, and then came the announcement that the day's play was washed out and abandoned.

Some way in front was James Braid, in his policeman's mackintosh trousers, no longer of Romford but of Walton Heath. The message reached him, but presumably in rather a vague form. At any rate, he did not wholly believe it, deeming it too unofficial, and so went on plowing his way through the rain-gushes. It must gradually have dawned on him that the news had been true, but, having once set on his voyage he continued and finished in 77 or 78, I think 78. It was a magnificent piece of golf in the conditions; one of the great rounds that do not count, which champions so often produce. Next morning, when he had to start again, he returned the very same score, and it seemed just about as good, though the rain had stopped.

Another famous stormy year was 1937, Cotton's year at Carnoustie. It was the last day of the Championship, as vile a day as could well be imagined, with a tempestuous wind and sheets of rain. It was obvious that there would be a grave danger of a washout. The first hole at Carnoustie is in a considerable hollow, which was sure to get full of water, and the green-keepers were kept busy cutting a fresh hole there, moving it ever further out of the hollow and up the bank. There were other greens, too, in great peril, and I have always had the feeling that, if anyone had protested, the day's play would have had to be abandoned. However, nobody did protest; I suppose they thought it was the same for all and they had had their chance; at any rate, they refrained from complaint in a very sporting manner, and the day's play was carried through somehow. I remember going out for a few holes with Reg Whitcombe at the very height of the storm and marveling at him, thinking that nobody could possibly play better; yet Cotton, with the tempest but little abated, did play better and gained half-a-dozen strokes on him in the last two rounds. One of the most vivid pictures in my memory is of Whitcombe trying to shelter under his umbrella while he wiped his hands and the grip of his brassie on a towel, before playing his second to the home hole and then lashing the ball home over the burn and onto the green.

The alarming thing about these storms is that the flooding of a single green may wreck the whole day's play, and it is sometimes the green that one least expects. I remember one year at Sandwich when there came a sudden squall that nearly ruined everything. I had taken shelter with Cecil Hutchison, who was then a member of the Championship Committee, in the green-keeper's tool shed close to the eighth green. There we had a view of the seventh green, as innocent a green as possible, so one would imagine. But it has little ripples in it and in one of those little valleys the hole was cut. The valley quickly became full of water, and a couple came up who could not hole out. Cecil rushed out to summon the green-keeping forces, and mobilized them with squeegees to sweep the water off the green. This they did, and the waiting couples, for there were more than one by this time, could go ahead and hole out. It would have been truly dreadful if that one little flood had destroyed a whole day's play, but that is the sort of thing that can happen. I remember, on that day at Carnoustie that I mentioned, a frantic message coming back to the Committee that a famous player refused to go on, and officials had to run out and pacify him and cut a fresh hole.

To return to Sandwich; it was the scene of a celebrated storm in, I think, 1938. It was not a storm of rain this time, but such a wind as I had never felt before. It blew down all the tents in the night and blew a good deal of money into the fortunate pockets of those who had backed the higher scores in a game, which I never fully understood, played on the Stock Exchange. The weather had been perfectly fine and easy for scoring and the scores had been very low accordingly; then came the tempest and they were blown to smithereens. I remember being quite unable to guess what sort of scores people could or would do. I went out with a friend to the ninth green to meet Whitcombe and Adams, who were playing together, wondering what we should hear. To our amazement we heard that Whitcombe was all fours and Adams very little worse. It is true that Whitcombe managed to take six to that hole by some ping-pong across the green; but even so he was out, unless my memory has gone astray, in 38, and the red book tells me his score for this third round was 75, truly miraculous in the circumstances. The wind really was tremendous: witness the fact that Padgham drove on to the eleventh green, where he rubbed it in by holing his putt for a two.

It seemed as if Cotton was going to do the most incredible score of all in the afternoon when he set out in pursuit of Whitcombe and Adams. It looked a hopeless business, but he played so supremely well that for fourteen holes it really seemed that he might do it. And then his iron shot up to the fifteenth hole was carried away over the little bank to the left of the green, and that meant a five. He could afford no more slips, and the sixteenth did it. I can still see his ball hovering high over the green before being swept into the left-hand bunker; the great spurt had been blown away.

The result of watching these tremendous events is, as far as I am concerned, a conviction that it is a mistake to believe that any storm will really defeat a great golfer; he will fight his way through it somehow. It will beat nearly all the field, but not quite all. The truly great ones will conquer, and it is unwise to bet against them.

Autumn Comes

Rubs of the Green
1936

The time of autumn golf has come, and it would be the pleasantest of the whole year if we could forget that winter golf was hard on its heels. The touch of wet on the grass, the freshness of the air, if they did not tell us that summer was over, would promise delicious rounds. It is the only defect of these October days that we have to snatch them; we must gather our mushrooms while we may.

Yet, considered from another aspect autumn is, perhaps, the most cheerful season of the year. The golfer has come back from his holiday, and it is then that he dreams the wildest dreams. The holiday itself is seldom a season for hope, because there is not time for hoping. It is true that the golfer on his holiday tries this and that, and often believes that he has got it at last, but disenchantment follows so quickly and so regularly on attainment that it loses much of its bitterness. He has scarcely had time to pin his faith to his elbow, before he has discovered the emptiness of all elbows and turned to his foot. Life is a long series of little disappointments, rather than a single great and tragic one.

When a man comes back to work on the other hand he has time for reflection; he has been wandering in a crowded mist of styles; now the mist clears and he sees exactly what he was doing wrong all the while. He can even remember the round in the middle of the holiday when he was on the very verge of the great discovery, only to be led away in another direction by some perverse will-o'-the-wisp. Yes, that was undoubtedly it, there was a feeling about that particular shot. It was stupid of him not to recognize a thing so obvious at the time, but better late than never. Therefore, the days that elapse between the return home and the first Saturday round are filled with hope, and, given a week, with no chance of sobering disillusion, hope can grow insanely high.

Again the golfer finds it at first pleasant enough to get back to his own course and meet his own partners and opponents. Their characteristic waggles had possibly grown a little tiresome after eleven solid months, but now after an interval he is glad to see them again and to play the old familiar holes. That is an entirely sane and rational pleasure, but here also insanity lurks waiting for its prey. As a rule, the home course is something shorter and easier than the seaside one where the holiday was spent; it is not afflicted by those winds which are, as Mr. Guppy would say, "enough to badger a man blue." Consequently for the first round or two, golf may seem a comparatively simple game; the gentle suburban breeze does not sweep the ball a hundred yards off the line; if that ball is blown into trouble it can be got out again and is not battered in vain against the remorseless walls of Strath or the Hill bunker. The poor fool actually comes to believe that he has improved and that his holiday resembled a visit to one of those spas which undeniably make a man feel like a limp rag at the time, but are alleged to make him feel like a young Greek god when he gets home again.

This autumnal hopefulness is, in reality, only that which buoys up many golfers from Sunday night to Saturday morning all through the year, but, owing to its slightly exaggerated form, it may endure throughout October with no more than the ordinary ups and downs. With November comes a crash; the golfer finds that he is getting shorter and shorter. If he would accept the fact, which is patent in the case of his friends, that the ground accounts for it, he might be tolerably happy; but the experience of many Novembers has not convinced him, and he goes out practicing in the secret dusk in search of that vanished length. There is a particular part of a particular London course that is haunted for me by the friendly ghost of an old gentleman, who was puzzled by this autumnal mystery every year till he was over eighty, and never solved it at last. Let us hope that on Elysian courses there is neither deceitful run nor disillusioning mud.

With regard to this painful subject of mud, I met the other day the sternest and most conscientious of all parents. His home is in a country of clay, so that except on his yearly visit to the greatest of seaside courses he scarcely hits a ball. Not only that but he will not allow his small boys to do so, lest their swings should be corrupted by delving in the mud. I can testify that they swing like dashing young angels, and I look forward to tottering round on a shooting-stick to watch them in future championships; I wonder if a little mud would really hurt them. I recall such good fun in such squelchy fields in my own boyhood that I feel a little sorry for them. I wish they might be allowed just once, on Christmas afternoon, let us say, when they are full of plum pudding. If they solemnly promised to play winter rules and tee the ball they surely could not come to much harm. There is something worse than muddy golf, and that is no golf at all.

A Mid-Winter Night's Dream

Rubs of the Green
1936

Epithets are important, though it is doubtless still more important to do without them. We have to be particular at this season about the epithets for Christmas and the New Year—the one merry and the other happy. It would never do to transpose them, since we would scarcely wish our worst enemies a whole year of merriment. If we played golf on Christmas Day it is to be hoped that we put into it a reasonable amount of the carnival spirit; but imagine twelve whole months of backslapping, leg-pulling, cheerio-drinking, four-ball matches. The mere thought sheds a melancholy upon the soul, and so we must be careful to wish each other a happy golfing New Year.

It is, of course, a vain wish. The only golfer that could truly be called happy would be some poor gentleman who went round the links with a keeper under the delusion that he was Bobby

Jones. Short of that there can only be different degrees of unhappiness. At this moment I almost believe myself to be happy, because I hope to be playing golf on New Year's Day. Yes, if all goes well, I shall be snuffing the sea breeze and teeing my ball at just about the hour when suburban trains, having possibly been delayed by fog, are disgorging their freight of toilers at some bleak terminus. Yet I do not say this in any gloating or offensive spirit. Those black-coated golfers, though they may not realize it, will be happy for a longer period of the New Year than I shall. Not till the Saturday morning will their hopes be blasted, whereas the gorgeous fabric of my dream will have been unraveled by lunchtime on Tuesday.

The best I can wish any fellow golfer is that at this the last weekend of the old year he may discover a something, no matter what, which is to make him a new man forevermore. Let him discover it not while waggling a delusive poker in his room or even at practice with a club and ball in his garden. Let it be while he is playing a real game against a flesh-and-blood opponent; and I would pass him the further hint that he had better light on it as late as possible, so that it may last out the round. Then he can think about it continuously as he smokes his cigar after dinner on Sunday night, and spasmodically, so far as his workday avocations permit, during Monday, Tuesday, Wednesday, Thursday, and Friday. After that the deluge; he will at least have enjoyed the maximum of unclouded happiness during the New Year.

Is there any other game which produces in the human mind such enviable insanity? Does, for instance, the Rugby football player, as he goes to bed on the 31st of December, hug to himself the belief that he will never again miss a place-kick at goal because of some nonsense or other that has just been revealed to him? A place-kick right in front of goal is rather like a short putt, and many a golfer on New Year's Eve believes that he will never miss a short putt again. I do not know, but I very much doubt, if the football player shares this touching conviction. There is, to be sure, a difference between the two cases. The golfer is entirely dependent on himself, and so it is enough if he have complete faith in himself. In the case of the football player and his kick there is the other fellow who lies on his stomach in the mud and may place the ball with tremulous and bungling fingers. There are also those nasty rough creatures who wait beneath the crossbar ready to rush out; they, too, may interfere with the perfect kick. So the analogy is defective and there remains only the billiards player who may imagine that never again will he miss a half-ball loser from balk. At least, I suppose he may, but, having never yet learned where to tee my ball for that apparently simple shot, I find such a state of mind hard to conceive.

The golfer may be more at the mercy of this mid-winter night's dream because he can have a new club or even, in these prodigal times, a whole set of new clubs. The football player has no weapons but those Nature has given him, and I cannot think—perhaps this is mere ignorance or prejudice—that a new cue or bat or racket can flood the mind with the same glow of madness as does a new club. Only the other day, I met a distinguished golfer of my acquaintance who takes the game, as a rule, in the spirit of a philosopher at once lighthearted and cynical. Yet it was with a radiant face and almost a blush that he told me that a set of wooden clubs with extremely springy shafts had given him a fresh lease of life and that he had gone round his home course in sixty-nine. Now it happens that this particular golfer has also enjoyed a second blooming as a cricketer. He does not, however, attribute that pleasing fact to a new bat, but to sitting at the feet of a wise man. A bat can be a very good bat, but even on New Year's Eve, when fairies are abroad, it cannot pretend to be a magic wand.

Perhaps, then, I ought to add to my New Year's good wishes to the reader that somebody may give him a new club. There was once a small girl who on being promised a puppy as a present asked whether she might get under the table to think about it. My imaginary reader may not wish to go to that length, but, if the club be a putter, he can at least practice with it at the legs of the table. If he does not fall into the vulgar error of not hitting hard enough he will be sure to hit them, and his five days of beautiful, foolish, pathetic hopes will thereby be made if possible more beautiful than ever.

The Frozen Player

Playing the Like
1934

In winter, too, when hoary frosts o'erspread
The verdant turf, and naked lay the mead,
The vig'rous youth commence the sportive war,
And, arm'd with lead their jointed clubs prepare.

So sang a Glasgow poet, Mr. James Arbukle, in 1721, and I hope he enjoyed his game. For my part, I hold that there is nothing more detestable than golf in a frost, and that it ought to be put down by law. "No golf. Ping-pong weather"—so ran a telegram that I received, a sadly long number of years ago, when on the eve of a golfing weekend, and how cheering it would be if someone would send me one now. The extreme poignancy of my feelings is due to the fact that on the very day on which this pusillanimous words will appear in print I have pledged myself to play in a golf match—not a mere game which I could unblushingly shirk, but a match against "vig'rous youth," who are presumably at this moment preparing "their jointed clubs" for the purpose. The war against them will not be "sportive"; it will be wholly and entirely beastly, and, what is more, when once it has begun it will go on to the bitter end. Just now there came a flurry of fine, powdery snow against the window and I prayed that it might grow ever thicker, but it has stopped and once more the prospect of golf looms bleak and horrible. O "vig'rous youth," how at this moment I do hate you!

I cannot deny that I have played frozen golf. There comes back to memory a whole week of it, two rounds every day with an east wind blowing all the time. That wind blew more or less straight up and down the course, inspiring a certain spurious joviality on the way out and cutting like a knife all the way home again. It seems incredible now and yet we almost enjoyed it. I believe that the mere fact of reaching non-reachable bunkers amused us. We believed—heaven forgive us!—that such stupendous hitting could not be altogether due to the wind and the ground; we must have discovered something. At least each of us believed that about himself; the others were deluded victims. It would almost be worthwhile to be such fools again and play in that frosty paradise.

In my present gloomy and disillusioned state there seems to me only one possible thing to be said for frozen golf. There is a certain impish satisfaction to be extracted from trying quite deliberately to jump the bunkers. It becomes a positive delight if we do it in playing the odd and then see our enemy in the like play precisely the same shot but with less good fortune, so that his ball just catches the top of the bank and falls back into a footmark in rock-like sand. It is again not wholly unpleasant to see the pitcher's skill rendered unavailing. We clumsy scufflers go no farther over the green than does the master of backspin. These, however, are but mean and shameful joys, and evanescent ones at that. It might be maliciously amusing to see Lindrum playing billiards on the table in the village institute, where the ball rattles as it goes, but the amusement would not last.

No, if we must play golf in this weather let us putt upon the carpet, either at the coal shovel or at the legs of tables and chairs. The shovel provides probably the better education, the table leg the more flattering fun. There is the highest authority for this pursuit, for Mr. Horace Hutchinson recommended it in the dear old *Badminton*, in order that the student might discover how to keep his club on the line. I must copy out the words, which I know almost by heart, because I love them as old friends. "For a player to find out for himself how best he may accomplish this is a problem that can be solved more readily in a drawing-room without a ball—by seeing how the putter head may be best induced to move along a straight line of the carpet pattern—than on the putting green. We give this advice to adepts and tyros alike; for we are very sure that practice of this kind is a better lesson for true hitting of the ball with the putter than any amount of outdoor play—though it, of course, teaches nothing of strength."

Fired by rereading these words, I actually got my putter and began to explore the various carpets in the house, but they were most disappointing. One room has got nothing but rugs with drunken zigzag patterns that would do more harm than good. Beneath them, moreover, is a hard, shiny floor which makes the ball rattle as on that village billiard table. The carpets proper are entirely devoid of patterns, but they are not devoid of invisible borrows, and who can allow for a borrow that he cannot see? One might as well, like poor Hubert in "Ivanhoe," "shoot at the edge of our parson's whittle or at a wheat straw or at a sunbeam." I am afraid I am past being educated and I found I was not amused.

At this point I laid down both pen and putter and walked to the golf course in order to get a club mended against the possibility of having to play in the match. It was not agreeable—far from it; the wind tweaked my nose and I slipped and slithered, but there were compensations. I saw two benighted persons trying to play golf and thought that I was not as they were. Better still, it *was* snowing—not a tremendous par snow, but a mild, persistent Bogey snow that effected its purpose; some of the greens were positively getting white. A little more and there would be no golf. If only the date of the skating championship is not too ostentatiously fixed I have now distinct hopes.

A Christmas Story

Playing the Like
1934

I heard a little argument the other day as to the proper definition of an amateur. There was an idealist who declared that an amateur should be defined as one who played for love of the game. "That won't do," said the cynic, "for there are many of us who hate golf like poison and yet go on playing it."

That is not at all the right sort of story for this time of year, and I will try to tell another more appropriate. It is that of a golfer whom I know very well. Let me call him Gabriel Grub, after that morose, sulky old party of whom Mr. Wardle told the story on Christmas Eve. Gabriel sometimes hated golf bitterly, and never more so than on one afternoon just before Christmas. He did not want to go out, and would have preferred to stay sulking and dozing in front of his fire. However, he forced himself to take off his nice fluffy slippers, put on his boots, and go out on to the lawn with a mashie and a few old balls. He put them down drearily in a row and played them to the other end; he walked drearily after them and hit them back towards the house. How he did hate it, to be sure! If he hooked a shot going down the lawn, the ball always just carried the wire, pitched on the hard tennis court, bounded miles in the air, and disappeared in an impenetrable wilderness beyond. If he hooked coming back, the ball pitched in a little turnabout house and the people sitting there were so absurd as to resent it. If he sliced he went into a tree (another lost ball), and if he topped he nearly hit a black dog who, out of pure friendship, would always stand and wag a Christmas tail exactly on the line.

These anxieties made Gabriel apt to take his eye off the ball, so that he played rather worse even than usual and actually socketed one shot and lost two balls in the bushes. He plodded up and down several times, hating it all more and more, and then he could endure it no longer and came in and sat down again before his fire, sulkier than ever. He reflected how horrid the course would be at Christmas if he played, which he certainly would not; how muddy and sticky, how crowded with hearty persons whom he did not know and did not want to, all drinking each other's healths, all playing four-ball matches and missing the globe and keeping him waiting in the cold wind. He shut his eyes and thought what fun it would be to go out all alone on Christmas Eve and dig a bunker somewhere that should catch the best drives of all those odious creatures.

The bunker grew deeper and deeper in his malicious imagination, and then, suddenly, just as befell the real Gabriel Grub, he found himself in a large cavern in the ground with the king of the goblins and all the attendant goblins mocking at him. "You hate golf! You are a miserable man!" said the king of the goblins, and a cloud at the end of the cavern rolled away and disclosed a green and pleasant view. There seemed to Gabriel something familiar about it. Surely he had seen before that narrow strip of turf between the sand dunes on one side and the railway on the other, with the big, brown, bracken-covered hills beyond it. There was a strong east wind blowing and the sea, when he could just catch a glimpse of it, looked gray and angry. And here were some fools actually trying to play golf. One of them stood up to address the ball for a mashie shot with all the natural grace of a Vardon, but when he came to hit it he threw up his head too soon, so that the club stuck in the turf and the ball only trickled a few feet. The other stood very close to his ball, whirled his club up very fast, with his right elbow high in the air, and leaped off both feet. It was an awe-inspiring sight, but the results were inadequate, for the ball either proceeded along the ground to short-leg or soared into the air, high, indeed, but in a malignant curve towards cover-point. Yet the odd thing, as it seemed to Gabriel, was that they neither of them seemed to get angry or to dislike the game, but enjoyed it amazingly, being so amused at their bad shots that they must have in their own breasts some unfailing materials of happiness.

It was rather surprising to see that these two players had attracted a gallery of one. The spectator was clad so strangely that for a moment Gabriel thought he must be dreaming. He wore a black coat, of which the tails fluttered in the wind, and on his head was a very small cap, blue with yellow stripes, which Gabriel recognized as the Quidnunc color. He had apparently hurt his arm, so that for the time he could not play, but he enjoyed watching the others and trotted to the flag for them and helped them to fish for balls in large lakes of casual water, and kept up a pleasant commentary upon their shots. By the way, Gabriel noticed that there were no caddies and the course was very long, but the players did not mind, and toiled along with astounding cheerfulness under their burdens. And when at last it was all over they clambered up a steep hill in uproarious spirits and had apple jelly for tea.

"What do you think of that?" said the king of the goblins, and Gabriel murmured apologetically that it seemed a very nice game indeed. "Show him more," said the goblin, and the cloud came and went again. This time there was no sea and no sandhills, but a flat expanse divided by a line of dark fir trees. The wind here blew still more fierce and cold, and it seemed to him, as he hugged his coat round him, that this wind must come straight and un-stymied from the Arctic regions. Moreover, the expanse was not green; it was white with snow. Yet even here there were golfers; they were younger than those in the first vision, and in one of them Gabriel thought he saw a likeness to himself as he had once been. They were actually playing golf with red balls, although by the time they reached the greens the red ball had become a white snowball. They were trying very hard too, and the one who reminded Gabriel of his old self appeared to grow exceedingly cross when he could not get his snowball into the hole with an odd little lofted cleek.

It looked the most nonsensical game, but they played it out to the bitter end, and after that they had to walk down the railway line in the dark, listening for the train lest it should run into them, and they went home in an abominably cold third-class carriage, stopping at every station. Yet they seemed to be glad they had gone. As the train stopped at the last station, Gabriel woke up with a start. He was lying on his shoulder-blades in his chair, very stiff in the back, and the fire had almost gone out, and he thought that he would die if he did not have tea at once. Luckily it was just ready; when he had had some he felt an altered man, and decided that, come what might, he would play golf at Christmas after all.

Nailed Shoes Over Waterloo Bridge

The Times
1925

It is to be hoped that at this time of year a number of people read once more the account of the Christmas journey to Dingley Dell. At any rate, I do; I find it does something to fortify me against the festive rigors of the season. When I was thus reading it yet again, it occurred to me to describe a winter journey that hardy golfers used to make, not once but many times. It may not appear much of a one; yet it came back to me with a sentimental thrill, and since it was before the days of motorcars, and even of tubes, it seems fully as distant as any coach drive. It was the journey that we used to make to Woking on wintry Sunday mornings towards the end of last century.

How easy it is to get there now, or to its pleasant neighbors Worplesdon and West Hill, in somebody else's motorcar! It was then an event in itself, made up of several adventures. First of all there was the getting to Waterloo at an inclement hour. In his book

Fly-fishing Lord Grey of Fallodon gives a quite delightful account of going early to Waterloo, bound for the Itchen or the Test. He saw with the eyes of true romance that the hansoms then to be found "seemed quite different from the hansoms abroad at more lively hours." I did not take a hansom, but, since I lived in the Temple, I walked over Waterloo Bridge, and I do not think it is a purely romantic memory that the pavement on that bridge was of a character different from that of all other pavements. It was of granite, which to one who walked in nailed shoes was of an icy slipperiness. If Mr. Wordsworth had worn nailed shoes and walked over Waterloo instead of Westminster Bridge, he never could have written his sonnet, for he would have been wholly occupied in not tumbling on his distinguished nose. To be late and to have to run for the train, clubs in hand, was a very definite adventure.

Trains were still trains, even in this era of romance, but there is something of old enchantment in the memory that we got cheap blue tickets for half-a-crown and no more, and traveled in dear, varnished second-class carriages with red cushions.

The journey itself was sociable and friendly enough, but when we had passed Byfleet and set down our cargo of golfers bound for the pinewoods of New Zealand, we began to fret in our seats, to get our clubs down from the rack, and to look on our neighbor as our natural enemy. Once we got into Woking Station it was a case of *sauve qui peut*; there was a wild rush for the brake and devil take the hindermost. I can see in my mind's eye one particular pair of coattails flying down the platform. The owner always wore them, I think, as a badge of divided allegiance; he hunted with the Whaddon Chase on the Saturday and played golf on the Sunday. How pleasant it would be to see them again flying away from the first tee! They always got there first and certainly never kept anyone back; it was their partner who had the hard time of it. I remember to have taken an eminent golfer for his first visit to the course, of which he has since become a permanent feature. He looked with a certain placid surprise at the flight down the platform, and remarked, "It is beneath the dignity of a Scottish gentleman to run." So we walked, and had the last and slowest cab all to ourselves.

Even if we condescended to run and thus got a place in the brake, the journey was by no means over, for we could not drive up to the clubhouse, or indeed anywhere near it. We were turned out by the roadside and scrambled up a slope across a tract of heather, then across a railway bridge, then through a little wood of hollies, and then we were there. It was possible by great activity to gain some places in this flight across the heather. There was a pleasant sensation of catching and passing exhausted adversaries in the last lap of some imaginary three-mile race. The coattails alone were invincible. They were always in the van.

Moreover, all these processes had to be repeated on the way home. It was a wrench to turn out of a nice warm clubhouse and paddle across the heather in the dark to where the brake lamps awaited us. The main path was flanked, if I remember rightly, by ditches, and there was even a legend of one who fell in and had to be rescued. That was after a match played there by the team of "Scottish Gentlemen" who used to invade us, but I daresay it is not true, or only true in a Pickwickian sense. At any rate, by the time one had squeezed into the brake and rumbled to the station, and stopped at Byfleet, Weybridge, Walton, Esher, Surbiton, Wimbledon, Clapham Junction, and Vauxhall, and tumbled back over the granite bridge, one felt one had done a good day's work.

It *was* a good day's work, but there were many people anxious to do it. The star of fir trees and heather had not then arisen to lighten the darkness of London golfers. Men judged things by Tooting standards, and we and our neighbors of New Zealand were unique. It was rumored that the waiting list at Woking was so long that when at last the Committee proposed to elect a candidate he was generally found to be dead. So to be a member was to be fortunate, and the course was just as pleasant as it is now. Some of the greens have been moved farther on; the holly trees have been cut back from the second hole; the long, bare stretches of "Harley Street" have been broken up with bunkers, whereby the hole has become far easier, but the old charm is still about it. It is still worth tumbling into a ditch to play there, and I have written this dull little account of it to please myself and in the faint hope that my friend of the flying tails may read it and like to remember.

A Christmas Sermon

Country Life
1913

A friend who is a recent and zealous convert to the game of golf has provided me with the text for a sermon which is, on the face of it, admirably adapted to a season of peace and good will. Whether a general following of its tenets would, in fact, be productive of those blessings I am not so sure. Briefly, my friend complains that golfers are not what Mr. Yellowplush called "beneviolent"; they never tell him what he is doing wrong in his shots, nor do they tell each other. Indeed, he had been so much impressed by this universal minding of their own business that he had come to believe that to tell a fellow golfer of his faults was contrary to the "etiquette" of the game, a dread code of which he stands very properly in awe. He declares that, if better players would more often go out of their way to help worse ones by pointing out their errors and the appropriate method of amending them, it would make for the general happiness of the world.

It is always interesting to know how institutions and societies to which we have been long accustomed strike a perfectly fresh mind, and there is a good deal in the contention of my eminently Christian friend. The sad part of it is that he will probably lose all too soon this first bloom of benevolence, and a year hence, if I tell him that he appears to me to be committing some crime or other, he may snarl at me that it constitutes a deliberately considered part of his style to which he attributes the successes that have attended him on all but that particular day.

The undoubted fact is that many of us do not like being told of our golfing mistakes any more than we do of those we make in more serious walks of life. We say we do and think we do, but in truth we very often do not like it at all. I think this is not wholly on account of extreme sensitiveness or extreme annoyance. We have so often been given counsel that did us no good whatever that it makes us both incredulous and irritable. I can remember personally, with profound gratitude, certain pieces of advice, given to me when my game was in a parlous description, that put me on the right track at very useful times, but I can remember infinitely more that consisted of the deadliest truisms. Therefore, as a general rule, the benevolent person should know something of the game of his victim and should be tolerably certain that he has something worth saying before he says it.

Most people have a certain delicacy in offering advice unasked upon any subject, and this is particularly true in golf. The superior player fears that his doing so may savor of patronage, the inferior of impudence. Though a mouse may help a lion, yet, on the whole, the inferior player exercises a wise discretion in remaining silent, but the superior should not be too self-consciously afraid of his motives being misunderstood. Needless to say, he will conduct himself with ordinary discretion; there are colonels and generals and other ferocious old gentlemen to be found on the golf course to whom it would be as much as his life was worth even to hint a fault. But in the case of milder persons, so long as he makes some modest preface to his remarks, he will very likely earn much gratitude and no resentment.

There is, of course, another reason why the offering of advice is a rather ticklish affair. It is a well-known fact that quite admirable golfing instruction which will ultimately bear good fruit may, and often does, for the first moment, reduce the learner to complete impotence. There is, moreover, nothing so disturbing to the right match-playing frame of mind as the trying of experiments in the middle of the game. Therefore, to attempt to coach an adversary is one good way of beating him. I suppose those who have reasonably clear consciences are not afraid of incurring the suspicion of trying deliberately to "put off" our opponent; but they may be justifiably afraid of achieving the same results with the highest of motives.

The more distinguished is the adviser, the greater the weight of his words, and, if a champion says nothing more original than "Keep your eye on the ball," we listen reverentially and proceed to look at the ball with so tremendous and concentrated a glare as to preclude all possibility of following through. So the champion who is kind enough to throw a word to us must remember, if he be a conscientious man, that a great responsibility rests upon him. It scarcely matters how nonsensical his advice, if we have confidence in him we shall hit the ball for a while; but when the next bad time comes, as come it must, his lightly spoken word may do great harm, because we shall persist in following it with blind, unquestioning faith. So, whatever the great man says, he should add, with all the emphasis of which he is capable: "The moment you begin to hit the ball, forget what I told you and never think of it again."

I did not discover with certainty whether my friend desired these good offices to be tendered only by a player to his adversary or whether the system should extend to all members of the club. Personally, I should only agree with him in the first case. When a perfect stranger shall tap me on the shoulder and say: "Excuse me, sir, but you would play much better if you did not tie yourself into such a ridiculous and complicated knot," then, even though it be Christmas time, I shall think that the system of promiscuous benevolence has gone too far.

The Last Round

Playing the Like
1934

To persons of an imaginative and so, of course, futile temperament, the last round of a golfing holiday is dreadfully important. It may color in the retrospect all its predecessors and all the weeks that have so swiftly evaporated. It can make of the holiday either an unsatisfactory problem play, or a good old-fashioned drama in which all the characters are summoned before the curtain for a happy ending.

In any case, to be sure, there must be something melancholy about it, for each hole is in itself a goodbye; we shall not play it again till next year. Yet this is a gentle, almost a pleasant, sadness. When, for instance, my ball from the ninth tee sped straight as a homing pigeon into the bunker on the left of the green, I felt that I had done, from a sentimental and artistic point of view, the right thing. My partner doubtless did not share this opinion, but she—*O fortunatam nimium*—was staying on for ages, so that I could justifiably be selfish. All through the holiday, save for a short surcease in the middle of it, I had plunged into that bunker; that I should do so yet again made an appropriate finish.

Neither was there cause for lamentation in the fact that the foursome was lost by a considerable margin. We did not play well, and we did not even say afterwards that we had. For that matter we knew that it would have been useless to do so. There is a lady who sits in front of her house, perched high on the hillside, looking down upon the links. Her eye ranges far and wide, and she is prepared ruthlessly to contradict those statements which are usually accepted among golfers with a certain charity. If one of her flock asserts on coming home that he has played well, she retorts, "Anyhow, I saw you take a five at the fifth"—a short hole. If he says that he did the fourth in four, she remembers that he was given the putt, and this giving of putts she regards, with all the rigor of a Sarah Battle, as "one of the worst features of the game."

To get into bunkers, to lose the match on this last round is nothing. What does matter is that we should finish respectably on the bye or even the bye-bye, that the last tee shot should be hit, the last putt holed; that systems which have stood by us, more or less, during the holiday should not break down at the very end, leaving us drearily puzzling. It was, therefore, the bye—by no means a short one—that made me really anxious, and I thank whatever golfing gods there be that all went tolerably well on it. The last two tee shots were straight; the one at the fifteenth was even—we all have our modest standards—long. The spoon shot to the home hole was at least adequate, and all three of these strokes marked a reversion to the system of the day before and were not due to any new, tomfool discovery. Finally, the ultimate putt, a good seven feet long, was holed for a four. All the earlier horrors were blotted out, and the holiday wrapped forever in a golden haze. As for my partner, whom I had rather unchivalrously forgotten during those last four holes, had she not happy weeks ahead of her in which to do unforgettable things?

Thus it came about that there was no unendurable bitterness in the next morning. That the station abuts on the links had its consolations. Those brutal creatures who were driving off had troubles of their own. In the pocket of each of them lurked two ghastly cankers, a card and a pencil; and they were setting out not merely on eighteen but on thirty-six holes of score play. So the grapes were hardly sour; it was with almost a single heart that I could profess myself thankful not to be in their shoes, shoes soon to be full of the sand of those isolated and malignant little bunkers, the existence of which we only discover on a medal day.

As the competitors passed along the platform to the clubhouse, I told them that I hoped they would enjoy themselves; I made crude jokes about the tearing up of cards; I told the young soldier champion, who had done a seventy-two the night before, that he had had his ration of putts for a month. They tried to parry my gibes as well as they could. For instance, the international personage, who had only arrived overnight, when told that he would find the putting tricky, answered with a mirthless laugh that he had been playing cricket and all the greens would be the same to him. Only the retired headmaster and the county court judge had indisputably the best of it. Each declared that he had not lived so long in the world or attained to his present eminence without knowing better than to play in a thirty-six-hole medal. Brains will tell, and I do not think either of them would have won.

The fatal train has torn me away long since. The holiday has become nearly merged in the glimmering company of those that have gone before it; I have been home for several days and not once yet have I taken my driver out of my bag to indulge in speculative contortions. A little putting on the lawn perhaps, but a man must do something. It only shows how important it is to hit the last shot of the last round on the last day. I believe nothing else really matters.

VI

Fields of Play

Architectooralooral

Playing the Like
1934

Joe Gargery, it may be remembered, was disappointed when on his visit to London he went to see the blacking warehouse; he thought that in the pictures of it which he had previously seen it had been "drawd too architectooralooral."

There are some who would, I fancy, if they knew it, apply this word of Joe's to the designers of golf courses. They think that these gentlemen have become a little too ingenious and too subtle, and are inclined to yearn for the simpler architecture of old times. On very rare occasions, as regards some particular piece of cleverness that has a little missed its mark, I agree with this view, but on the whole I most decidedly disagree with it. I have a great admiration for our golfing architects, and when we are inclined to criticize them or their works it would be well if we paused to consider what sort of a hand at it we should make ourselves. There was a time when the nearest professional player was deemed fully qualified to lay out a new course, and any body of retired colonels, constituting a green committee, thought that they could at the very least make a new hole. This state of pristine innocence is not often to be found today, but I doubt whether the average golfer even now fully realizes that the professional architect is not merely likely, but certain, to do the job infinitely better than the casual amateur just because it is his job, that he is paid to think about it, and has thought about it a great deal.

Those who laid out courses when the first great golf "boom" came did not presumably think much, neither had they very suitable equipment for thinking purposes. They had the material for thought in certain famous holes on famous courses, but they entirely failed, if they ever tried, to analyze the qualities of those holes and to discover wherein their merits lay. They took, as a rule, the way of least resistance; if they saw a hill they drove over it, and a hollow was clearly designed by Providence for a green, although oddly enough that same Providence had put most of the greens at St. Andrews upon plateaus. It seems to me that the great and primary virtue of the modern architect lies in the fact that he did analyze: that he went back to the classic models, and especially to St. Andrews, and insisted on discovering why golfers had for years particularly enjoyed playing particular holes. It is obvious by way of example that nobody ever gets tired of playing the sixteenth hole—the Corner of the Dyke. In what does its peculiar charm lie? Certainly not in the fact that the Principal's Nose punishes a bad shot because as a rule it punishes rather a good one, in the sense of a shot that is more or less cleanly hit. The charm is in the fact that the hole keeps us, unconsciously perhaps, thinking, that we have always got to make up what we are pleased to call our minds; that we have to decide between, on the one hand, a highly dangerous but highly profitable course that may lose us several strokes but may gain us one invaluable stroke, and, on the other, a comparatively safe, easy course that ought not to lose us much but may just lose us something intensely important. Their discoveries came, I think, very briefly to this, that golf at its best is a perpetual adventure, that it consists in investing not in gilt-edged securities but in comparatively speculative stock; that it ought to be a risky business.

Here was something of a new belief founded upon old holes. How those old holes attained the form in which we know them no one can tell. Assuredly it was not owing to the genius of some one heaven-sent designer whose name has unjustly been lost. It was rather through good fortune and a gradual process of evolution. The holes changed their forms many times according as whins grew or were hacked away, according as the wind silted up sand here or blew it away there, according as the instruments of the game changed so that men could hit farther and essay short cuts and new roads. Yet they possessed some indestructible virtue, so that, however they changed superficially, golfers united in praising them and loved to play them, gaining from the playing of them some pleasing emotion that other holes could not afford. To define that emotion and the cause of it was really to make a discovery, and to proclaim the discovery was to proclaim a new faith.

It was Mr. John Low who first put this faith into memorable words, and they are so excellent that I will set them down again here. He is defending the little pot-bunker that is very nearly on the bee-line to the hole and, he says, "The greedy golfer will go too near and be sucked in to his destruction. The straight player will go just as near as he deems safe, just as close as he dare. Just as close as he dare: that's golf, and that's a hazard of immortal importance! For golf at its best should be a contest of risks. The fine player should on his way round the links be just slipping past the bunkers, gaining every yard he can, conquering by the confidence of his own 'far and sure' play. The less skillful player should wreck himself either by attempting risks which are beyond his skill, or by being compelled to lose ground through giving the bunkers a wide berth."

Those words were written in 1903, and it was just about that time, I think, and, generally speaking, in accordance with the beliefs so proclaimed that the two leaders of the new school of architecture, Mr. H. S. Colt and Mr. Herbert Fowler, were doing their work. Yet if one hole has to be taken as typifying these beliefs, it is not one designed by either of them, but by a distinguished amateur. The hole is the fourth at Woking, which is familiar to all who look out of the railway carriage window as they go from Waterloo towards Southampton, and its designer was Mr. Stuart Paton, who is well known to all who ever played on the Woking course, and has even been designated by an irreverent writer its Mussolini. This was, when I first knew it, a comparatively commonplace hole. The tee shot had to be played between the railway on the right and the heather on the left, and there was a sufficiently wide stretch of fairway between them. The green was guarded by a cross bunker which covered its entire width. A tolerably straight drive and a tolerably adroit pitch were wanted, and nothing more.

Mr. Paton, presumably reminded by the railway line of the sixteenth hole at St. Andrews, saw his opportunity and proceeded to plant a Principal's Nose in the shape of a double bunker in the middle of the fairway. He reduced the cross bunker, I rather think by stages, until nothing was left of it but one small pot in the middle of the edge of the green. Thus the man who courageously lays down his balls between the first bunker and the railway line gets a clear run up to the hole on the most favorable possible terms. The more cautious one who drives to the left can still get his four, but, owing to the contour of the green, he has a much more difficult approach to play. He will find himself hampered by that second central bunker. If he pitches over it, he will have hard work to stop his ball from running away into trouble; if he dare not pitch but plays a running shot, he will often leave himself a long, nasty sloping putt.

From being a cut-and-dried affair, the hole became an uncommonly interesting and provocative one, and one which a man is always glad to leave safely behind him in a medal round. Moreover, since it was certainly one of the first, if not the first, of its kind in southern architecture, it roused plenty of hostility and plenty of argument. Its enemies said that the drive that was caught by the bunker in the middle of the course was invariably a very good drive, and that therefore the bunker was unfair. Its friends replied that the bunker was there, that the player knew it was there, and that it was his business to avoid it. The drive might have been a very good one if there had been no bunker there; as things were it was not a good enough one. The argument goes on to this day; people still abuse the hole, and if any further evidence be required of its merits it is to be found in that persistence of calumny. All the great holes and great bunkers of the world have their puny enemies.

I have mentioned this hole not only because it came something before its time and so shared the fate of zealots and reformers in being abused. It had in another way an effect impossible exactly to measure on modern golf. It plays something of the part in the story of a distinguished architect which the cakes are supposed to have played in the story of King Alfred. One day Mr. Simpson, who was then a good golfer but had never designed a hole in his life, went over to Woking for a game of golf. The day turned pitilessly wet and golf was out of the question. Whether the conversation among those stormbound in the clubhouse actually turned on the fourth hole or whether Mr. Simpson had heard such talk before I am not certain. At any rate, he determined to go and look critically at that hole. So out he went in solitude and a mackintosh, and, with the rain pouring off him, devoted his "immense and brooding spirit" to considering the purpose of that little bunker in the middle of the course. When at last he came in again, wet but presumably happy, he had found a new interest in life. He became, as all the world now knows, a golfing architect, one of the straitest sect, of an almost diabolically ingenious mind, who loves to see what the thoughtless golfer calls a good shot go bang into a bunker which is ready to receive it. As we ply our niblicks in one of his creations let us remember with gratitude what we owe indirectly to Mr. Paton and the fourth hole at Woking!

No man can be a good architect unless he has a wide experience of many courses, a most observant eye for the weaknesses of his brother golfers, and red-hot zeal for his art, so that he is more interested in seeing other people play holes than in playing them himself. And beyond this he must possess that indefinable, instinctive something that may be called an eye for country. There are some courses which may be said to lay themselves out in so far as this, that the rough outline at once suggests itself to any experienced golfer. Even so that is not very far on the road to success, and the experienced golfer would generally fail to get the best, or anything like the best, out of his ground. As a rule, however, the circumstances are not nearly so favorable; the architect finds himself plumped down in the middle of a wood and can go north, south, east or west as it pleases him. The ordinary person would feel himself lost, throwing up his hands in despair, and it is then, I suppose, that the natural instinct of the born architect comes to the rescue.

I have at different times spent very interesting days with eminent architects upon the sites of their labors when those labors had scarcely begun—with Mr. Colt at Stoke Poges and St. George's Hill, with the late Mr. Abercromby at Coombe Hill and Addington. I have called those days interesting; I should have said awe-inspiring, so bewildered was my own state of mind, so lucid and determined was that of my companion. I would be shown a thicket so dense that we had to struggle through it with a motion of men swimming, and be told that this was the line to the first hole. The line might, for all I knew, have just as well been in a precisely opposite direction. Yet I fancy that if two architects had been set to work, their instinct would have guided them to start through that particular thicket and no other; indeed I am told, though I cannot give chapter and verse for it, that the experiment has been tried, and the two consultants arrived independently, not merely at the same beginning, but at much the same entire round.

The piece of architectural vision which most of all impressed me is today represented by that admirable short hole, the seventh, at Stoke Poges. When I first went there with its creator, Mr. Colt, all that met my vacant gaze was a steep uniform slope thickly covered with wood running down to a small stream. To have seen concealed in that apparently most unpromising material a long, narrow, plateau green with a bunkered slope on the one side, and a deep drop into the perdition of the stream on the other still strikes me as an effort of genius.

In such cases there is nothing for it but to reflect humbly that, after all, it is the architect's job, and that it is only natural that he should do it better than a mere casual student. Yet these confounded architects can sometimes put us to shame when we really do think that we are as good as they are. When Rye had to be altered, I was one of a Sub-Committee to consider possible changes. We thought hard and long: we devised a scheme and then we got Mr. Simpson to come and polish it up for us. We were particularly well pleased with our new first hole, and a very good hole I venture to say it is, but the humiliating part of the business was this, that Mr. Simpson had only to move a half-a-dozen yards or so from the place we had designed for the green to find one obviously much better. We had pored over the site and he had not. Why had we not discovered that place that was plain for all to see, when it was pointed out? I do not know, and whatever I might admit on my own account I hesitate to say that all my companions were stupid. The fact remains that we had not. So I must needs say, "Hooroar for the architects."

I imagine that this altering and remodeling of courses is in fact a more delicate and difficult task than that of laying out a new one. The architect has neither so free a hand nor such agreeable privacy; everybody can see what he is at and can criticize accordingly. Moreover, he is sure to find himself opposed to vested interests in the shape of holes that have long and often undeservedly been regarded with love and veneration. This is particularly the case with blind one-shot holes which belong perhaps to the gutty era, when they were, at any rate, much more formidable than at present. I can still remember my feelings when a good many years ago I accompanied Mr. Colt on his advisory visit to Aberdovey. The third hole—it was then the fourth—is Cader, and the fact that it is the only hole habitually called by a name and not a number is eloquent. It calls for some sort of iron shot over a sandhill crowned with sleepers on to a hidden green with not unkindly sides. What would my companion say? He maintained a tactful silence that meant more than any words until he reached the far end of the green, when he said, "Take that back wall away." Then we passed on towards the next tee and, incidentally, that back wall is still there.

I have myself, I confess, a certain affection for Cader. I do not want it altered, and it is at least a far better hole than is the Maiden of Sandwich, possessing much more alarming trouble and a much smaller green. As compared with the Sandy Parlour at Deal, it is a perfect pearl among short holes. Will those more famous holes ever be altered? I gravely doubt it. Some little while ago there was a proposal to alter the Maiden by playing across the present green to a plateau perched high on the hilltop. There was, I believe, some prospect of the proposal being approved until an old friend of mine made a speech full of the most moving "sob stuff" about the dear old Maiden. The proposal was thereupon instantly and indignantly rejected, I do not say that either my friend or my fellow-members of the club were necessarily wrong, since I have in my own composition a good deal both of sentimentality and conservatism. I am only giving an illustration of the fact that reforming architects have to go warily.

They do go very warily, being as a rule monuments of tact. They can see deep into the frailties and vanities of the human heart, and can bamboozle green committees into doing their will. In short, they are great men, and they will have need to show themselves greater than ever in the years to come. It is their task to make golf courses no harder for the ordinary mortal, and yet a good deal more exacting and less monotonous for the man who can regularly drive untold yards and as regularly follow his drive with a high pitching shot with some lofted variety of graded iron. They have tackled it with courage and ingenuity, but it would be flattery to say that they have wholly succeeded, since the modern ball and the modern golfer's power of hitting it are in combination sometimes too much for them. A good illustration was to be found during the Open Championship of 1935 in the first hole at Muirfield. Here there has been made a highly ingenious little bunker some little distance in front of the green rather on the right-hand side of the fairway. Its object is to make the player place his tee shot to the left. In doing this he has to run an appreciable risk of going into a bunker, but, if he succeeds, he gets a clear run in to the hole with his second shot. If, on the other hand, he drives to the right, he must either carry that little bunker with his second or slice the ball skillfully round it. Everything goes according to plan for ordinary mortals, especially if the turf be not too keen and fast. The hole is then a good "two-shot hole," demanding accuracy as well as length. In the Open Championship, on the other hand, that little bunker entirely wasted its sweetness and might as well not have existed. With a light wind behind them player after player drove three hundred yards or more, and I saw, with my own eyes, Mr. Lawson Little hit a drive computed to be three hundred and sixty yards. The second shot became a pitch with a mashie-niblick, and whether or not it had to carry the little bunker was of no importance whatever. The ball and the hitter between them had rendered nugatory a very clever piece of architecture, and it is my present impression that, unless something be done to the ball, this combination will generally prove one too many for the architect.

The architects never say die; they return to the charge again and again with unimpaired bravery, they approach nearer and nearer to the kind of difficulty that is called "unfair." At the time when I am writing, the new course at Sunningdale, as altered by Mr. Simpson and Mr. Paton, is only just in play, and I can only write about it as I saw it in the rough. They seem to me to have gone further than anyone has gone yet in insisting on the "laying down" of the tee shot in a particular place; they have certainly made some admirable and interesting holes, but it remains to be seen how far they have succeeded, and whether or not the ball will beat them after all.

As far as I can see, the architect's strongest and most faithful ally in this perpetual battle is the plateau green. It cannot prevent the length of a hole being spoiled and its character impaired, but it can prevent its becoming child's play. The best example I can think of is the long hole in, the fourteenth, at St. Andrew's, universally recognized as one of the few great long holes. If we are to see it at its best, the player must skirt the Beardies with his tee shot down the Elysian Fields; play his second to the left of Hell bunker and as near as he dare to it, and so attain the ideal position for his third, a run-up shot. If the ground is hard and there is a following wind, the long driver upsets all these well-laid plans; he drives miles and miles down the Elysian Fields without bothering his head about Beardies, and goes straight for the green with his second, carrying far over Hell, probably with an iron. The old game of going from point to point has gone; "geography has been destroyed," as I have heard Mr. Robert Harris exclaim in a passionate tirade; but there does remain that narrow plateau green with a steep bank in front of it, a run-away at the back, and hills, that will make a fool of almost any shot and any player, on its right-hand side. Even if the long driver plays his second with a mashie, he will have hard work to stay on the green; he is at least as likely to take five as four. That is small compensation perhaps for the destruction of the true beauty of the hole, but it is at least some amends. The hole's character may be changed, but the hole is not conquered; it still defies the player.

I am conscious that I seem to be writing as if I had a hatred of long drivers and was suffering from a disease to be briefly described as "sour grapes." This is not really so. I am the last person to want golf to become a less athletic game. Long driving is not merely a matter of youth and strength; it is essentially a matter of skill and deserves every fair advantage it can gain. At present it is doing more than that; it is spoiling the beauty and interest of the game. In consequence there seems to me a real danger lest architects should conceive an unjustifiable enmity against the long hitters and should be driven to be too subtle and too malignant in their efforts to curb the slasher. A hole can be too clever and so can defeat its own end. I do not know many examples, but I think I could name one or two. We decidedly want golf courses to be tests of accuracy and forethought, and even perhaps a little low cunning as well as of mere straightforward hitting, but we do not want the game, as described in "The Golfers' Manual," of "oldsters spooning a ball gently on to a table of smooth turf when a longer shot would land them in grief."

The architects have done nobly; they have fought the good fight, but it ought not to be a fight. The fact that it threatens to become so is the fault of the ball. Whether or not the ball can ever be brought back to its proper limits is another story, but unless it can, the architects will be forever fighting an uphill battle.

In the Rough

American Golfer
1922

There are no two expressions more frequently in the mouths of golfers than "fairway" and "rough" and there always seems something surprising about the fact that neither of them is to be found in the rules of golf. That most dreadful enemy, the rough, which probably slays its tens of thousands, has no legal existence. In law it is exactly on a footing with the smoothest and most beautiful piece of turf in the very middle of the course.

This seems today surprising and yet, without sounding too terribly old, I can remember the time when "the rough" was neither a regular expression nor a regular thing. In the 1880s and early 1890s it was quite the exception to find clear-cut areas of rough grass or other destructive vegetation on either side to catch the erring ball. I recollect that when I played at Woking, which was the first of our courses to be carved out of heathery country, those parallel and menacing lines seemed decidedly novel.

That was only twenty-five years ago. Seaside links had clumps of gorse or bushes here and there and there was of course plenty of bent grass on the sandhills, but there was no hard and fast middle way; if there were bents on the right there was open country on the left. As to inland courses, certainly I played, in the University match, on Wimbledon Common where there were some terribly narrow drives between gorse bushes but the three courses with which I was perhaps most familiar, had no rough of any kind. Two were on the Downs; the lovely springy turf stretched for miles on either hand and, apart from a chalk pit or two and a few hurdles, you could drive where you pleased under the vast dome of Heaven.

The third was of a type fortunately rare. It was a flat, muddy Common, where the wretched golfers of Cambridge were condemned to play. The only trouble consisted in a few black and ill-scented ditches. Here lurked troops of black, ill-scented little boys who either recovered your ball from the water for a penny or, if they deemed it a more profitable speculation, stamped the ball into the oozy mud and then, when you had passed on, stole it at their leisure.

I am not holding up these latter courses for admiration—far from it. I only use them as illustrations of the fact that clear-cut lines of rough have not always been with us. My experience is far too small for me to generalize but I did not see a course in America that did not have them. Nearly all our inland courses today have them. Only on some of the seaside courses do the old, more varied conditions exist. At St. Andrews, for instance, there is certainly a rather broken line of rough country to catch a slice on the way out but that is all. For the most part you are trying to avoid a particular bunker from the tee or obtain a certain strategic position for your next shot; you are not trying to go down a groove.

The same thing is true of Westward Ho! There are indeed plenty of tall and spiky rushes, but they are not, as it were, formed up in regular battalions but dotted irregularly here and there about the battlefield. It would be possible to give other instances but I think, even on sensible courses, there is more definite rough than there used to be. Muirfield for instance, where Mr. Gardner fought his great fight with Mr. Tolley, resembles in this respect an inland course more than a links and even Sandwich has given us narrow alleys whereas before we wandered o'er the steppes.

It seems to me that golfing architects might sometimes with advantage compromise between the two systems more than they do at present. There is, I suppose, not much doubt that the parallel lines of rough make the better educational school because they insist on rigidly straight play. Indeed, if St. Andrews does not turn out so many good golfers as it used to, it may be because the young golfers there, having too much license in the matter of erratic driving, do not sufficiently curb their traditional, loose, slashing style. On the other hand, the sensation of being perpetually set in a framework of rough is a monotonous one and the golf tends to become monotonous.

It may be immoral, from the highest golfing point of view, that at St. Andrews a very wild hook may go scot free and a nearly perfect shot be trapped, but it is the endless variety of possible lines to every hole, changing with every little change of the wind, that make the unique charm of the great course. People often get annoyed with St. Andrews but they do not get bored with playing there. Where there is a definite fairway and definite rough, there is less variety. Bang, bang, bang—right down the middle: that is the only game. There is little strategy of tactics: no flanking movements, only frontal attacks.

There should as a rule be two degrees of rough, purgatory and hell. It seems unfair but it is often the case that the man who goes one foot off the course lies in the grass just as thick and tangled as he who goes twenty or forty. The moderate sin should only entail purgatory—there should be some chance of a startling recovery. And apart from grounds of abstract justice, hunting for lost balls is a sad nuisance both to ourselves and those who play behind us. That is another reason for not having the rough one uniform "hell."

Indeed, I think, uniformity is a thing to be avoided. I think the hardest hole I ever knew—it was played with a gutty ball—was a three shotter in which the fairway ran absolutely straight from tee to hole. On each side of it was a ditch of uniform depth and beyond the ditch heather of a uniformly damnable character. There was one small bunker exactly in the middle of the course and just in front of the green and that was all. I think, as I said, that it was the hardest hole, and I am quite sure it was the dullest.

The Heart of a Rabbit

Playing the Like
1934

It is today an accepted principle of golfing architecture that the tiger should be teased and trapped and tested, while the rabbit should be left in peace, since he can make his own hell for himself. Broadly speaking, it is an excellent principle, but I wonder, nevertheless, whether those who enunciate and act upon it do not sometimes a little misunderstand the rabbit's heart.

Rabbits are tolerably sensitive animals. Do they not feel a little hurt that the architect thinks so meanly of their powers that he will put nothing in their way? I fancy them like the burgesses of Deptford when their architect did not want to let them even have a shot at the pronunciation of Avignon. "We are not aware," so runs in my mind their imaginary manifesto, "that the lofting of a ball over a cross-bunker a hundred yards from the tee presents any insuperable difficulties to the members of this club with handicaps of fifteen or over." They must sometimes resent the implication that the attempt to trundle the ball in inglorious safety will give them more than all the trouble they want.

If I may express an unpatriotic doubt, I question whether the British variety of the genus rabbit is quite so earnest, so set on self-improvement, as is the American. At any rate, I am sure that the American rabbit does not appreciate too much kindness and consideration. Pine Valley, near Philadelphia, is generally deemed the hardest course in the world, or, at least, the course holding the greatest possibilities of disaster. It would be inaccurate to say that I played round it for the first time in a large number of strokes, for I took no definite number; having played ping-pong indefinitely across the eighth green, I picked up my ball. After that chastening experience I said to my host, "How do your fat old gentlemen (for we were all younger and thinner once) like this sort of thing?" He answered that they were "tickled to death," since if they could go round in a hundred and fifteen instead of a hundred and twenty they felt like striking the stars. Not many of our rabbits can emulate, perhaps, this nobly ambitious spirit, but in their own way they do like to live dangerously.

Our architects are, of course, not only very skillful artists but very cunning persons, and they often contrive to make the rabbit believe that he is living more dangerously than in fact he is. There is one particular device employed to this end, though discretion forbids me to name particular courses. On one side of the green is a precipice full of bunkers, deep, cavernous and horrible; on the other side is a broad way of safety which coaxes the ball towards the flag. When we have played the hole successfully, we look shudderingly down upon those bunkers and think that there, but for the grace of heaven, we might have been. In our hearts we know that only a singularly atrocious stroke would have taken us there and that the bunkers are largely "eyewash"; but we cannot restrain a little thrill of pride and pleasure.

Easily as he is bamboozled, the rabbit, having played such a hole many times, comes to suspect that it is a simple one, and must long for something to surmount more genuinely perilous, more directly in his path. He welcomes now and again the possibility of swift and utter destruction, and likes to cry in his heart, even as he waggles, "Victory or Westminster Abbey." Better a nine with four niblick shots in it than a six all along the ground.

Some years ago a gentleman of my acquaintance wrote to me, in a very natural state of elation, to say that his majority at a recent election had been 5,454. Did I not think, he asked, that there was a noteworthy resemblance between these figures and the beginning of a score at golf? Certainly it is a beginning for which many of us would be thankful on a medal day; but there seemed something rather pedestrian about it; it hardly offered a fruitful or picturesque topic. Only the other day I mentioned it to one who had also been a victor in the same election. He said that his majority had consisted of figures far more dramatically suggestive of a medal round—1,327. Nobody, to be sure, has ever, to my knowledge, started a round one, three, two, but the seven at the fourth hole—how well we all know that! It is bitterly true to golfing life.

And yet "bitterly" is not quite the right word. Perhaps I ought rather to have written "fascinatingly" or "seductively" true, because I suppose golf would be a dull game if we did five, four, five, four to all eternity. I think the rabbit enjoys his sevens or even his tens so long as they come from one sudden catastrophe rather than from a slow frittering away of strokes. He has very little to complain of; indeed, he ought to be intensely grateful to the modern architects who are forever considering him, whereas their predecessors planted ramparts with a ruthless lack of imagination. Still, he would prefer their consideration tempered with a little frightfulness and not too obvious. Did not Abraham Lincoln say in effect that you could not fool all the rabbits all the time?

Aberdovey

Tee Shots and Others
1911

The golfer is often said to be a selfish person. He deserts his wife for days together; he objects to the presence of bank-holiday makers upon the common, where he desires to play his game; he commits various other crimes. He is almost certainly selfish about the festival of Christmas, in that the kind of Christmas which other people want is to him hateful beyond words. For the Christmas which English people are at any rate supposed to enjoy there are necessary, besides mistletoe and plum pudding, which do no one any harm, a fall of snow and a good hard frost—two things which, it is superfluous to observe, are wholly inimical to golf. The golfer likes to read of the typical "old-fashioned" Christmas, such as Caldecott drew, or dickens described, but in reading he likes to translate it, as it were, into his own terms.

For instance, one of the most delightful pieces of literature in the world, and the one most redolent of Christmas, is the account of the Pickwickians' journey by the Muggleton coach, on their way to Dingley Dell. There is Mr. Pickwick watching the "implacable" codfish squeezed into the boot; Mr. Pickwick begging the guard to drink his health in a glass of hot brandy and water; the horses cantering, and the wheels skimming over the hard and frosty ground; the meeting with the fat boy who had been asleep "right in front of the tap-room fire." All these things are perfectly heavenly, but it is one of the disadvantages of having a mind warped by golf that one cannot help remembering that this journey was a prelude to Mr. Winkle's skating and Mr. Pickwick's sliding, and where there is ice, there is no golf worthy of the name. So I have to translate this glorious journey to myself into my own language. It may sound lamentably prosaic; there will be no cracking of whips and tooting of horns, but this journal of mine is good to look forward to, nevertheless.

Before the journal comes the packing, a thing usually loathsome, but on this occasion positively delicious, more especially the packing of clubs. All the clubs are taken out one by one, looked at with a gloating eye, and then stowed triumphantly into the bag. Of course, I shall take more than I really want, just for the fun of packing them. There are one or two wooden clubs from my reserve which must certainly go. There is one brassy that only wants just a drop of lead let into the head to make it an enchanter's wand. There is an iron that I have not used for some time that will be just the thing for carrying the mighty sandhill, crowned with ominous sleepers, that guards the fourth green; and then, of course, one must take a spare putter or two, against the almost unthinkable event of going off one's putting. Also there is a large umbrella, though it can never be that the fates will be so unkind as to make one use it.

So much for the packing, and now for the journey, which will begin, not in a coach, but in a cab, which will take me to Euston, most dear and romantic of stations. I shall instruct a porter as to the label to be affixed to my bag, adding quite unnecessarily, but with an additional thrill of joy, "On the Cambrian Railway, you know." I shall not ask him to drink my health in brandy and water, but in the enthusiasm of the moment I shall probably give him sixpence. I shall take my seat in the carriage and that almost certainly a corner seat, because in my excitement I shall have reached the station absurdly early. Then I shall start. I shall not read the paper that I have bought, because I shall be looking out of the window at the golf courses that I pass on my way and thinking, without any disrespect to them, how far pleasanter is the course to which I am bound.

The stations will whirl past. Bletchley, Rugby, Stafford, Wellington, and at last beloved Shrewsbury. So far I shall have been alone, but at Shrewsbury will be encountered my two kind hosts and other golfers bound for the same paradise. We shall greet each other uproariously, behaving in an abominably hearty and Christmas-like way, and then we shall pack ourselves into another carriage, for the second half of our journey. Our talk, surprising as it may appear, will be about the game of golf—whether there is casual water in the Crater green, and how many of the new bunkers have been made. I should not be surprised if we even attempted to waggle each other's clubs in the extremely confined space at our disposal.

More stations will go by us. They will not whirl this time, for the trains from Shrewsbury to Wales are not given to whirling; they will pass in leisurely order. Hanwood, Westbury, and now the Welsh border is crossed; Buttington, Welshpool, Abermule, Montgomery, Newtown—I forget their order, but love to write down their names. The train comes into a country of mountains and jolly, foaming, mountain streams; it pants up a steep hill to a solitary little station called Talerddig. Near Talerddig there is a certain mysterious natural arch in the rock, and it is a point of honor with us to look for it out of the window. However, since we never can remember exactly where it is, and the twilight is deepening, we never see it. Now the train has reached the end of its painful climb, and dashes down the hill into the valley, and by this time we feel as if we could almost smell the sea. There is a pause at Machynlleth (let any Saxon try to pronounce that!), and we have tea and listen to the people talking Welsh upon the platform. Then on again through the darkness, till we stop once more. There is a wild rush of small boys outside our carriage window, fighting and clamoring for the privilege of carrying our clubs. *Nunc dimittis*—we have arrived at Aberdovey.

Escaping with difficulty from this rabble of boys, we clamber up a steep and rock road to where our house stands, perched upon the hillside, looking out over the estuary and at the lights of Borth that twinkle across the water. We have our annual argument with an old retainer of Scottish ancestry and pedantically exact mind, who points out to us that it is clearly impossible that we should all be called at precisely eight o'clock in the morning. We suggest as a compromise that one should be called at two minutes to eight, and another at two minutes past, and to this course, though still unconvinced, he grudgingly assents. Then next day, when the hour of his calling has come, we wake, if all is well, to one of the most seraphic of imaginable winter days, for be it known that Aberdovey is called by the local guidebook the Madeira of North Wales, and that one hardy schoolmaster played there on two successive New Year's days in his shirtsleeves. Warm, still and gray, with no dancing shadows to distract the more fanciful of our party—that is how I like it best, and that is how, in a good hour be it spoken, it generally is. Yet there are exceptions, and I remember almost painfully well one Christmas, when it was indeed a "fine time for them as is well wropped up." This, it will be remembered, was the soliloquy of the polar bear when he was practicing his skating, and we who were practicing our golfing heartily endorsed the reflections of that arctic philosopher. Yet even so we played our two rounds a day like men, and that says something both for us and for Aberdovey.

The ground was iron hard with frost, the east wind blew remorselessly, and we were certainly very well wrapped up indeed. Spartan persons who had never yielded before were glad to nestle inside Shetland waistcoats, while at the same time reluctantly admitting that mittens did restore some vestige of feeling to the fingers. It is indeed dreadful to contemplate life in wintertime without that blessed invention the mitten, or, to give it its technical name, the muffetee. A mitten proper has a hole for one's thumb, and so comes too far over the palm of the hand to allow a comfortable grip of the club. The muffetee, which is made of silk, if one is extravagant, and of wool, if one is economical, only encircles the wrist with a delicious warmth that in a surprisingly short space of time permeates the wearer's entire frame.

There are still a good many people who will not believe that this is so. I have come across this willful blindness among my own relations, who are of a highly scientific and skeptical turn of mind. They allege the most futile and irrebuttable reasons why the warmth of the wrist should have no connection with the warmth of the hand, but there is a measure of consolation in the fact that they suffer agonies from cold fingers, and, better still, top their mashie shots in consequence. Of course, when they have once tried the experiment they have to give in and own churlishly enough that there seems to be something in it. Even the most distinguished of golfers are sometimes to be caught without mittens. I have twice played the part of Sir Philip Sidney and lent mine to eminent professionals when they were playing quite important matches on the most bitterly cold days. Those that I lent to Taylor were, needless to say, returned to me permanently enlarged, and ever afterwards hung loosely upon my puny and attenuated wrists. If, however, they are no longer very useful as mittens, they are as precious to me as were the three cherrystones to Calverley's young lady, from having "once dallied with the teeth of royalty itself."

I believe that there is a Brobdingnagian kind of mitten to be bought which reaches from the wrist to the elbow. I have never yet had a pair, but some day I shall certainly try to afford one. Meanwhile, the ordinary woolen mitten is within the reach of all, since a pair costs, if I remember rightly, no more than sevenpence halfpenny. They will do more towards winning you your winter half-crowns than all the curly-necked clubs in the world, or even, I suspect, than the patent putter for which the advertisement used to claim that it "made every stroke practically a certainty."

This rhapsody on mittens has carried me far away from Aberdovey, where we were left battling with the elements. It is a curious game, that golf on frozen ground and in an easterly gale, for one reason because, after a few days of it, it is hard to remain entirely levelheaded about our driving powers. The ball goes such portentous distances that we really cannot believe that it is entirely attributable to the weather. In our heart of hearts we half believe that some subtle change has come over us, and that we shall drive just a little farther ever afterwards. Thus, when we came into lunch after our morning round—and oh! how good lunch was—we each had our little boast of some green reached, some bunker passed. We fully appreciated that the shots of others were mere accidents due to the ball falling upon a particularly frozen spot; but as to our own, there must have been just a little extra sting behind those—we thought we detected a new and wonderful use of our wrists that accounted for it.

Needless to say, at that Christmas time of bitter memory the obdurate wind took a rest on Sunday, as did the golfers. There was a cloudless day, without a breath of wind; we could have kept quite warm, and our approach shots would not have skipped like young rams upon the green, ere they buried themselves in a bunker fifty yards beyond it. All we could do was to bemoan our luck, and look at the view, a very beautiful one truly, for the Dovey estuary on a fine winter's day can show hills and woods and bracken as lovely as may be. Then one round in the thaw on Monday morning, just to rub it in that we were going to leave the course at its best, and so home to a singularly depressing London of slush and drizzle.

I have written of Aberdovey in winter because it is then, I think, that it is at its best, perhaps because I love it so much that I selfishly like to have it to myself. It is good in summertime too; good even in August when the rain too often comes pitilessly down, when the hand of the great midland towns lies heavy on the course and a pitched battle rages daily between the outgoing and incoming battalions in the narrow space that lies between the Pulpit and the Crater hole. September is a divine month there, when there are but few people left, and so is June, when there are none at all. It was in June that I paid my last summer visit there, and that on a somewhat sacrilegious errand, for I was to aid in the altering of old holes and the making of new bunkers. The committee had decided to call in a highly distinguished golfing architect to set their house in order, and I was asked to attend him as *amicus curiae* or bottle-holder, or clerk of the works—in short, in a menial capacity of an indefinite character. This task I undertook with alacrity, but after the first day's work I was a physical and mental wreck and felt a positive loathing for my architectural friend. Yet this I must say for him; like Rogue Riderhood, he does "Earn his living by the sweat of his brow." I never saw anyone work harder. Save for a wholly insufficient interval for lunch, we were on our legs from 9:15 in the morning to 7:30 at night. As a warning to others who may lightly undertake this kind of work, even at the risk of too wide a digression, I will shortly describe our day.

We started out first of all with two caddies. One of them carried our two waterproofs and a large plan of the course nailed onto a board. The other carried my clubs. The architect himself did not take any clubs, but stated that I should hit balls for him when required. My sensations rather resembled, as I should imagine, those of one who accompanies a water diviner. The architect behaved in the same mysterious and interesting manner. Sometimes he would come to a full stop and remain buried in thought for no ostensible reason. Then he would suddenly turn round and retrace his steps to the tee. Then he would pace a certain distance, counting his paces aloud in a solemn manner. Finally he would give a cry of joy, make a dash up to the top of a little sandhill, and declare with triumph that it would make the most perfect plateau green in the world, and that why in the world those who had originally laid out the course had not discovered it he for one could not conceive.

By slow stages the first two holes, which the members had always considered rather good in a humble way, were completely transmogrified. The greens were moved in the architect's mind's eye from their then reasonably open and easy-going positions to the most devilish little narrow gullies surrounded by sandhills and bents, where only a ball that flies as straight as did an arrow from the bow of Robin Hood might hope to reach the green. Beautiful holes they were, both of them, and would make a magnificent beginning to the course, but I could not but feel an uneasy doubt as to whether all the long-handicap members of the club would appreciate them at quite their true value. Nothing much happened at the third hole, and then we approached the fourth, over which I personally felt rather nervous. The club is proud of this fourth hole, which consists of a rather terrifying iron shot, perfectly blind, over a vast and formidable hill shored up with black railway sleepers, on to a little green oasis amid a desert of sand. Now, the hole is really a sacred institution (it is one of the few holes on the course that is known by a name and not a number), but it is also one of the type of hole for which I knew my architect to feel a most utter contempt. I wondered uneasily whether he would want to do some horribly revolutionary thing, and I reflected that if he did I should certainly be lynched by the committee for his sins. However, he merely cast a withering look at a grass bank behind the green, commanded that "that back wall" should be taken away, and passed on, deeming the hole unworthy of any further notice. I will not enter into further details of this our first progress round the course. At intervals I was ordered to drive a ball from a specified place, and my efforts were commended as being admirably adapted for showing where the normal, short, bad driver would get to against the wind: this when I was driving with a fairly strong breeze behind me. To cut a long story short, we finally got round in something over three hours, and fell ravenously on our lunch.

I had faintly hoped that in the afternoon we might relax our labors so far as to play a friendly round, but as a matter of fact, what

I had undergone in the morning was the merest child's play to the afternoon. After lunch we started out again with a large cart driven by a sleepy boy, and pulled by a sleepy horse. In the cart were about 200 stakes, commandeered from a neighboring sawmill, for the purpose of marking the sites of proposed new bunkers. We started about 2:30, and we stopped about 6:30, and I cannot help thinking that those two small caddies who hammered in stakes with violent blows and a heavy mallet, must have been very stiff after their labors. Personally I grew infinitely more faint and weary than I have ever done even at a picture gallery, which is generally believed to be the most exhausting thing in the world. To give the devil his due, my architect was wonderful, and filled me with admiration. Like a comet, he left a shining tail behind him—of white stakes gleaming in the sunlight. The speed with which he would decide on the position of a bunker was really astounding. While I was feebly wondering what a certain stake was for, he had decided that the right policy was to make people play at the green from the right-hand side: to make a series of bunkers all along the left of the fairway so as to drive them towards the rushes: to dig out that hollow close to the green, and so on, and so on. He is really a wonderful person, but it is a fearful thing to do a day's work with him, even though it be in the service of the course one loves best in the world.

The Links of Eiderdown

The Times
1934

Given exactly the right conditions, there are few pleasanter things than a day in bed. We must not be rank imposters; we must be just ill enough to be sure that we shall be nearly well next day or, indeed, quite well so long as we have not to come down to breakfast. We must feel equal not to gross roast beef but to a whiting sympathetically eating its own tail and to a rice pudding, not forgetting the brown sugar. Tobacco, though sparingly indulged in, must not take on the flavor of hay, and though wholly incapable of answering a newly arrived letter, we must be well able to read an old book.

It is best, if possible, to feel some warning symptoms the night before, so that we may be assured that it would very unwise to get up next morning. Thus we have the joys both of anticipation and of fruition. That such joys are selfish it cannot be denied. The telephone bell rings in the distance and we cannot answer it. The bell rings for luncheon, and there are sounds of scurrying feet as of those late in washing; we are taking a little holiday in that respect and our lunch comes up on a tray. With what heavenly malice do we hear a strange motorcar crunching the gravel under the window. Callers—ha, ha! The new neighbors—ho, ho! We shall be told later that they proved to be very agreeable people and we are perfectly ready to take it on trust. With a last thought of them sitting ranged round the drawing room, we drift away into a beautiful halfway house between sleep and waking without fearing any of the misery that ensues if we do the same thing in a chair. We shall come to ourselves as bright as a button and ready for another go of *David Copperfield.*

This was my admirable choice last week, and I was so drowsily happy that I found even Agnes "pointing upward" not unendurable. Only one thing disturbed my serenity. In my warped mind's eye I continually saw golf holes designed on the "land of counterpane" before me. It is not an uninteresting one, this links of eiderdown, and is laid out on what an ingratiating prospectus would call fine, undulating country. Moreover, by undulating himself in bed the patient can in a moment change the contour of his course. In the ordinary way there is a broad hog's-back ridge extending down the middle of the course. It is doubtless possible to use it in several ways, but I always saw a long plain hole running nearly the whole length of it, slightly downhill with a fall to perdition on either side for the slicer or the hooker. It seemed to me, if I remembered the number aright, rather like the 13th hole at Liphook. There were no bunkers on it of any kind; no "lighthouses," as the more ferocious of architects scornfully term them, to guide the eye of the tiger and make superfluously wretched the rabbit's life; nothing but a wide expanse on which it would clearly be very difficult to judge distance.

When my eyes dropped to either side of this ridge I felt that I was in another country. Was I at Formby or Birkdale, or perhaps at the 6th hole at Prince's, Sandwich? Here, at any rate, was one of the holes that run along a narrow valley with slopes on either hand—on one side, to be precise, the patient's leg, and on the other the outside edge of the eiderdown. I have always had rather a romantic affection for such holes. I have heard with pain from those same "highbrow" architects that they are not really good holes, because the mere fact of the banks (which will kick the ball back to the middle) give the player confidence, whereas the architect's duty is to make him hesitating and uncomfortable. I began to think that these irritating views were right; the valley might be narrow, but I felt as if I could drive straight down it, whereas when I looked at the ridge I did not feel nearly so happy.

There were other holes on the course, but they were hardly so satisfactory. There was, to be sure, a big, blind tee shot, to a one-shot hole as I imagined it, over a comparatively noble hill, made by my toes, but somehow it lacked subtlety; and when by a swift piece of engineering I moved the hill to see what the green was like on the far side, it proved flat and featureless. By separating and then adroitly manipulating my two sets of toes it was possible to make a crater green, with visions of the ball running round the side wall and back wall to lie dead at least for an unmerited three. That brought back sentimental memories. I knew a beloved course once that had three such greens running, and many years ago I had three threes running there and won a medal thereby. Still, the sweetness of such threes has a cloying quality. No doubt it is all for the best in the most testing of all possible worlds that there should be no more greens like that nowadays.

To roll over on my side had a disappointing effect on the links. In fact it was obviously not a links any longer, but a mere course: one of those courses on downland which I have the misfortune to dislike, with long, steep slopes, equally tedious to play up or down, and too often adorned with "gun-platform" greens. When tea came, however, the course took on a new aspect, for the tea tray was on a bed table and the bed table had four legs. The course was now one cut out of a wood, on which the architect had wisely allowed a solitary sentinel tree or two to remain standing in the middle of the fairway. The valley holes instantly became far more interesting, for each of them had one tree, acting in some sort as a Principal's Nose, for the tee shot, and another, like that capital tree at the first hole at Frilford, bang in front of the green. I spent some time trying to resolve on which side of those trees to go. At one hole it seemed best to try the right-hand line, because if I went to the left I might hook on the floor, which was clearly out of bounds. At the other hole an exactly converse policy was indicated, but even with the banks to help me the shot was far from easy.

Now I am, as Mr. Littimer would say, "tolerably well" again, and *David Copperfield* is finished. I have no reasonable pretext for not getting up for breakfast, and indeed it is rumored that there are to be sausages tomorrow morning. The links of eiderdown are fast becoming of the fabric of a dream. I have tried to fix the holes before they elude the frantic clutches of memory and fade away into one another.

St. Andrews in August

American Golfer
1923

I have just finished a round at St. Andrews with a feeling of profound thankfulness for not having committed infanticide. From the last tee my ball leaped lightly over the left ear of a small and daydreaming boy who was walking along the road that crosses the links and leads to the shore. All day long there is a procession along it of motorcars, perambulators, children and old ladies and the golfer, learning perforce to be callous, drives over, round, or through them from the first and from the last tees. Mr. Horton in his box periodically shouts "Fore" at the people in a voice of thunder or rather he makes some horrific sound with no distinguishable consonants in it, but nobody pays any attention and, which is more surprising, nobody is killed.

St. Andrews in August is distinctly different from St. Andrews in September. September is the month of the public vase and the

Medal when "Everybody as is anybody" feels bound to come here and meets all the golfers one ever knew in the clubroom. In August there are plenty of members here, but it is preeminently the season of the golfing day-tripper from Edinburgh, from Glasgow, from all over the place. Most of them play golf and all of them putt. Excluding the ladies' club putting course which is select and genteel, where you must be accompanied by a member and must play with a putter of wood on the sacred turf; excluding also the children's links on the far side of the road by the seventeenth green; there are three public putting courses.

You pay twopence or a penny. You hire a putter, if you need one, and a ball from which the vestiges of paint have long since vanished, and you putt. These greens are just outside the white railing between the shore on one side and the fairway to the first hole on the other. One of them is in considerable peril from the sliced drives from the first tee, and I apprehend that on this one you only pay a penny, because of the enhanced risk to your life. The greens are not very good (how could they be with the constant tramping?), but they are very amusing and there is something extraordinarily friendly and jolly about the whole performance. You feel that putting is not the solemn and agonizing business that you have so often imagined it, but a popular pastime with vast scope for rollicking humor, like going on a roller-coaster at Coney Island.

Of course, there is plenty of solemn golf too. At this present moment there is a big open tournament on the Eden course with so many entries that the qualifying rounds take two days. In it are playing such well-known golfers as Mr. de Montmorency and Mr. John Caven, both of whom have played for Britain against America, and a host of those artisan golfers with whom Scotland abounds—golfers who from lack of time and means seldom go far from their home courses but who have all the dash and style of the professional and want only something of his steadiness and experience. There are big crowds watching the play, for the Scots never tire of watching golf, but this does not seem to diminish by a single man, woman or child the crowd that is playing on the Old Course and on the New. They were hard at it when I looked out of my bedroom window at 8 o'clock this morning and they will still be hard at it when in a few minutes I strike across the edge of the last green to dress for my dinner at 8 o'clock in the evening. And nearly every match is a four-ball match because it takes three hours to get round and to play a single is to become a martyr to impatience on every tee.

Nothing demonstrates so well the unique fascination of St. Andrews as the fact that golfers who might go anywhere else come here year after year and gladly suffer all the slowness and all the inconvenience in order to play on the Old Course. That is the magnet. The New Course is a very fine one. If it were anywhere else in the world except under the shadow of the Old, it would be very famous. It is even argued that judged by orthodox standards of architecture it is as good as the Old. Yet everybody wants to get a place in the ballot for starting times on the Old and nobody but regards the New as a *pis aller*. The Calcutta Cup foursome tournament is played on the New Course. Yet I remember that two years ago, not one single player took the trouble to go for a preliminary round of exploration on the New. They just played it "blind" because they would not spare one precious moment from the delights of the Old. There is nothing like it anywhere else, though I am sure I cannot explain why. The best reason I know is George Duncan's that "You can play a d___d good shot there and find the ball in a d____d bad place!"

Muirfield in Winter

American Golfer
1935

A great many American golfers have been to Scotland in summer, but I suspect very few have been there in winter. Neither, I have now come to believe, have many Englishmen. Till lately I myself have been nothing but a summer tripper and when a kind friend asked me to come and stay in February I told several English golfers rather shamefacedly that I had never been to Scotland in winter before. To my surprise most everyone answered, "No more have I," and I began to be less ashamed of myself. The going was a great romance and I thought of little else for several days beforehand. Now I have come home again; I am hugging to myself the memory of three of the most delightfully friendly and sunshiny days of golf I have ever had in my life and, however tiresome I may be, I cannot help talking about them.

My friends and my family prophesied the gloomiest things for me. They said that it would probably snow, that it would certainly freeze hard, and they urged me so strongly to take all the thick clothes I had ever possessed that I began to feel like an arctic explorer. In vain did I quote my host's letter that his wife had lately picked a bunch of roses in her garden at North Berwick. This statement was received with ribald Saxon merriment. I dined at my club before catching my night train and when I rose to go with the statement that I must be off for Scotland I was overwhelmed with that kind of sympathy which takes a pleasure in its friend's misfortunes. Well, I have the laugh of them all now, for it froze and it snowed in London while I was basking in my Riviera of Muirfield.

It is always an exciting moment to wake up in Scotland, to look out of the window and to see everywhere the running waters; they were streams in England and now they are burns. It was more than ever thrilling this time and, Heaven be praised, there was never a patch of snow even on the hills, and not as much as a puff of bitter wind to ruffle the trees. By half past ten o'clock I was in the delicious solitude of Muirfield, with the sun just coming through a thin veil of mist, playing golf, and without my waistcoat. There was to be sure a little frost in the ground and our early putts behaved rather eccentrically while our driving powers were flattered.

By noon the frost had all gone and for the rest of my three days the weather was perfect. I really mean perfect because to my mind winter golf in fine weather on a seaside course is the best that life has to offer, and worth a hundred rounds on summer days. There is a freshness about the turf as about the air which summer cannot give, and the holes are of the right length. We cannot reach the greens by means of senile shuffles which send the ball much further than they deserve. The ball "maun be hit," we hit it as well as we can and if ever we succeed how great is our reward and our joy. The Open championship is at Muirfield this year and doubtless the professionals will be compassing the "two-shot" holes with a vast driver and then a flick with some much lofted club. In winter, they might occasionally have to use a wooden club for their second shots and lash out like men to get home.

I went to Scotland not only to play my games but to be a guest at dinner of that venerable and illustrious club, the Honorable Company at Edinburgh Golfers, whose home is Muirfield. The members dine periodically, make matches—nearly all of them foursomes—and if they have a mind to it bet on them in moderation. There is at once great friendliness and a pleasant air of ceremony and tradition. Several members may rise simultaneously to catch the eye of the Captain in his red coat who sits entrenched behind the Silver Club, with silver balls depending from it. "Mr. So and So," says the great man, whereupon Mr. So and So delivers himself as follows: "Mr. Captain, with your permission Mr. A and I propose to play Mr. C and Mr. D on Saturday, the ninth of February." There ensues a few minutes of babel in which bets are made and then the Captain hammers on the table with his mallet of office, silence falls, the recorder rises and says, "Sir, the match is Mr. A and Mr. B against Mr. C and Mr. D," and reads out all the wagers that have been laid. Then more people leap respectfully to their feet, another match is read out and so the match-making goes busily and cheerfully along. Let me add in modest parenthesis that a match was made for me and that with a stout partner I managed to win it.

I could enlarge forever on the beauty of those days, on Gullane Hill and the view over the misty sea and the mystery of Archerfield wood with its gnarled fir trees permanently heeling over under the wind, the wind which comes into Robert Louis Stevenson's great story, "The Pavilion on the Links." However, this is not business and since Muirfield is the scene of the championship, in which I hope we shall have some American champions playing, I may say that the course has been in several ways changed and improved since Walter Hagen won there in 1929. Incidentally, Hagen himself has caused one change, for he exploited an ingenious short cut to the eighth hole, by way of the rough, which was not rough enough, and now they have planted a hedge there to stop such antics.

A variety of unsightly and superfluous bunkers have been filled up and one or two small but dominating ones put in. The first hole, for instance, which was dull and straight, with rows of bunkers on either hand, has not the most ingenious little fellow in front of the green. The man who drives to the left has a straight run for his second. The man who drives to the right will have to play his second with an extremely skillful slice. Then the bunkering has been altered at the home hole, which is now closely beset and makes a splendid ending.

Most important of all the horrid, ugly little thirteenth, which looked as if it came out of a suburban garden, has been done away with and a really fine, dangerous, uphill, one-shot hole substituted. I admit the old one did cause dramatic disasters, but it was a scurvy little beast and I am thankful it is gone. Altogether I think Muirfield will make a fine battlefield when the day comes, but it never can be quite so good again as it was on those winter days "sent from beyond the skies."

The Old Course

Golf Courses of the British Isles
1910

Really to know the links of St. Andrews can never be given to the casual visitor. It is not perhaps necessary to be one of those old gentlemen who tell us at all too frequent intervals that golf was golf in their young days, that we of today are solely occupied in the pursuit of pots and pans, and that Sir Robert Ray, with his tall hat and his graduated series of spoons, would have beaten us, one and all, into the middle of the ensuing week. Such a degree of senile decay is fortunately not essential, but one ought to have known and loved and played over the links for a long while; and I can lay no claims to such knowledge as that. I can speak only as an occasional pilgrim, whose pilgrimages, though always reverent, have been far too few. . . .

There are those who do not like the golf at St. Andrews, and they will no doubt deny any charm to the links themselves, but there must surely be none who will deny a charm to the place as a whole. It may be immoral, but it is delightful to see a whole town given up to golf; to see the butcher and the baker and the candle-stick maker shouldering his clubs as soon as his day's work is done and making a dash for the links. There he and his fellows will very possibly get in our way, or we shall get in theirs; we shall often curse the crowd, and wish wholeheartedly that golf was less popular in St. Andrews. Nevertheless it is that utter self-abandonment to golf that gives the place its attractiveness. What a pleasant spectacle is that home green, fenced in on two sides by a railing, upon which lean various critical observers; and there is the clubhouse on one side, and the clubmaker's shop and the hotels on the other, all full of people who are looking at the putting, and all talking of putts that they themselves holed or missed on that or some other green. . . .

St. Andrews never looks really easy, and never is really easy, for the reason that the bunkers are for the most part so close to the greens. It is possible, of course, to play an approach shot straight on the beeline to the flag, and if we play it to absolute perfection all may go well; but let it only be crooked by so much as a yard, or let the ball, as it often will do, get an unkind kick, and the bunker will infallibly be our portion. . . .

Let not the reader hastily assume that his only difficulty at St. Andrews will be to keep out of the clutches of the bunkers lying close to the greens; he will find plenty more stumbling blocks in his path. There is the matter of length, for instance. The holes, either out or home, do not look very long . . . with the wind behind . . . , but it is an entirely different matter when we have to play them . . . with the wind in our teeth. . . . There are a great many holes that demand two good shots, as struck by the ordinary mortal; there are three that he cannot reach except with his third, and there are only two that he can reach from the tee, of which one by common consent is the most fiendish short hole in existence. Thus we have two difficulties, that the holes are long, and that there are bunkers close to the greens; now, for a third, those greens are for the most part on beautiful pieces of golfing ground, which by their natural conformation, by their banks and braes and slopes, guard the holes very effectively, even without the aid of the numerous bunkers. . . . Finally, the turf is very hard, and consequently the greens are apt to take on a keenness that is paralyzing in its intensity.

Having by alarming generalizations induced in the unfortunate stranger a suitably humble frame of mind, time has now arrived to take him over the course in some detail. The first thing to point out . . . is the historic fact that there were once upon time but nine holes, and that the outgoing and incoming players aimed at the self-same hole upon the self-same green. That state of things has necessarily long passed away, but the result is still to be seen in the fact that most of the greens are actually or in effect double greens, and consequently the two processions of golfers outward- and inward-bound pass close to each other, not without some risk to life and much shouting of "Fore!"

With this preliminary observation, we may tee up our ball in front of the Royal and Ancient Clubhouse for one of the least alarming tee shots in existence. In front of us stretches a vast flat plain, and unless we slice the ball outrageously onto the sea beach, no harm can befall us. At the same time we had much better hit a good shot, because the Swilcan burn guards the green, and we want to carry it and get a four. It is an inglorious little stream enough: we could easily jump over it were we not afraid of looking foolish if we fell in, and yet it catches an amazing number of balls.

The second is a beautiful hole some 400 yards in length, and with the most destructive of pot-bunkers close up against the hole. Here is a case in point, when the attempt to shave narrowly past the bunker involves terrible risks, and it is the part of prudence to play well out to the right . . .

The fifth is the long hole out, when we shall need our three strokes to reach the green, which stands a little above us on a plateau of magnificent dimensions, were we rub shoulders with the incoming couples who are plying the "Hole o' Cross." In ancient days, when the whins were thick and flourishing on the straight road to the hole, the only possible line was away to the left towards the Elysian Fields. It was from there, so Mr. James Cunningham has told me, that young Tommy Morris astonished the spectators by taking his niblick, a club that in those days had a face of about the magnitude of half-crown, wherewith to play a pitch on the green. Till that historic moment no one had ever dreamed of a niblick being used for anything but ordinary spadework. . . .

At the eighth we do at last get a chance of a three, for the hole is a short one—142 yards long to be precise—and there is a fair measure of room on the green. So far the golf has been very, very good indeed, but with the ninth and tenth come two holes that constitute a small blot on the fair fame of the course. If they were found on some less sacred spot they would be condemned as consisting of a drive and a pitch up and down a flat field. What makes it the sadder is that ready to the architect's hand is a bit of glorious golfing country on the confines of the new course. However, we had better play these two holes in as reverent a spirit as possible and be thankful for two fairly easy fours, because the next is the "short hole in," and we must reserve all our energies for that.

The only consoling thing about the hole is that the green slopes upward, so that it is not quite so easy for the ball to run over it as it otherwise would be. This is really but cold comfort, however, because the danger of going too far is not so imminent as that of not going straight enough. There is one bunker called "Strath," which is to the right, and there is another called the "Shelly Bunker," to the left; there is also another bunker short of Strath to catch the thoroughly short and ineffective ball. The hole is as a rule cut fairly close to Strath, wherefore it behooves the careful man to play well away to the left, and not to take undue risks by going straight for the hole. This may sound pusillanimous, but trouble once begun at this hole may never come to an end till the card is torn into a thousand fragments. . . . It is a hole to leave behind one with a sigh of satisfaction.

The next hole would in any case fall almost inevitably flat, but the thirteenth, the Hole o' Cross, is a great hole, where having struck two really fine shots and escaped "Walkinshaw's Grave," we may hope to reach the beautiful big plateau green in two and hole out in two more. . . .

Although home is now in sight, there are yet two terribly dangerous holes to be played. First of all we must steer down the perilously narrow space between the "Principal's Nose" and the railway line—the railway line, mark you that is not out-of-bounds, so that there is no limit to the number of strokes that we may spend in hammering vainly at an insensate sleeper. We may, of course, drive safe away to the left, and if our score is a good one we shall be wise to do so, but our approach, as is only fair, will then be the more difficult, and there are bunkers lurking by the greenside.

The seventeenth hole has been more praised and more abused probably than any other hole in the world. It has been called unfair, and by many harder names as well; it has caused champions with a predilection for pitching rather than running to tear their hair; it has certainly ruined an infinite number of scores. Many like it, most respect it, and all fear it. First there is the tee shot, with the possibility of slicing out-of-bounds into the stationmaster's garden or pulling into various bunkers on the left. Then comes the second, a shot which should not entail immediate disaster, but which is nevertheless of enormous importance as leading up to the third. Finally, there is the approach to that little plateau—in contrast to most of the St. Andrews greens, a horribly small and narrow one that lies between a greedy little bunker on the one side and a brutally hard road on the other. It is so difficult as to make the boldest inclined to approach on the installment system, and yet no amount of caution can do away with the chance of disaster. . . .

After this hole of many disastrous memories, the eighteenth need have no great terrors. We drive over the burn, cross by the picturesque old stone bridge, and avoiding the grosser forms of sin, such as slicing into the windows of Rusack's Hotel, hole out in four, or at most five, under the critical gaze of those that lean on the railings. . . .

VII

Crossing the Pond: The Atlantic Monthly *Dispatches*

The Golfer's Emotions

The Atlantic Monthly
JUNE 1928

I

All games have their moments of anguish, and golf can certainly claim no monopoly. Not for the most enduring but for the most acute agonies I am inclined in my insularity to claim preeminence for an English game, cricket. I feel the profoundest pity of all for the young batsman going in to play his first innings in his first big match at Lord's. It is such a terribly long walk out to the wicket, he is such a terribly small speck in the big arena, there are so many people looking at him, and at nothing but him, and he feels in the very marrow of his bones that they are looking. And then if he fails there is that same long walk back, this time not with mingled hope and fear in his heart, but only despair. Cricket is such a cruel game because it does not, unless you are lucky, give you another chance. You have been tried and found wanting, and you will probably have nothing to do for several hours but sit and ponder over it.

The football player waiting for a ball high in the air, conscious of his enemies' fierce rush coming ever nearer; the runner poised on the mark in a hundred yards' race wherein a good start or a bad one will make all the difference; the baseball player, as I should ignorantly imagine, running under a mountainously high catch (though to be sure they never seem to miss them)—all these and several others must have a horrible cold sensation at the pit of the stomach, and feel as if their knees were made of brown paper. Their misery, however, is momentary; it comes and goes in spasms and is swallowed up and forgotten in violent exertion, but the golfer's suffering is long drawn out; it may endure from the first tee shot to the last putt and there is no swift movement to make him forget it; he is on a slow fire. Those who gloat over his tortures—the hard-hearted spectators—are quite close to him all the while; there is scarcely a twitching nerve they cannot see, not a stifled groan they cannot hear. Thus the student of game-playing psychology finds his richest field in golf, and there is probably no game in which temperament plays so important a part or is so constantly discussed.

Especially is it quite openly discussed by the ghoulish clan of reporters, of whom I am one. It was not ever thus. I remember when we used to read such a sentence as "At this point (perhaps all square with one to play) *X* unaccountably missed a short putt." Now if the man who wrote such a sentence really believed what he wrote, he must have been an insensate idiot. "Unaccountably"! Why, there is nothing that could be called unaccountable at all square and one to play, no act of terror-stricken folly of which a golfer would be incapable. However, I prefer to believe that the writer was not an idiot but a kind-hearted man, who did not want to hurt the player's feelings. Today the pendulum has swung the other way with a vengeance, and we read how the unhappy *X* approached that critical putt "trembling like a leaf." Perhaps it has swung too far, for after all it is as well to remember that to miss a putt is not a criminal offense and does not prevent a man from being an excellent husband, father, and citizen.

II

Still, this brutal frankness does make accounts of golf matches more interesting, and does present a truer picture. If the reporter has some experience and imagination he can nearly always put his finger on the event which was the turning point of the match, the thing which caused one player to strike the stars with uplifted head, the other to feel a broken man. It may come quite early in the game or it may come late; it may be a piece of pure good or bad luck, or it may be some one tremendous thrust not to be parried. Whatever it may be, it is not easy to mistake. An experienced watcher looking at a match will generally be able to say at a certain hole, "That's done it; it's all over now," and he will seldom be wrong. The strain of a hard match is for most people a very severe one. Something happens which lightens the strain for one side and makes it unendurable for the other. That something counts two and indeed much more than two on a division.

I remember a friend, who was once in the Oxford eight, telling me of a certain sculling race which he won. He was behind and so could not see how his enemy was faring, but he himself felt as if he were in his death agony, as if he could not pull more than another half-dozen strokes to save his life. Suddenly someone shouted to him from the bank that the enemy had capsized. Instantly he sat up, feeling perfectly at ease, and finished more or less as fresh as paint, sculling in excellent form. The same thing happens at golf. The strain suddenly lightens and we play as if we were walking on air, having but a moment before felt leaden-footed. It is interesting—horribly interesting sometimes—but it is not in the least "unaccountable"; the reason of it is plain for all to see.

Some golfers collapse easily under the strain, others have great powers of endurance, but none are immune; there is no one who has not "cracked" at some time or other in his career. In particular there is no one who has not been overwhelmed by the "holes dropping away like snow off a dike." To have what appears a winning lead and to see it dwindle and dwindle—this is what no one can bear with perfect equanimity; and it is all the harder to bear just because the adversary's spirits, which but a little while since were at zero, are now so obviously and rapidly rising. When one of these sudden landslides of holes has occurred, it is not infrequently said or implied that the leader had become slack or overconfident. Generally speaking, I do not believe a word of it. No doubt there are some who feel pleasantly lazy when they are four or five up at the turn, but they are not many and they are not of the kind that collapse when one or two of those holes slip away. Overconfidence may have slain its hundreds, but overanxiety has slain its tens of thousands. We are in such a desperate hurry to win quickly and so be spared the strain of the last few crucial holes. We are not content to let victory come gradually in its own good time; we want to accelerate it, and there is no better way of putting it off forever. We look too far ahead; we hear in imagination the band playing "See the conquering hero" and feel our friends patting us on the back.

When things go wrong and we realize that after all the match is going to be what the Duke of Wellington called the Battle of Waterloo, "a d_____d close-run thing," the disappointment unnerves us altogether. If once we can arrest this panic rout, we may recover ourselves, and the enemy's counterattack may die away, but it is so difficult to arrest it. In such moments our ambition seldom soars beyond a halved hole; we play too cautiously, and the half just escapes us again and again. Sometimes the best thing for us is to lose all our lead and be done with it. As long as one hole remains to us we are still banking to some extent on our reserve, feebly trusting to the chapter of accidents rather than to our own efforts. When the last hole is gone, we awake to the fact that our back is against the wall, and then at last we fight.

This particular phenomenon is often noticeable when a match in a tournament is halved and the players have to proceed to the nineteenth hole. *A* has been perhaps three up with four to play; he has hurled victory away with both hands. *B*, on the contrary, has fought with a tigerish courage of despair and has pulled a hopeless match out of the fire. Surely and obviously, you would say, *B* must be the man to back at the nineteenth hole. Yet, in fact, *A* wins it quite as often as not. It is his now to experience the blind courage of despair, whereas *B* has begun to think. During those last four holes *B* did not really think or hope, he just fought. Now he realizes that after all he has a chance—a great chance—of victory, and it often unmans him.

What is the cure for this horrible tendency to collapse on the threshold of success? I know of none save to try to play each hole as if it were a new and separate match, looking neither forward nor backward; and that is advice easy enough to give and—ye gods!—hard enough to follow. As a corollary may be quoted a remark of General Briggs, not a great golfer, but a great character, who used to play for many years at St. Andrews. "When I am six up," he said, "I strive to be seven up. When I am seven up, I strive to be eight up." These are brave words and contain a piece of sturdy, "common-sensical" wisdom—not to be content with halves when we have got the lead.

III

If this game of golf is so severe a trial of the nerves, what is the right kind of man to play it successfully? The obvious answer seems to be, "The man who has no nerves." "The more fatuously vacant the mind," wrote Sir Walter Simpson, "the better the play. Alas! we cannot all be idiots. Next to the idiotic, the dull unimaginative mind is the best for golf. In a professional competition I would prefer to back the sallow, dull-eyed fellow with a quid in his cheek, rather than any more eager-looking champion." There is much in what he says. The word "eager" implies that dreaming of triumph before it has arrived which I have already reprobated. Yet I do not believe that Sir Walter's is altogether the right answer, and I do not believe in the man with "no nerves." He, the "dull-eyed fellow," may do steadily, but he will not do the great things. I do not know how it may be with other people, but I distrust myself most profoundly on the days when I feel that I do not care. It is an unnatural lull before a brainstorm and I feel sure that on a sudden I shall come forward to caring too much. As far as outward appearances go, there has never been quite so apparently phlegmatic a golfer as James Braid, but I have heard him say that he likes to feel "a little nervous" before starting a match. Give me the highly strung man with self-control, the nervous man who can conquer his nerves.

Of this truth, if it be a truth, American golf can supply some admirable illustrations. There was the late Walter Travis, for instance. When he was playing he looked cold, calm, inscrutable as the Sphinx; there was something positively inhuman about him; yet those who knew him best always declared that he was really wrought up to a high pitch of tension. Then—a still better example—there is Bobby Jones. Here is a highly nervous player who has had to conquer not only his nerves but a fiery temper as well. As we know from his own delightful account of his sensations in *Down the Fairway*, he still longs now and again to throw his clubs about. Yet he is at once a model of outward suavity and a most gallant fighter. I do not believe that there is a golfer alive who suffers more over the game than he does, partly from nervous tension, partly from his own extreme fastidiousness as an artist, which makes him rage inwardly at any stroke not played with perfect art. He has told us that he regularly loses I don't know how many pounds in weight in the course of a Championship. Yet he has conquered himself and he has conquered the world. Had he been placid and lethargic I do not believe he would have accomplished half as much.

Yet another example is a golfer whom I should rate as at least as good a match player as I ever saw—Jerome Travers. He too had to conquer something in himself and has confessed that sometimes his nerves were so "raggedy" that it was all he could do to keep them under control. Yet his frozen calm and his power of pulling matches out of the fire were proverbial; they not only won him many matches but frightened many other people into losing them. If I had to pick out one of Mr. Travers's "temperamental" qualities for praise, it would be his power of putting aside and forgetting. He was never afraid of showing momentarily his annoyance over a bad shot, just because he was so sure of himself and knew that he would instantly regain control. But the best example of this power of forgetting was shown in his wrestlings with his wooden clubs at a time when they betrayed him so seriously that he had to drive with an iron from the tee. When I saw him win the Championship at Garden City in 1913 he was constantly trying his driver, losing his lead in consequence, and then putting the peccant driver away again and taking to his iron. Other people might possibly have won while driving with an iron, but they would have had to stick to the iron from first to last. To be able to try those antics and then settle down again, not once but several times, in the course of a match, seemed to me a miracle of concentration, of obliterating from the mind everything but the one hole, nay, the one stroke to be played next.

There is another very great American golfer whose temperament seems to demand some analysis, and that is Walter Hagen; but him I do not profess to understand. Does he feel nervous? I imagine that he does, because I cannot believe that he could rise to such heights if he did not; but I certainly have no evidence to bring forward in support of my views. He impresses one beyond everything else as really enjoying the fight. Because he is a great showman as well as a great match player, he has clearly cultivated this quality in himself for all it is worth, but it must, to begin with, have been a natural one. There are two kinds of fighters: those who actually want to be in the ring and those who will fight bravely when they find themselves there, but would instinctively prefer to keep out of it. The former is the happier class, and Hagen is at the very head of it. With this rejoicing in the battle he seems to have cultivated another quality, that of an eminently sane philosophy. He has not the point of view of Bobby Jones, as he has not his flawless art.

He is always likely to make a bad mistake or two in the course of a round, and accepts them as natural and inevitable, not to be resented, only to be compensated for. Bobby is always trying to do *the* best; Hagen tries to do his own best.

IV

I feel that patriotism demands of me that I should give at least one example of great fighting qualities from among British golfers, and there is one at any rate ready to my hand. That is the now veteran champion, J. H. Taylor, and never was there a better example of a highly strung man capable of keeping a hold on himself and rising to the occasion. It has been said—and perhaps rightly, on the whole—that the poetic temperament is a bad one for golf; but there never was a man with a more palpably poetic temperament than Taylor. He is a man of strong emotions. When I think of him I always remember some words from Mr. Jarndyce's description of Lawrence Boythorn in *Bleak House*: "It's the inside of the man, the warm heart of the man, the passion of the man, the fresh blood of the man. . . . His language is as sounding as his voice. He is always in extremes; perpetually in the superlative degree. . . . He is a tremendous fellow." Taylor is a tremendous fellow and so a tremendously exciting golfer. He fights himself and the fates and furies of golf and every other man in the field, all at the same time. He confesses that he has tried the plan of "letting up" between whiles and then concentrating fiercely on the stroke in hand, but it is not in him; he must be boiling and bubbling all the time. All this pent-up or partially pent-up emotion takes it out of him most prodigally, and yet no man can last better in a crucial finish up to the very last putt. However great the agony, wild horses would not draw from him the admission that he hates it. He would despise himself if he did. No, in his own way he loves it, and if there is one thing that rouses his ire it is a young golfer who professes not to enjoy the fight.

Such a temperament has the defects of its qualities, and occasionally, very occasionally, "J. H." may have beaten himself; but much more often he struggles and wrestles with adversity until he overcomes it, and then, when a great stroke or a piece of good luck has turned the tide for him and things begin to go right instead of wrong, he is far more dangerous than any more placid or phlegmatic person. I remember sometimes to have watched him when things have been going badly and to have felt that I should not dare speak to him for a thousand pounds. I have wondered what would happen if some ill-advised spectator did speak to him, half hoping, half fearing that it might happen, like a small boy who knows that there is a firecracker in the fireplace behind his master's coattails and wonders when and how it will go off. I remember particularly one such occasion in an Open Championship at Deal years ago now. For nine holes or so Taylor, who had started favorite, was pursued by every kind of adversity and he looked like a powder magazine about to explode. Then, I think at the tenth hole, a long putt went in for three and from that moment he was positively scintillating, a man inspired; there was no need to look any further for the winner of that Championship.

Perhaps the most famous match player we have ever had in England is John Ball, who won the Amateur Championship eight times. He is of a different type, outwardly dour, silent, unruffled—a man, you would say, made of granite. Yet I have seen Mr. Ball before the beginning of a big match stripping the paper off a new ball, and his fingers almost refused their office. Assuredly his is no "dead" nerve.

The interesting thing about him as a match player is that, though he is so doughty a fighter, he does not seem to make a personal fight of the match. He tries, I think, deliberately to forget about his enemy, bending his whole mind to doing his own duty and getting the hole in the right figure. He has one mood for both medal and match play, and one simple object—namely, to do his best. Today this principle is called "playing against par," and the adoption of it is said to have strengthened the one slightly weak place in Bobby Jones's harness. Obviously it is a good plan, but much determination is needed in order to adhere to it. The best of plans can be too inexorably pursued and there are occasions in which it is a tempting of Providence not to pay attention to the enemy's plight. When a five will certainly win the hole no sane man takes a very big risk in pursuit of his par four. On the other hand, hundreds and thousands of holes have been thrown away by thinking too much of the adversary and so playing overcautiously. Once we begin to approach the green too consciously on the installment system, to take irons from the tee and to putt round bunkers for fear of pitching into them, there is no end to the strokes we can fritter away. It is the height of folly to credit our opponent with supernatural powers, but at the same time we must not forget that the most utterly crushed and downtrodden enemy *may* hole a long putt. Carefulness has lost infinitely more holes and more matches than have ever been lost by temerity.

I have been talking chiefly of match play because it is the more clearly dramatic: it possesses the elements of a battle; it provides an interesting clash between two diverse temperaments. But in any article which tries to deal with the emotions of the golfer it is quite impossible to be altogether silent on score play. The card and pencil are infinitely more terrifying to the average golfer than any flesh-and-blood opponent. They can turn many a stouthearted match player into a little whipped cur. Familiarity can breed a measure, not of contempt, but of passive endurance toward these twin engines of torture; but in England, at any rate, the average golfer does not play in enough scoring competitions ever to grow familiar with them. So every time a medal day comes round he is just as frightened as he was before.

At least one of the causes of this terror is this: that on a medal day golf loses, or appears to lose, one of its kindliest and most charitable qualities. In match play it is always giving us another chance. The worst of errors can but lose us a single hole; but in medal play it is possible—or so it seems, at any rate, to our jaundiced imagination—to make an error of so appalling a character as to ruin us once and for all. This is seldom really so; the rules have always limited our liabilities even in the most hopeless of situations and are more forgiving now than they used to be; but still on a medal day, "All hope abandon" seems to be written in the sands of great bunkers. Consequently strokes that in the ordinary way do not cause a twitter of the pulse become horribly alarming. The man who usually thinks nothing of the big sandhill with the black-timbered face says suddenly to himself, "Heavens! Suppose I topped it!" Or he visualizes, long before the time comes, the splash of the ball where that simplest of little pitches has to be played across the corner of the lake. Hydrophobia is a disease that may attack almost any man on a medal day, and on no other day are there so many people to be heard simultaneously explaining in the clubhouse that they have done something which they have never done before in all their lives.

The worst thing, however, and the commonest that can befall us on a medal day, is an attack of shortness. The way to win a medal is, for most people, to say *Aut Caesar aut nullus*, to recognize the fact that someone is sure to do a good score and that the only way to beat him is to go out for everything in reason. Yet in fact we do just the opposite. We carry the installment system to its extreme limit; we are most cramped just when we ought to be most free, and as to our shortness on the putting green—well, let any spectator count the approach putts that are past the hole on the first green on a medal day; his ten fingers will, it is likely enough, suffice him for all his reckoning even in a big field. There is some malign power that positively holds our putter back, and the brave ring of the ball against the back of the tin is seldom heard.

V

If golf is so dreadful a game, "aye fechtin' against ye," as the old Scottish golfer said, why do we go on playing it? I have often wondered, but I have never—no, not even for the bitterest instant—dreamed of giving it up. I can only recollect one man who quite deliberately thought the matter over, came to the conclusion that he would be happier without golf, and acted upon it. He was gifted as a games player altogether beyond the common run of men. He was a cricketer and a tennis player and took to golf like a duck to water. In about a year from his beginning, his handicap had come down to "scratch," which did not mean what it would today, but yet stood for a respectable standard of play. And then he found the game a cause of such intense exasperation that he gave it up and took instead to a little peaceful domestic practice with the bow and arrow. There must have been moments when he regretted it, but he never admitted this. It amused him to see other people play, and now and again at long intervals he would try a shot with a friend's club, much as a long-reformed drunkard might trust himself occasionally to drink one glass of beer. He knew himself and in that knowledge was probably wise, but for the rest of us, surely, both the manlier and pleasanter course is to go on trying and hoping.

For myself, I am convinced that were I to give up golf there would come to me a series of revelations, and I should know how to exorcise the chronic slice, the dancing of the toes, the shortness of the putts which had afflicted me all through my golfing life. And then it would be too late.

The Perils of Golf

The Atlantic Monthly
NOVEMBER 1931

I

" 'Crumpets is wholesome, Sir,' says the patient. 'Crumpets is *not* wholesome, Sir,' says the doctor, wery fiercely. 'But they're so cheap,' says the patient, comin' down a little, 'and so wery fillin' at the price.' 'They'd be dear to you at any price; dear if you wos paid to eat 'em,' says the doctor. 'Four crumpets a night,' he says. 'vill do your business in six months!' "

Substitute golf for crumpets, and that passage from the immortal *Pickwick* summarizes very fairly the opposing views as to the healthy or the lethal qualities of the game.

Here by way of example are two extracts which I tore out of my newspaper on two successive days on my journeys to and from London.

On the first day the *Evening Standard* shouted, "Heart strained at golf," in reverberating capitals. "Washington, Friday," it went on: "Mr. Edward B. McLean, the publisher of the *Washington Post*, is stated by his doctor to be seriously ill. The diagnosis is myocarditis (inflammation of the muscles of the heart) caused by overexertion on the golf links." Here was a pretty business at Washington, Friday. I had to play in a golf match—two rounds, hot weather, and formidable opponents—on the following day, and had serious thoughts of telegraphing that I couldn't come. However, I decided to brave it, and on the Saturday morning the *Daily Mail* heartened me up with this: "New Woman Golf Champion. Tribute to the game as Health Builder." There followed an account of the victory of Miss Enid Wilson in the final of our Ladies' Golf Championship. I skipped hastily over the rows of fours and threes with which she had pulverized her adversary to find these remarkable words: "Her father, Dr. Wilson, told me that when she was born she weighed four pounds. In her early childhood he applied her to golf for the benefit of her physique. She now weighs more than thirteen stone and stands six feet high, a wonderful example of athletic girlhood."

So I went happily on to my destination, lost, as I hope, a little of my own thirteen stone in two hard foursomes under a broiling sun, won them both, and came back feeling agreeably tired but, unless I am deceived, all the better for my day.

When I got home again I seemed to remember something that should come pat to my purpose as to the great Bobby Jones. Turning to *Down the Fairway*, I found that Bobby had begun life "with an oversize head and a spindling body and legs with staring knees" and something the matter with his little inside that puzzled half a dozen doctors and prevented his eating "any real food" till he was five years old. Then his father and mother began to play golf on the East Lake course: he naturally imitated them, and lived fat and happy ever afterwards.

So far, so good: and golf certainly seems to have benefited these two infant phenomenons, but that does not altogether dispose of that affair at Washington, Friday. Moreover, I have a friend in the United States who in his turn has a friend; and this friend collects news of all deaths on the links and makes the flesh of elderly golfers creep by publishing the most appalling statistics. There must be—and indeed I am sure there are—two sides to this question, and golf, if it can do good, can also impose a strain on both mind and body which is not good at all. I cannot write about it as "Specialist" or "Harley Street Physician," a *nom de plume* which covers as a rule one who is not a doctor but a journalist, and lives not in Harley Street but in Brixton. I can only write as one who, having begun the game at nearly as early an age as Bobby Jones and being now something over fifty, still tries to play in pretty hard matches in pretty good company and finds it sometimes pretty hard work.

II

Let me take first those whom I know most about—the illustrious persons, not yet very old, whom I watch in championships. That they, especially the more highly strung of them, undergo a severe strain no one can doubt. A friend of mine, an experienced Scottish golfer, said the other day that too much was now talked and written about this question of strain. He admitted that with the increased competition and higher standard of play, the enormous crowds and the enormous number of columns in the papers, championships were more exacting than they used to be. Still he stuck to it that the older generation of players did not even in proportion suffer the torments that the modern ones are alleged to do, and that it was a pity that this aspect of the game should be overemphasized. Golf, he said, was intended to be "a contemplative game, like bowls."

I imagine that bowls can be an agonizing game to those of a nervous temperament who play in serious competitions. However that may be, my friend was certainly right in saying that this question of the mental strain is emphasized today. Once upon a time those who reported golf—to be sure, they did not always know much about it—used to state that Mr. So-and-So missed a short putt "inexplicably" or "unaccountably" or "presumably owing to carelessness." Nowadays we—my ghoulish colleagues of the press and I—are more likely to say that the poor man was trembling like a leaf and palpably could not hold his club. Similarly, if in the old times Mr. So-and-So lost a match after being, let us say, four up with seven to play, he was alleged to have taken matters too light-heartedly. When he loses that match now, we trot out the old quotation as to "holes dropping away like snow off a dike" and add that there is nothing so paralyzing as the dwindling of an apparently winning lead. Because the descriptive method has changed, I am not at all sure that there has been a change in the emotion underlying the events described. If today, when he is sixty, you talk to that great golfer, J. H. Taylor, about some of his past struggles, he will tell you, with much shaking of the head and jutting of the chin, that he suffered the tortures of the damned, nor can you doubt that he is telling the truth. There have always been agonized golfers as there have been comparatively phlegmatic ones, but the agonies used to be more decently covered up. I agree with my Scottish friend so far, that it is bad for the golfer that this side of his nature should be written of with such freedom; but, as one of those who have to do the writing, I submit that there is something to be said for us and that the psychology of golf is horribly interesting.

Let me go to Bobby Jones's *Down the Fairway* again for an example. When in 1926 he won both the British and the American Open Championship he tells us that after his last round at Columbus, before he knew whether or not he had won, he "blew up completely." "Anyway," he adds, "I never sat down and cried before." Well, I defy anyone to say that is not interesting; it makes a very human champion of him.

Take also a little scene which I saw in this year's Championship at Carnoustie; I have described it before, but will risk it again. In the last round Tommy Armour was going "great guns" and had a score of two under fours for the first eleven holes, so that he had high hopes of catching Jurado. At the twelfth he hit a really wonderful second shot right on to the green and then missed a tiny putt for his four. That obviously shook him, and he played a bad tee shot to the short thirteenth and his ball was not on the green; he could not afford to lose another stroke and *must* get his three. He knew this so well that when he came to play his chip he simply could not play it. Up and down the line he looked with a quick turn of the head, backward and forward he waggled his club, until I thought that the stroke would never come and turned away my eyes in sheer distress. At last he conquered himself, played the shot, got his three, and went on his way rejoicing. I felt like one gloating over an execution, but I had seen the crucial moment of Armour's championship.

All the famous players do not feel as acutely as these two that I have cited. It is impossible to imagine James Braid, for instance, breaking into a storm of tears. He once told me that he liked to feel "a little nervous" before a championship started, and if he ever did feel more than that, assuredly no one can produce evidence to prove it. No one was every more to be trusted in a close-run finish than that man of granite, but as a rule I fancy that the highly strung men are the greatest finishers if—and of course it is a big if—they can master themselves. To be a bundle of quivering nerves under control is to be capable of greater things than is the champion whom Sir Walter Simpson preferred, "the sallow, dull-eyed fellow with the quid in his cheek." But the imaginative golfer may well wear out quicker, for he pays the heavier price. With use and wont the strain becomes the more endurable, but it can hardly be good for him. Last year at Hoylake I was sitting writing in the room where Bobby Jones was waiting to hear whether MacDonald Smith's great spurt had caught him or not. I thought then that it was almost time that he retired from the arena, and when some months afterward he announced that he was going to do so I was almost glad. The point had come when the game was scarcely worth the candle.

III

So much for the champions, and now for the ordinary mortals. That golf has done good to many of them is obvious enough. The praises of fresh air and exercise, of change of scene and occupation, need no singing, but there is the other side of the picture; there is the man who makes himself so miserable over the game that at the end of a golfing holiday he ought to begin another holiday both from golf and from work.

I venture to speak with some little experience, for I believe I have—more shame to me—made myself as unhappy over golf as most men. I can truthfully say, as did the little boy who made himself sick with smoking, "Yes, but I like the feeling." At the same time, if I had to get myself, in order to save my life, into a state of the greatest possible fitness, I would not play golf; I would do something more bovine that would not make me so often angry and desperate, even though it brought no compensating ecstasies. Some people can more skillfully divide their lives into compartments. There was a man of my acquaintance, of great ability, and one of the sanest, calmest, most sweet-tempered of mortals in every department of life save one: as soon as he began to play golf, or any other game, he suffered from the belief that of all men in the world he had been chosen by Fortune as a butt for her arrows. He was almost entirely miserable while he played, but as soon as he finished he ceased to repine until the next time, and did not chew the cud of his bad, or rather his unlucky, strokes. It may be supposed, therefore, that his golf did him good, but he was surely an exception.

Another comes to mind who had a natural genius for games, and, after playing golf a little more than a year, attained the proud handicap of scratch. The standard of handicapping was less exigent in those days, but this was an astonishing achievement. Within another year he had achieved something greater still, for he found that golf so chafed and exasperated him that he gave it up and contented himself with purely domestic archery and croquet. Once or twice afterward at long intervals he played a game of golf and came to no hurt, but he resolutely refused ever to let the dreadful game get hold of him again.

Against such a story as this there are no doubt thousands of others to be set. Great men of affairs are constantly telling the newspapers that they find in golf the perfect relaxation, because while they are at it they think only of the game. In that case, presumably golf is much better for them than the taking of a walk, because on a walk all the troubles of the world would still be running through their heads like a millrace. Presumably also they do not take their golf too solemnly, so that no ghosts of peccant elbows haunt them at night or distract them from their serious labors. They really do what so many of us pretend we do, and play the game "for fun." *O fortunatos nimium!*

Apart from the question of mental anguish, golf is at once a very tiring and a very untiring game. It is untiring in the sense that we walk a number of miles that we would not always face without a club in our hands, that we take in addition a good deal of exercise in the matter of hitting and yet are tolerably fresh at the end of it. It is tiring, as it seems to me, in the sense that it goes rather too slowly. In hot weather, at any rate, we undergo a process of slow grilling which is, or at least seems, more prostrating than violent exertion at, let us say, lawn tennis.

American readers who habitually play in hot weather may not agree, but we in England are very limp golfers as soon as the sun really begins to blaze: we are apt to grow scandalously lazy on the gorgeous days, if we ever get them, of June and July and August, and postpone our rounds till the cool of the evening after tea. We have put away our ancient prejudices against coatlessness and play as lightly clad as need be, but we are still rather frightened of the sunshine. Some of us, at any rate, almost prefer mittens and frost to shirtsleeves and apoplexy.

Despite what the statisticians may say, I have only known personally one golfer who died of apoplexy. He was a fat, cheerful, hearty old fellow—an admirable subject—whom a party of us met ages ago at a tournament in Wales. To one of us he confided that he did not think much of the course, which was flat and insipid; on his course, where he had been bred, there were sandhills so towering and noble that he always took a tee "as high as this," and he indicated the generous glass of whiskey and soda at his elbow.

The rest did not believe this story, so we who had heard it indignantly undertook to make the old gentleman say it again. We duly conspired, we ordered him a handsome drink, we brought the conversation round to sandhills, and he did say it again, correct to the letter. He must have been a little surprised at the torrent of laughter, but he was radiant and jovial and suspected nothing. I never saw him again, but I remembered his name, and years afterward I read in the newspaper that on that very course of mighty hills he had fallen down dead "from excitement at a golf match"—a happy ending of which, after all, no one need be afraid.

IV

For my part, if such a fate ever overtakes me, I fancy it will not be in some terrific moment in a match, but rather after exhausting hours of practicing. Practice is not only very good for our golf; it is a joy in itself, but it can be extraordinarily tiring. Let anybody try to bang balls into a net for twenty minutes and he will find his hands in blisters and his mind and body in a state of collapse. That is altogether too exhausting; moreover, it always seems to me that one should practice with no human eye to overlook one's antics and experiments; even the presence of a caddie to retrieve the balls is for me the rose leaf that keeps the princess from her sleep. But in that case one must walk after the ball between shots and must search for them in the rough, and looking for golf balls is surely one of the most infuriating and prostrating of all human activities.

I have one friend—nearer seventy than sixty, as I suppose—who has a pious and peculiar way of spending his Sunday afternoons. He sets out on his lawn fifty "peg" tees in a row and perches upon them fifty balls. Then he stations in the field beyond the railing four small boys from the village as retrievers, and sets to work at the beginning of the row of balls and goes right through them with the rapidity of a machine gun. He wastes no time in waggling, but just lashes the ball away, occasionally altering his stance and direction according as he thinks that one small boy is overworked and another is being starved. When all the balls have been hit, they are brought back by the largest boy, who acts as sergeant major, and they are teed and hit off again. Sometimes he will even go down the line a third time before the boys are recalled and brought into the house, where on four plates in the hall there are set out for them four sixpences and four slices of plum cake. I am not sure whether this is good for his golf; it appears to be good for him, but then he is a remarkable person in other walks of life. For myself I had to stop and rest, enduring his contempt as best I might, after hitting a paltry twenty-five or so.

If I had the temerity to advise the middle-aged and elderly golfer, I would suggest to him that he make a habit of playing foursomes, and by that I mean foursomes proper, with but two balls a side and alternate strokes. I know that the American golfer is possessed of so fiendish an energy that he seldom if ever plays this game. Yet I venture to think that, as he grows older, he would find it good for both soul and body and a delightful game into the bargain, which has in it more of the spirit of partnership than any other. On purely physical grounds it is obviously less tiring than the single or the four-ball match. There are but half as many shots to play, and then think of the short cuts and the saving of the legs! There are those who carry this leg-saving to a fine art and declare that they propose to drive at the odd holes or the even, according as there are fewer long walks to the teeing grounds.

Let my elderly reader by all means hit his own ball in the morning, but for the second round, after lunch or after tea, do let him try a foursome. If he will do that I will undertake not to resent his calling it a "Scotch foursome." I am sure he will enjoy it as much as did a charming old Scotsman who once wrote a manual on golf. He was a foursome player and rejoiced in his match with three "oldsters," as he called them, "the quotidian round enlivened with varied conversation." Listen to his parting benediction: "Then gentle sprite! Whose Empire is the dark green links, and whose votaries wield the bending club and speed the whizzing ball, art as dear to us now in the sere and yellow leaf as when first we flew to share in thy health-inspiring rites with the flush and ardor of boyhood."

I am sure he lived to a hundred, and no gloomy statisticians could make any capital out of him.

Bad Manners in Golf

The Atlantic Monthly
JULY 1938

I

"When a man looks to see if he has laid me a stymie I consider it an impertinence." These formidable words fell from an old friend of mine, a good golfer in his day, a man of great kindliness but some austerity of manner, one who loves the rigor of the game and was brought up in its strictest tradition. They may at first sight seem almost too stern for the offense in question, and yet I am not sure.

It is irritating enough to have a man lay us a stymie, but it is infinitely more irritating to have him step in front of us as we are brooding over it, take a quick glance at the line, and then leave us to it, with an ill-concealed smirk of triumph upon his face. If in addition he should so far forget himself as to say, "It's not a stymie—there's room to get past on the left," then there is nothing malicious or revengeful that we are not disposed to do to him.

Proof of those words having been uttered would make it impossible for any jury of golfers to bring in a verdict of murder, and I doubt if they would even agree on one of manslaughter.

Yet the object of our hatred has probably acted in perfect innocence. He has not done it to annoy. He has only forgotten his golfing manners for one fatal moment, or even, perhaps, has never learned them.

The golfer is admittedly a hypersensitive creature, and many things goad him to fury which would seem harmless to the outer and uninitiated world. A very famous English judge once said to a young barrister, "I am afraid I did many improper things when I was at the bar. In fact, I know I did"; and few of us who have played golf for any length of time can altogether acquit ourselves of breaches of the unwritten code of golfing manners. We have all said things to our opponents which would have incensed us if they had been said to us. The words have passed the barrier of our lips before we were aware of them. We have been very sorry afterwards, and then perhaps we have done the same thing again when the same set of circumstances have presented themselves.

I am not thinking so much of the offenses which are particularly mentioned in the etiquette of golf—the talking or moving on the stroke, the standing, as it is called, "behind the player's eye," and so on. Of these we have all been at times guilty through sheer inadvertence. I am thinking rather of the things that we say to our opponent, and which would so much better have been left unsaid.

One friend of mine regards as constituting almost the blackest crime in the whole golfing calendar the six simple words, "You let me off that time." It is so hard not to say them sometimes; they represent such a natural outburst of relief. The other fellow has two putts for the hole, his ball is but a few yards from it, and hope has died within our breast. He does not lay the first one quite dead, and our drooping spirits revive a little; it seems just possible that the impossible may happen. He misses the short one, and our pent-up feelings find expression in the forbidden words. It is eminently natural, and even the greatest and most benevolent of men have fallen into a like error.

"A double, sir," said Mr. Pickwick, after winning a second rubber against the fat gentleman, whose partner had committed various crimes. "A double, sir," and we cannot doubt that he smiled as he said it. "Quite aware of the fact, sir," replied the fat gentleman sharply. I suppose he forgot his manners, too, but we can sympathize with his remark.

And now that we have approached the subject of short putts, what a rich cause of offense they are! What a chance do they give for bad manners! The other day I was watching a foursome tournament of some importance, and there came beneath the eyrie where I was perched a match between two prominent amateurs on the one side, a world-famous professional and an amateur on the other. What had happened before, I do not know, but here, on the twelfth green, they were holing out putts of six inches and less with a grimness of demeanor which baffles all description. I never learned exactly how it had started or "who began it," but there was no doubt that all four were now playing in a state of cold anger.

Of course we may say, and we constantly do say, that no one has any right to resent being asked to hole a short putt, but the fact remains that there are putts so short that it is vexatious to be asked to hole them, and when one party begins, the other determines to play him at his own game. This is a fundamental weakness in golfing human nature; nor, as far as I can see, will any legislation eradicate it. The law cannot insist on *A* holing his putt when *B* has picked up or kicked his ball away and given up the hole.

Of course, as I say, we ought not to get cross, and I do not think we do unless there is something indefinably defiant and offensive in our opponent's manner as he stands watching us hole out the six-inch putt. If he stands still and in silence, we have no real cause for complaint, but suppose he waits a perceptible moment of time, looks at our putt, and then says, "I think I'll see that one in"—only blanks and asterisks can express our just indignation. The words are permissible only in the most lighthearted of palpably postprandial games, and then they are better not spoken. In the case of any opponent who does it more than once, we are justified in having a permanent engagement should he invite us to play again.

The converse crime is that of the man who makes as if to knock the ball in one-handed and says, "Will that do?"

"Halved hole," says the foe, but "No"—I say, "No";
"Putt it out, mine enemy!
"You're dead, but not buried." He's shaky and flurried;
O! a terrible miss makes he.

A terrible miss he often does make if we have the moral courage to say "No," and we are entirely justified in saying it. Only the question is whether life is long enough for these little unpleasantnesses. We had better either make the best of it as "pretty Fanny's way," or not play with that particular adversary again.

There are variants of this last formula, such as "Do you think I can miss that one?"—to which the suggested answer is "I don't know, but I hope so." These are things seldom said in a match that can be called serious, but there is a thing occasionally said in a very serious match that is deserving of severe punishment—namely, "I should like to give you that one, but I am afraid I ought not to." I once heard that said at the last hole of a championship match, and the man who was bidden to hole the short putt missed it and the man who had said the dreadful words won, by the unjust workings of Providence, at the twentieth or twenty-first hole. The obvious inference is that it was said on purpose, but I am not dealing with deliberate "propaganda," and in this particular instance I believe him who said it to be as honest a man and a golfer as need be. It was simply one of those unutterably foolish things that we may say in moments of excitement, and for which, let us hope, we suffer remorse in the watches of the night.

I remember once when I was playing in the semifinal of a foursome tournament. My partner and I were dormy one, and he laid the third shot within the comfortable distance of a foot from the hole. The enemy had a putt of some six feet for his four, missed it, and then said to me in a tone of concentrated venom, "I meant to make you hole that one." It was rather futile and not very gracious, but how easy it is to be magnanimous in the moment of victory! Indeed, I am afraid that my satisfaction was maliciously enhanced. Besides, I am sadly conscious of having spent my golfing life in a glass house and am very wary as to throwing stones.

II

There is one clear moral to be drawn in this matter—namely, that the less we say the better. I was once playing with a great and wise golfer, now dead, when I apologized to him for some childish outcry over my ill fortune. He himself had suffered in his youth from a fiery temper and was very kind and sympathetic. He said that he had found it a good rule to try to make no comment either on his own shots or on his adversary's. It is an admirable rule, and, though I have wholly failed to follow it, I have never forgotten. Of course it has exceptions, and an occasional "Hard luck" is surely not only permissible but laudable; but it should be reserved for a calamity to the enemy which really does come under that head—a fine shot trapped by inches or an unfortunate kick.

The adversary will not, unless he be a very simple fellow, believe that we are anything but glad at his misfortune, but he will be a little grateful to us nevertheless. There is some value even in the obviously base coin of an unfelt sympathy. He knows that we cannot be sorry, but, unless he is a very fierce realist, he likes us to pretend that we are. However, we must not pretend too much or too often. Can anything be more infuriating to a golfer, who is putting badly, than his foursome partner's parrot cry of "Well tried"?

One golfer of my acquaintance complained bitterly the other day of an opponent that "the brute did not say 'Sorry' when he laid me a stymie." Doubtless he was both illogical and exacting, for we are not, save in very exceptional circumstances, sorry when we lay the enemy a stymie and, moreover, we have not done it on purpose. Yet it has become a regular if empty form of politeness to say "Sorry," and we say it not altogether for his sake but also for our own. We feel sometimes, and quite unreasonably, a little mean when we have laid a stymie, and salve our consciences by this fiction of apology. It is a foolish custom, and yet it is probably both wise and civil to yield to it now and again.

Too much butter, like too much sympathy, is to be deprecated, but occasional praise of the opponent's shots is only decent. Yet we must beware of asking him in humble admiration how he does it, for if once he begins to think on that subject he may be able to do it no more. The illustrious Mr. John Ball had (and has, when he plays—all too seldom) a curious and characteristic grip of the right hand. Between the rounds of a championship a worshiper, in the innocence of his heart, approached him and asked if he would demonstrate this grip. "No, no," said the great man, "I've been had that way before—I'll show you after the round." There never was a less self-conscious golfer than Mr. Ball, and if he was afraid of being made to think, how much more easily will others fall into the fatal pit of thought!

Sir Walter Simpson (Robert Louis Stevenson's companion of the *Cigarette* and the *Arethusa*) has given a pleasantly immoral description of the baiting of such a trap. "He [the opponent]," he says, "is thoroughly stretched, supple, confident, and consequently out comes one of those extra-long shots. If you and he both leave him alone, he takes no heed, and other extra ones follow at intervals. But, if you are a cunning player, flatter him about his shot, point out that his next is as long, and, if he takes the bait, the third may be long too; but your experienced eye will detect that he has staggered and overexerted himself to produce it. It is a question of your tact against his sense, whether you get him broken down altogether, or whether he returns to hitting steadily and without prejudice."

Here, however, I am verging on the realms of propaganda. In that debatable—or perhaps it is not debatable—land there have dwelt great men. That mightiest of all cricketers and most delightful and kindly of men, Dr. W. G. Grace, had his own standards of conduct. A friend once told me how he and W. G. were playing in a foursome match and one of the opponents began with several very long, straight shots. "George," said W. G. confidentially, "this man's driving too well for me. You watch me talk him off his game." "Oh, I hope that may not be necessary, Doctor," said George, with some natural compunction, but he saw his partner put his arm round his enemy's neck and tell him a series of stories with great bursts of Homeric laughter. The enemy, flattered by these friendly attentions, was reduced to a state of giggling futility, and the spiky gorse bushes became his grave.

However far we may get away from it—and I am conscious of meandering—we always seem to come back to the point that the less we say, the less harm we can do. Of a set and serious combat, Mr. Horace Hutchinson wrote that the most we can expect of an opponent is that he "should play in silence and as badly as possible." Yet fortunately all games—indeed, most games—are not of such deadly character; there is a gradation in these matters, and good championship manners are something too grim and formal for the friendly foursome of every day. When all is said, golfing manners are good or bad much as are manners in general. We can all think of the perfect partner or adversary, the cheerful, unselfish fellow who wants to enjoy his game and wants to make everyone else enjoy it too, who wins without exultation or patronage, who loses without rancor. Some nameless quality shines out of him, so that it is a positive pleasure to see him play, whether in a big match or a small.

I can still vividly remember a match in the Amateur Championship at Deal in 1923, now fifteen long years ago. Two of the American Walker Cup team, Mr. Francis Ouimet and that excellent golfer from California, Mr. Jack Neville, had the misfortune to draw one another and so cut one another's throats in an early round; it may even have been the first. It was a good and close fight, which Mr. Ouimet won, but the point was not in victory or defeat;

it was in the manner of the playing. The two did not talk much to one another; each played as hard and as keenly as he could, and yet that match radiated a delightful and friendly atmosphere. Nor was it I alone who was thus impressed. Everybody who had watched said afterwards what a joy that match had been to see. There was something indefinably pleasant in the spirit of the combat. Here was an example of how two gentlemen should play golf, for others, however faintly pursuing, to follow.

It is not given to many to play the game in that way. It would be easy to name others who have, as regards all outward forms, perfectly good golfing manners, and yet exude an atmosphere of hostility. They are by nature and instinct killers; that is the way they are made. Their manners can only be good in a negative sense, and no one has the right to ask any more of them; but they cannot give the same pleasure in the watching. Perhaps I may be allowed to quote an admirable description of a typical killer in another game, Spofforth, the Australian bowler, once known far and wide as "the Demon." The writer, Mr. Neville Cardus, is looking at some pictures of the famous bowler: "They were taken long after his days in the sun were over, yet there lurks in the pictures of the man a sense of sinister power. The bowling action is spring-heel-Jackish; the form of him lithe in an inimical way; his face set in hard, predatory lines. He was the Australian of Australians, a stark man that let in with him the coldest blast of antagonism that ever blew over a June field."

There are such players in all games, and we can appreciate their qualities; nor is there anything to be said against them, save only that they do not add to the enjoyment of the game; indeed, "game" becomes in their presence an inadequate and inappropriate word. Killing can be done in different ways. There was no greater slaughterer of his enemies than Mr. Bobby Jones at his zenith, but there was nothing unpleasant in seeing that carnage. He never appeared for an instant to be reveling in blood; corpses must needs bestrew his victorious path, but he did not trample on them. He was the highwayman who was forced to take his victim's purse, but took it with the courtliest of bows. In short, he was the proof that it is possible to have the competitive instinct developed in the highest degree and yet remain the perfect opponent.

III

Manners and customs are not, of course, one and the same thing, but different customs can beget different codes of manners in different countries. For instance, in England we usually play four-ball matches on the principle that the partner who is palpably out of the hunt at a particular hole should not continue to the bitter end. He is regarded as something of a selfish nuisance if he does so. In America, on the other hand, the players have generally, in my experience, some wagers as to their individual scores for the round, very likely with others who are playing in a separate match. Therefore they very properly hole out, although they cannot affect the result of that particular hole. I recall playing a four-ball match on a course near Chicago in the year ever memorable as Mr. Ouimet's, 1913. At the first hole my partner was near the hole in two; I, doubtless deservedly, was in a bunker by the green in three, and picked up my ball accordingly. Thereupon my kind host assured the few onlookers that such was the English custom, lest they think that I had abandoned the struggle in a tantrum. That mild little story is an illustration of the fact that what are good manners in one country may be odd ones in another, and vice versa. It is simply a question of not impeding the players behind, and depends on what is called the pace of the green.

I think that, owing to the universal popularity of four-ball matches and the general holing-out, the average pace of the green is slower in America than in England, and yet, in my experience, the average American golfer plays more quickly than his English brother. Certainly those who have come over with Walker Cup teams set us a good example in this regard. In England we have been suffering from an epidemic of drearily slow golf among those who ought to know better. I hope that it has now passed its peak, but there is still much room for improvement, still too much dawdling and pottering, still far too many stomachic prostrations—if I may so term then—in the studying of putts.

A few years ago there was a competitor in championships who, owing to a nervous affliction, could not bring himself to hit the ball until after some seventy waggles. In one tournament he drove two successive victims to the verge of madness. The third, being forewarned and extremely strong-minded into the bargain, took out a deck chair and a newspaper and won his match. Who shall decide as to the exact quality of his manners? Desperate diseases require desperate remedies.

His was a case for some sympathy, but there are others who deserve none. Dear me, into what a malignancy of hatred we can be worked up as regards those whom we know only as "the people in front"; and yet it is very often not their fault, for they have other people in front of them, and so on *ad infinitum*. At St. Andrews, when the full tide of summer golf is surging, we always take three hours to get round, and the best are as the worst, for they all travel at the pace of the green. Yet I have personally been driven to the point of frenzy there by a bishop in front of me, whereas, had he been a golfer, I should have remained placid. I am afraid we are snobs in this matter and do not mind being kept back by a champion.

Yet snobbishness is a venial sin as compared with some of those of which we are guilty, at any rate in desire, in this matter of keeping back. It is worse even than that of short putts in producing bad temper and bad manners. There are golfers who will go to almost any trouble in order to avoid what they deem the indignity of being passed; they will run, they will pick up the ball, they will ruin their own pleasure in order, as it appears, to ruin that of somebody else. They will lose a ball, reluctantly signal to their pursuers to come through, and then, on finding the ball, dash forward again. That is unspeakable; once the signal has been given, it must be abided by, even though those who are coming through make the most deplorable bungle, as players anxious to pass invariably do.

It is often a sore temptation to drive into those confounded people in front, but, whatever the provocation, we put ourselves in the wrong if we do. In my boyhood there was more latitude, and so far more squabbles, sometimes even pitched battles, on this point than there are today. The "etiquette" of golf now lays it down that "no player should play until the party in front are out of range." The elder tradition was that those behind were entitled to play when those in front had played their seconds; and if it was acted on literally, as it sometimes was, the lives of short-driving old gentlemen were in the gravest peril. Occasionally the party driven into would declare open war and drive the invading ball into the sea. Alternatively, if hidden by a sandhill, they would adopt guerrilla methods and stamp it into the ground. Either plan was likely to lead to an explosion, and I think golfers were altogether more explosive fifty years ago.

Where is that race of peppery colonels, now only to be found in works of fiction, before whom caddies fled aghast, who threw their clubs into the waves and then were nearly drowned in rescuing them? If they throw their clubs now, is it into the Styx? Where is that most delightful of Scottish golfers who said to his putter, "Don't you presume on my good nature any longer," and battered it to death against the stone wall at Prestwick? The wall has gone, and he with it. It is some years now since I saw a shaft cracked across an infuriated knee; I have not even cracked one myself. There is for everything a time and a season. Those colonels are dust and their niblicks rust,

Their souls are with the saints, we trust.

Something of picturesqueness has doubtless departed with such barbarous customs, and doubtless also it is all for the best. As the golfer said, in response to his wife's consolations, "I know it's only a d____d game!"

The Ailing Golfer

The Atlantic Monthly
MAY 1939

I

Never was the golf doctor so busy or so prosperous as he is at present. His consulting room is full to bursting, and prospective patients must needs put their names down weeks in advance for a treatment. A gathering of golfers is not unlike the daily meeting at the pump room at some famous spa, where the victims compare notes as to their ailments and the various baths, cures, and diets which their respective doctors have prescribed for them. There is scarcely a golfer who is not "under" some specialist, so that the few who are not conscious of more than normal frailty, and play the game as best they can with reasonable success, are quite out of it. Hitherto rather proud of their ignorant robustness, they now feel crude and ashamed in that they do not, in the old phrase, enjoy bad health.

To drop the language of metaphor, nearly everybody today has golf lessons—lots of lessons—and this is not only true of the struggling and middle-aged, the inglorious proletariat of golf. The good young golfers who have played almost from their cradles and used enviously to be spoken of as "natural" golfers are the most assiduous of all the learners. It is my possibly old-fashioned view that they are included to overdo it. However, these young gentlemen are relatively few compared with the great body of players who are the backbone of the game. Let us leave them alone for a while and turn to this rank and file who are not young, who have not a great deal of time for golf, and whose humble ambition, if they have one, is to break a hundred.

Doubtless all of these would be the better for a little doctoring in their golfing infancy. At the same time, the golfing beginner ought at the outset of his career to have one important piece of knowledge which nobody can give him: he ought to know himself, or have at least a notion how golf will take him. Of course he will say that he is going to play for fun, but what is the precise kind of fun that he is going to get out of the game?

There are some who will simply enjoy the fresh air and the friendliness, who will be perfectly content with the sensation of an occasional and accidental clean hit, an occasional long putt holed, and will have no ambition to play any better. It may be that they are the happy warriors, and it would be futile to urge on them any system of teaching; by all means let them thump and be happy. But theirs is the exceptional case. The average beginner may be pretty sure that golf will arouse some ambition in his breast, if it is only that of hitting the ball as far as possible. He will be happier if he attains a certain modest standard of skill, and his best way of doing so is to begin with lessons. Our beginner may say in effect, "I don't know whether this game is going to get me or not. Let me make a start and see. If I find myself growing keen, then I will have lessons." The answer is that by this time a good deal of harm may have been done which might have been prevented and may never by wholly undone. Unless he is something of a natural genius, he will very likely have acquired tricks that will stick to him like burrs through all his golfing life.

Take one point, which probably seems to the beginner the simplest of all—that of holding the club. He thinks that he cannot go wrong if he holds it in a way that he calls natural and comfortable, but alas! he can. Experience shows that what may be a capital way of holding a battle-axe is not adapted to a golf club, and, however natural and comfortable he may feel, he may be pretty sure that he looks neither; in fact, he often looks distorted to the point of agony, and his hands are obviously warring against one another. If he had allowed a teacher to make him feel unnatural and uncomfortable for a little while those sensations would soon have vanished, but by the time his bad habits have grown even a few months old they will take ever so much more exorcising. And since, as I said, he is sure to want to hit far, let us bribe him into virtue by telling him this, that the grip which feels to him at first the most powerful and least cramped will probably turn out in the end prohibitive of all real power or freedom.

Again, it is worth pointing out to him the obvious truth that he cannot see himself. The malleable small boy can learn by imitation; the grown-up, as a rule, cannot. He may have visions of himself resembling the lissome professional. Yet, sad to say, to any impartial observer he resembles an ancient cab horse in the throes of paralysis. Having been told something of the virtues of "slow back," he may think he is taking the club back slowly, and so in a sense he is; but it is with the slowness of a man, in Sir Walter Simpson's happy phrase, trying to grab a fly on his ear. There never was such a game for self-deception. We are always fancying ourselves as doing one thing when we are doing almost the exact opposite. A teacher can at least see us with clear eyes and, if he has some gift of mimicry, can hold up the mirror to our contortions. This last service, however, will not be required by the beginner in his earliest stages, because he has not yet acquired contortions. He is apt to be stiff, wooden, and unhandy, but he has not got tricks; he has nothing to "get out of," and that is why these early lessons may be so valuable. They may save him from so much.

The average golfer does not begin in this virtuous manner. He thumps his way along for a while by the light of nature, and then is suddenly stricken with the desire for improvement. He will have got tricks and must suffer the more in trying to get rid of them, but in the end he will be the happier man for some teaching. After all, it must be a mistake to set out to do something in a way in which it cannot possibly be done; yet that is one which many people commit, especially in the short game. There are some things about golf that seem unnatural, and one is the fact that the way to get a ball up with an iron is to hit it down. A walk round any crowded golf course will show us many victims of the scooping theory of iron play, and they may scoop forever if somebody does not make them experience in their own persons the delicious and surprising sensations of the stroke properly played.

This is but one elementary example of what a lesson can do. It shows the pupil that his teacher is not a magician but only a man doing a thing in the best possible way, and that something at least of this way can be acquired. There are many golfers who have never hit a ball truly in their lives. The moment in which they first do so can afford an ecstasy akin to that of first wobbling unaided on a bicycle. They discover with the blinding shock of a revelation that the thing can be done.

I suppose that an enormous percentage of all the golf lessons given in the world are lessons in driving. That is what the learner wants to learn, and insists on being taught. It may well be that the teacher would prefer him to begin with some lofted iron, and learn the fundamental stroke of the game (R. A. Whitcombe calls it the "bread-and-butter shot") with that and so work up to the driver; but the teacher has his own bread and butter to earn and will not press his views unduly. So it is driving, driving all the way, and the learner is right in so far as there is no more exhilarating fun in the game; but he is dreadfully wrong if he thinks that there is nothing to learn about the iron.

Some men who are natural game players with good eyes and good wrists become more than respectable drivers and never understand their irons. I used something to play golf with the most famous of all cricketers, Dr. W. G. Grace. He had not begun till he was quite old, but, having a supreme genius for hitting a ball, he became an extremely straight and steady driver, as far as I know without any kind of lesson; but he never could manage an iron shot, and except for those who learn in boyhood by imitation I believe it is much the harder shot of the two.

As to niblick play, did anyone ever see a professional imparting its secrets in a lesson? Well, I did once. At a course in Wales many years ago we had no professional, but the foreman in a neighboring timber yard, himself a player of very moderate skill, would sometimes take a beginner in hand. We used to observe with joy his methods, which never varied. He put his pupil with a club and several balls in a certain sandy, stony ditch and stood over him while he tried to get out. In that case the pupil had no option. Those who have might do much worse than have a lesson with the niblick, but they think—heaven knows how erroneously—that in bunkers all men are equal.

II

So far I have been talking of golf teaching in its simpler forms for rather elementary players. Obviously, save for the happy thumpers, it is a good thing in moderation, especially as the professional of today has made a serious study of his business. Now I come to the players of a higher class, who are apt to have lessons to what I deem an immoderate extent. That some of them benefit I do not deny, but let us see what are the disadvantages. For one thing, the pupil who surrenders too entirely to his teacher is apt to lose self-reliance and the power of looking after himself. We all know that a teacher can have a magical effect upon us, as long as we are under his eye. He gives us confidence, and confidence is half the battle. It does not much matter for the moment what he tells us to do so long as we believe in him and consequently in his gospel. We slash away at the ball with perfect faith and so with perfect timing, and away it sails, sails all the more gloriously because we are probably not shooting at any precise mark.

There was once tried at Assizes a farmer charged with wounding a boy who had been robbing an orchard. His defense was that he had fired merely in order to frighten the boy. The judge began his summing up as follows: "Gentlemen of the jury, the prisoner says that he aimed at nothing. Unfortunately he missed it." At golf when we aim at nothing we generally hit it, in the sense that a drive, unhampered by any object save that of hitting, flies far and sure. So on the practice ground, with the professor's encouraging eye upon us, we perform prodigies and set out for the links next day full of hopes. Too often those hopes are delusive. We have no master to wish us well, we have an opponent to wish us ill, and we have the cramping limits of the fairway forever before us. We feel miserably alone.

Thus that utter faith in the master which is such a source of strength in his presence may be a weakness in his absence. The man who has no notion how to cure a golfing disease save by trying to remember what his master said—very likely about quite a different disease—can be a pitiful object. He is further to be pitied in that he misses some of the best fun that the game has to give. There must, I am sure, be many golfers who look back with the greatest pleasure to hours spent in solitary communion with a club and ball on some summer evening.

Personally I have a distaste for practice grounds. Give me the course itself, if only I can get it to myself. What greater ecstasy can there be than the making of a discovery in these lonely wanderings? How I have dashed after the ball in the failing light, "and in my heart some late lark singing"! How I have shouted "Eureka!" True, many of the discoveries made on these occasions turn out to be fallacious, but even so the delusion has been so pleasant that the subsequent disappointment is worthwhile. And just a few of them are genuine and abide. They can be recalled sometimes when they are badly needed.

It may well be that in many cases the solitary student could have taken a short cut to the knowledge thus acquired by consulting a professional; but I do not believe it is true of all cases, and there is a particular relish about something that we find out for ourselves, even as there is about the bread and cheese that we earn for ourselves. We get to know our own strength and still more our own weakness, and that knowledge, even if no more than a corollary to what we have been taught, will stand us in good stead. I do not agree with Sir Walter Simpson, who wrote, " 'Know thyself' may be good philosophy; it is bad golf."

There is another reason for distrusting overmuch teaching—namely, that, save in the case of people who are abnormally strong and gifted with little imagination, it takes away the dash and freshness and spirit without which the most severely "mechanized" golf will break down. I cannot help thinking that some otherwise excellent teachers work their pupils too hard.

Not long ago I watched for a few minutes a young lady of great promise who was hitting away scores of balls under the eye of a distinguished professional. He issued his commands in short, sharp tones, now to hit one with a slice, now with a hook, now high, now low, and in the intervals of these refinements he bade her "sock" them as hard as she could. She obeyed with skill, with docility, with apparent enthusiasm; it was rather like watching a performing animal at a circus. She had been at it for an hour or so; she was going on till luncheon; she was going to start again afterwards, and she had been doing this sort of thing for weeks. The lady is very young and very strong, and no doubt her professor has brought her on rapidly. So far, perhaps, it has been all to the good; but, putting on one side the question whether this is a reasonable manner in which to play a game, I cannot believe it will be to the good unless she soon calls a halt. I have seen other young players go the same way, and what they have gained on the swings they have lost, and more than lost, on the roundabouts. They may have become more mechanically accurate, at any rate in practice, but, they have lost something essential of fire and spontaneity, and their "temperament," once their strong point, has become their weak one. To have a swing well "grooved" is important—nay, essential—but it must not be grooved at the expense of mental weariness. Golf can never be entirely mechanized.

Too much golf "doctoring" can be more than usually perilous if it is in the hands of several physicians, either simultaneously or even successively. "Who is So-and-so under now?" is a question I have often heard, and the answer is that So-and-so began with *A*, went on to *B*, and now swears exclusively by the ministrations of *C*. I am not prepared to say that the last state of So-and-so is always worse than the first, but it very often is. The professor may all inculcate more or less the same doctrine, and golf teaching has become, so to speak, more stabilized since photography has shown the masters what they really do as opposed to what they think they do; but if they mean the same thing they assuredly say it in very different ways, and the pupil who goes from one to another is likely to grow sadly puzzled and muddled. He may think that, having sucked all the good that he can out of *A*, he can gain a further benefit from the fresh mind of *B*, a little final polish of the iron shots from *C*, and so on, but that is not the way in which it always works out in practice. He is more likely to resemble one of those hypochondriacal persons who are forever dosing themselves with patent medicines in a general and speculative manner.

And, apropos of medicine, the ordinarily sane person does not take medicine when he is in good health. He knows that he cannot be better than well and reserves the doctor for when he is ill. Too many golfers do not proceed on this principle, because they think that they can be better than well. So, well or ill, they go regularly to some golfing doctor or other, and he, poor fellow, does not like to turn money from his door. Besides, even the best and sanest of golfing doctors has some pet little theory of his own which he likes to try on his patients. There was a pleasant old jingle about the doctors who attended King George III, which has a golfing application.

Three doctors see our sovereign daily,
Willis, Heberden and Bailey.
All three wise and learned men,
Bailey, Willis, Heberden.
One of them quite sure to kill is,
Bailey, Heberden and Willis.

III

It must be remembered, of course, that golfing doctors and golfing patients both differ widely in kind. There is, for instance, the ordinary club professional, who is a good golfer but in no way famous either as a player or as a teacher. He corresponds roughly to the general practitioner, the workaday family golfer. Apart from those in the elementary stages who are taking a regular course, most of his patients come to him because they have been attacked by one of the mild and inevitable golfing ailments which correspond to a cold in the head or a pain in the stomach. Like the family doctor, he prescribes, as a rule, some well-known nostrum. It may be in the comparatively violent nature of a pill if he sees something in the system of play needing radical alteration. It may be, if he can diagnose no very obvious complaint, merely a dose of soothing syrup, such as the advice not to hit so hard. This will often be highly effective if backed up by a good bedside manner. In either case the patient pays his fee and goes back to ordinary life, nor does he return to the doctor until the next time he feels ill.

On a higher plane is the specialist, who has made a reputation both as player and as teacher and so attracts pupils from other clubs and courses than his own. Between these specialists there are considerable differences. Some try primarily to make the best of the patients' golfing constitution as it is. They have an almost uncannily observant eye for some small cause of mischief such as a foot a few inches too far forward or back. They put these little things right rather than attempt any radical change of system. Yet by insinuating small reforms—a little widening of the swing's arc, a little freer turn of the body and so on—they can often do remarkable things. There are others who have more trenchant views and are not so much interested in the mere patching up of their patients. They prefer to begin again at the beginning, and so their course of treatment is longer and more severe.

At the present moment in this country there is probably no teacher who has so many pupils from afar off as Henry Cotton, and certainly none who has probed more deeply into the mysteries of the golfing swing or tried out so many methods in his own person. He is an excellent and stimulating teacher, but chiefly, I think, for pupils who come to him, not for a temporary alleviation of a passing fault, but because they are fired with a noble ambition for general improvement. They are ready to put away all preconceived notions and to absorb the master's views from the very beginning. Their treatment is rather in the nature of a cure at a spa; it takes time, and the patient may very likely feel worse before he is better, but if he is enthusiastic and hard-working he does often emerge in the end very decidedly better, even to the extent of a whole class in golfing society. A cure of this comprehensive kind is chiefly for those who are young and strong and already reasonably good players. To be sure, hope springs eternal, and many a golfer has improved when his years seemed to forbid it, but a middle-aged dog can seldom learn wholly new tricks.

Besides professional golf doctors with whom the patient is as a role tolerably safe, as long as he sticks to one at a time and does not overdo the cure, there are some teachers who may be called quacks. They are as a rule amateurs, in the sense that they have never played golf professionally, and have taken to the game late in life. They have generally found some one movement which they believe to be the key to all golfing greatness, and a very excellent movement it may be; but they are apt to ride their hobby too hard with a pathetic enthusiasm.

I recollect being peremptorily summoned to a newspaper office by one of these enthusiasts, who declared that he had discovered the secret of the golf swing and could not wait a moment for fear that somebody else should discover it too. He was a stout patriot and particularly frightened lest America should anticipate him. He swore me and my colleagues to secrecy by the most solemn oaths and then demonstrated his discovery to us by hitting little paper balls about in the rather confined space at his disposal. He wanted no material reward for his secret; his single-minded ambition was to benefit British golf, and he was terribly disappointed when we would not give a page to his revelation in the newspaper. I recall one of my colleagues saying soothingly to him, "You know, Mr. So-and-so, you can't discover the secret of the swing as you can the North Pole," but he was not to be comforted. I felt a heartless beast, but at any rate my conscience is clear on one point: I can never violate my oath, because I have clean forgotten what the secret was.

Golf in a High Wind

The Atlantic Monthly
OCTOBER 1954

I

"If a ball at rest be moved or the lie altered by any outside agency except wind"—so begins No. 27 of the Rules of Golf and goes on to lay down that the player shall replace his ball without paying any penalty. But there is no such leniency in the case of the unsleeping and inexorable enemy, wind. It makes a plaything of the ball and its antics must be endured with constancy. The golfer must learn to hold his own as best he can in this eternal battle: he must not allow the wind to be his master; he must try to make it his servant.

We in Britain incline to believe that our golf courses are more violently attacked by this old enemy than are those in America. This may be a little harmless vanity on our part, since an American friend complains to me of the westerly breezes of September and the "storm wind of the Equinox." However, a larger proportion of our courses are by the sea and that is where the wind blows fiercest. I have felt it blow reasonably hard, unless my memory fails, on the National Golf Links at Southampton and I have no doubt that it can blow at Kittansett and elsewhere. I claim no superiority for British seaside winds as such; I only say that they play a greater part in our golf. There was a time when we believed that having been brought up to fight this foe, our men would do better on a windy day. Before an international match some deluded Briton might in nautical fashion whistle for a wind. We have long learned better from humbling experience. The man with the best method, who hits the ball most truly, will do best in a wind. If ever we uttered such arrogant prayers before a Ryder or a Walker Cup match, we do so no more.

At the same time each one of us is, I think, proud of his native gales. He is disinclined to admit that it can ever blow quite so tempestuously on another man's course as it does on his. I am not prepared to say that it blows harder at Hoylake, that nursery of great golfers, the home of the Royal Liverpool Golf Club, than it does elsewhere, but I know that the men of Hoylake think it does. Let the innocent stranger go there and rashly expatiate on the gusty buffets he has received. "Wind!" his hospitable friend will exclaim. "We don't call this a wind at Hoylake—this is only a gentle breeze." Well, I will admit he has a right to be proud; it does blow there, and this is emphasized by the constant menace of out-of-bounds territory. An old friend of mine, member of a distinguished golfing family, used to boast that he had been out of bounds at seventeen out of the eighteen holes at Hoylake. I can confirm him that it is a conceivable if difficult achievement, for I once put so many balls out of bounds at a single hole there that I had to give up the battle from lack of ammunition.

It was the winds of Hoylake, moreover, that had a hand in educating the greatest amateur golfer we here have ever possessed—the now almost legendary John Ball. It was he who, having returned an incredibly low score in a gale of wind, remarked, with delightfully modest understatement, that he happened to be hitting a ball of the right height for the day. The other great Hoylake golfer, Harold Hilton, was a master of using the wind, now with a hook and now with a slice, in a way seldom seen today and perhaps indeed seldom needed with the modern ball, which can bore its way through the storm. I do not intend to pose as a praiser of the past, but no one who did not play with a gutty ball has any real notion of what the wind can do. That now semi-venerable personage has got to be old, since Mr. Haskell conferred on golf the doubtful benefit of his rubber-cover ball about the turn of the century; but he need not be yet in his dotage.

A friend of mine once gave to a patentee a testimonial in the words: "Your club has added fifty yards to my slice"; but fifty yards represented a comparatively small slice. When the wind really got under the tail of a sliced ball it could whirl it to the ends of the earth. On a certain course in Wales, an obscure schoolmaster not otherwise famous made himself immortal by slicing onto the railway line at eight of the first nine outward holes. Could a man do such deeds with the pampering rubber-core? Perish the thought. The ball could be and sometimes was blown back over the striker's head. At Westward Ho there is a black and Stygian ditch some forty or fifty yards from the first tee, and on a medal day of mighty wind only one man carried it with his tee shot. At least so it was said, but that wind may have risen with the years.

Such a wind as that with a gutty ball had rather to be circumvented than encountered in open fight. An old golfer long dead, Mr. J. R. Hutchison, a good player of the elder school, told me how he had once been playing Sir Walter Simpson, the friend of R. L. S., author of that admirable book *The Art of Golf*. It was a day of furious wind by the sea and Mr. Hutchison was stealthily progressing by half cleek shots which kept the ball close to the ground. Sir Walter, never a great golfer though full of theories on the subject, was exposing his rather elaborate swing to the full force of the gale with calamitous results. "Look at Mr. Hutchison," said his caddie. "He's no playing a proud game."

There are hurricanes, no doubt, that can reduce golf to a farce. Not so a good, stiff wind, which emphasizes all the greater virtues of a golfer's method, his power of standing firm on his feet, his mastery of balance and rhythm and control. Such a wind in a championship separates the wheat from the chaff, the sheep from the goats. It did so most surely in the days of the gutty, but it always provides a touchstone of quality. I remember J. H. Taylor telling me once how he and James Braid were sharing a room at a championship. Braid was first out of bed in the morning and, looking out of the window, announced a fine day. "Well, that's a blessing anyhow," said J. H. Braid strongly demurred; such a day would make golf easy for plenty of people "who are far better putters than you and me." Taylor was certainly altruistic in his praise of fine weather, for if ever there was a great player in bad weather, he was the man. To see him pull his cap down over his eyes and plant his feet like to rocks on the ground was to see the defiance of Providence carried almost to the point of blasphemy. He made no adroit allowances; his ball flew straight through the gale, as if making a hole in it. If the wind was reinforced by sheets of rain, so that he could pitch his mashie shots right up to the flag on the sodden greens, then he was supremely happy.

Another who reveled in the wind was Arnaud Massy, a splendid figure of a man sprung from fisher folk and bred up at Biarritz amid Atlantic storms. Asked on the eve of a championship for his taste in weather, he expressed the hope that it would blow hard enough to blow down every tree in Sandwich.

I have watched many of our championships, both open and amateur, won by American golfers, but I cannot recall any of them being played in a real gale. A good strong wind there often was—notably, if memory serves, on the last day of Snead's Championship at St. Andrews—but nothing in the nature of a storm. I am not suggesting that it would have made the least difference to the result if there had been. Gene Sarazen in particular I should reckon a player second to none in a high wind—of just the right shape, so firm and compact, four-square, fronting the elements with so cheerful a confidence.

II

Seaside winds afford a fine education for a golfer, perhaps in all but one regard: I fancy they sometimes destroy his courage on the green. To be forced to give the ball the most timid of little prods lest it run away downwind far past the hole on an ice-keen green cannot be the best way to learn putting. What is wanted is an essentially free stroke, and that can probably be best acquired in still weather on reasonably grassy greens. Having once gained smoothness, boldness, and freedom, the player will not lose it in more testing circumstances. I remember playing with that delightful man and fine golfer, the late George Rotan, on his first round of the National Golf Links. There was a breeze, the greens were keen, and he could for a little while make neither head nor tail of the putting. He was used to the greens of his native Texas, which are, I believe, inclined to be slow and grassy. But he was a good putter and after a round he quickly adjusted himself.

In all other respects the wind must be a good teacher unless, indeed, it is in alliance with a ferociously narrow course. If the young player is too frightened of his ball being blown into impenetrable bushes, his hitting may become cramped and short. "I don't like to see a young one too careful," I once heard John Ball say, and I am sure it was a wise saying.

The golfing winds are as distinct from one another as are winds in general. When one did Latin verses at school and was well acquainted with Eurus and Boreas, Zephyrus and Favonius, one might have applied their names to the winds of golf. Since classical names have now grown dim, I think of them rather under four main titles in plain English; there is the wind against, the wind behind, and, of side winds, the wind on your back and the wind on your face. Of the four, three are definitely hostile; the fourth, the wind behind, intends, I believe, to be friendly but too often overdoes his friendliness. He is a rollicking, boisterous fellow, who really does mean to do us a good turn by bowling our ball along for huge distances in front of him. Unfortunately he applies the same principle to our approach shots and helps them forward so vigorously that they end in horrid places beyond the green. On the green, too, he is tactless in his good nature. He does not in the least understand the terrors of a downwind putt on a slope. It is all the same to him; with the very best intentions he just blows us to perdition.

The fact is that he is rather stupid. The same thing is mercifully true of the wind against. He is a completely honest foe, with nothing in the least tricky or shifty about him; he just tries to stop us as hard as he can. If we can persuade ourselves not to hit too hard—not, in short, to play too proud a game—much of his enmity will be wasted. When it comes to approaching, he is a positive friend if we can only make up our minds to bang the ball right up to the hole. Moreover, he gives us one of the most delicious of golf's sensations, that of a ball struck perfectly clean and flying low into the wind's eye.

The two side winds are in every way far less pleasant characters. They are crafty and evilly disposed creatures and essentially bullies. If they see that a man is frightened of them they are ruthless. The poor slicer aims farther and farther to the left, and the wind on his back, realizing that he has a coward to deal with, blows his ball farther and farther to the right. But if the slicer takes his courage in both hands, makes no allowance, and even stands boldly for a hook, the bully wind will often surrender on the spot. Conversely, much the same is true of the wind on your face, but as more of us are slicers than hookers, so most of us fear him the less. He tempts rather than precipitates us to destruction. Driving with a hook is a flattering amusement, since the ball seems to run forever. Sooner or later, of course, will come one hook too long into the heart of a gorse bush—but it was fun while it lasted. I said these side winds were bullies; and they are also snobs. When they meet a really great player who can master them, they grovel before him and slavishly do his will.

Yet another of the wind's unattractive traits is its low cunning. It has a habit of hiding behind a hill, so that the player on the tee feels himself in a blessed calm. Scarcely has the ball left the club, however, when out rushes the wind from its hiding place and sweeps the ball far away.

The wind has other knavish tricks that it can play upon us, admittedly of a minor character. It can flap the mackintoshes of spectators, if we are so fortunate as to attract any, in a manner extremely disturbing to the concentration. It is no doubt a rather ridiculous confession, but I can well remember a certain nineteenth hole in a certain tournament, when I believe my second shot was flapped into a disastrous place by an innocent mackintosh. I can still hear the sound of it in my dreams. For that matter, the wind can flap our own trousers as we are dealing with a crucial putt. And then it has a habit of whining through the anatomy of a shooting stick, with what Robert Louis Stevenson would have called "an infinite melancholy piping." It would be as absurd to complain of it as of the lark pouring out its song above our head, but it can be on occasions strangely disconcerting.

Now and again the wind can implant in our breasts some flattering beliefs. I once played a whole week's golf on a frozen ground in a strong east wind. It was bitter work even though there was benedictine after lunch and divine apple jelly for tea when we had climbed up a steep hill homeward. But heavens! how beautifully far the ball did go with that wind behind it. As we came in to lunch, each one of us had his little boast of some landmark passed, some inaccessible bunker reached. Of course this was but a touching delusion on everybody else's part. Poor old fellow! He would never learn to drive an inch farther. But, for ourselves, surely we had discovered a little something, hard to explain but impossible to have imagined, which would make us longer drivers forevermore.

Now that I can play no more I love to lie snug in bed or hear the wind rumbling in the chimney on the eve of some great match. The sight of the flags standing out straight and straining at their sticks gives the course on a medal day morning a fine relentless air. I might not feel the full charm of it had I still to hear my name called aloud by the cold, passionless voice of the starter and go out to face the tempest. Today when it is pleasantly still and warm, I incline to say disparagingly, "Oh—anybody can do a good score on a day like this." Yes, circumstances do alter cases, but still, play or watch, walk or sit, I shall maintain that golf would be a poor game without our old enemy. A reasonable wind gives a spice to golfing life.

Let me quote what a very wise golfer, John L. Low, wrote of it. "We must regard the wind as a friend that may be treated as a nodding acquaintance. We must recognize its presence, but not make obsequious obeisance when we meet it on our journey. If a ball be freely hit the wind will affect it but slightly; it is when we try either to use it too freely or to counter it in anger that we make our worst play." Those are words to be taken to heart, at once brave and prudent.

"The only argument available with an East wind," said James Russell Lowell, "is to put on your overcoat." The stouthearted golfer will hardly confess to so cautious, almost cowardly a policy. Mittens perhaps and a woolly waistcoat, for no wise man disdains armor for the fight, but a genuine stand-up fight it will be. He will never capitulate; he will hit through the wind low, piercing shots that shall be blown neither to the right nor the left. And when he has carried the last cross bunker, all the all the trumpets shall sound for him on the other side.

VIII

Valedictory

Giving Up the Game

Every Idle Dream
1945

Sometimes man gives up the game and sometimes the game gives him up. Very often the desertion is mutual. However it happens it is a sad wrench and its sadness does not depend on the distinction to which the player has attained, but rather on his love for the game and all the fun he has got out of it. Fortunately there is, as a rule, a merciful gradation and few of us realize when we have played our last round. We may suspect and, as time goes on, feel almost sure, but we shut our eyes and always have a hope either that Nature will vouchsafe some miraculous restoration or even, failing a miracle, that, on some particular occasion, and with a particularly kind and forgiving partner, we may yet take the field. It is true that for the more illustrious who formally retire there does come a definite break, a last race, a last championship, a last innings in first-class company. The batsman as he walks back to the pavilion, cheered all the way whether he has made a duck or a century, gives a sorrowful little flick of the head to take one last lingering look back before the chapter is ended. But it is only one chapter, if the brightest, and he still hopes to play many more innings in less exacting cricket and perhaps with a lighter heart. The abhorred shears have not made too clean and ruthless a cut.

"Vell, gov'ner, ve must all come to it, one day or another," as Sam Weller said to his father, and the golfer ought to take a long time coming to it. He has perhaps less cause to complain than anyone else. One evening, a good long while ago now, I arrived at Aberdovey, walked into the well-known room to find the expected company of friends and asked cheerfully, "Who's going to play me tomorrow morning?" The answer came in a chilling chorus, "Oh, we none of us play golf." It came as a sudden and depressing shock, a *memento mori.* I ought to have felt, and I hope I did feel sorry for them, but there was, I am afraid, in my sorrow something of rejoicing in my own still comparatively unimpaired powers. There still seemed so many years of golf left, and in fact there were a good many, if not quite such an unending vista as I then saw. The golfer ought to have plenty of sympathy to spare for other people whose pastimes make greater demands, for his is, in one sense at any rate, worthy of that blessed reproach, "an old man's game." He is first of all sorry for the runner whose time is terribly short, very seldom more than the span of two Olympiads, and not always that. Then he is sorry for the oarsman. His fame may be enduring and his time on the bank long, with his blue blazer growing tighter and tighter and more and more gloriously faded. But *exceptis excipiendis* his active days are cruelly brief. The Latin tag may be freely translated, "Schoolmasters don't count." They are well known to go on forever, and this perennial quality of theirs is noteworthy in another pursuit in which the ordinary man's time is short, football. It is an historical fact that one Eton master used to play the Wall Game at the mature age of fifty-six. If some of his energies were employed in haranguing the bully rather than joining in its mysterious rites, still he did play and that at a game by no means deficient in a certain static vigor. All men cannot be schoolmasters, and for the rest of the world a thirtieth birthday is as the bell which announces the last lap. After that, at least in the higher walks of life, selectors shake their heads over them. The cricketer has a much longer life, though his place in the field grows ever nearer the wicket, and so has the player of tennis. The famous Barre went on to some fabulous age even though he must lean panting against the dedans exclaiming of the then youthful Heathcote, "Mon dieu, mon dieu, il est si jeune." And now Heathcote in his turn—but the subject lends itself too easily to sentimental Thackerayan moralizing. Let it be enough then that, compared with all these players of other games, the golfer comes nearest to attaining a practical immortality and has much to be thankful for accordingly.

Whatever the game, many give it up when the decline of their powers is still a slow and gentle movement. I once asked the late Stanley Jackson whether he played much cricket nowadays, and with that perfect candor and the quality of taking himself for granted which made one of his great charms, he replied that he did not; "the fact is I don't play so well as I used to and I don't like it." Then he added something like these words: "I play once a year at Harrow and I generally go in and make fifty or sixty runs and then when I go on to bowl they won't take me off because they know I shall be so stiff that I could never go on again." I can see the spot where he said it, on a golf course in Cheshire, and it struck me as so simple and engaging that the words there and then burned themselves into my memory and I can almost guarantee their accuracy.

Nobody can like it, when he finds himself not so good as he was, but some dislike it much more acutely than others. Presumably the ideal is to dislike it so little, or to like the game so much more, that even an eighteen handicap or a series of ducks and missed catches make "a sundown splendid and serene"; but that is a great deal to ask. A little allowance must be made for the vanity of poor frail human nature, and in golf at any rate I have observed that those who go on the longest have had, as a rule, no very high standard of achievement from which to fall. The octogenarian foursomes, of which we sometimes hear, are seldom composed of old internationals. It is not, I hope, unbearably sentimental to say that there is something sad in watching a once fine player beginning to slip. I remember a conversation with Harold Hilton at Hoylake, on the evening when the side to play for England against Scotland was being chosen. He remarked that in a year or two people would be saying, "Hilton—h'm—is he good enough?" It sounded in my worshipping ears a kind of blasphemy uttered by a deity against himself. Could such a time ever come? And yet it did, as it now appears, almost in a flash. But that very great golfer continued to play the game when the little jump on to the toes and the follow-through seemed the same as before; only the remorseless, realistic ball refused to go.

That is the braver course and surely the happier, but this "menace of the years" affects different people in different ways and sometimes in, to me at any rate, unexpected ways. Those whom I imagined going on forever make a sudden break, and those who, as it seemed, could hardly bear the descent, go philosophically topping and slicing down the hill. I can recall one whom I should have thought as nearly as might be untouched by vain regrets, and yet he gave up early and utterly. He never tired of looking on, with a club under his arm, but only the far distance, when he believed nobody by, could he be seen now and then to play a shot with it, nor, I think, would it have been tactful to admit that one had played the spy on his privacy. More enviable was another, a great player in his day and one of perennial keenness, who went on playing in a green old age, hardly realizing what had befallen him. He still experimented with clubs of vast weight, because some lusty young driver used them; still walked on and on expecting to find his ball, long after he had passed it. He must have been puzzled now and then, but I doubt if he ever clearly drew the painful deduction from the obvious facts. Dickens once wrote a story called *A Child's Dream of a Star*. I think that old friend was happily dreaming it till the day of his death.

There was one golfer whom in this regard I admired more than any other, and since I have nothing but praise to give, why should I not name him? This was the late Mr. Mure Fergusson. In his prime he had not suffered bad players very gladly, but when he was old and stiff and full of rheumatism, and had to receive many strokes from those to whom he had once given them, he went on his way round the links with a dour cheerfulness. He recounted with grim enjoyment how his small caddie had declared that he might yet become a player if he could learn not to drop his shoulder. He even adopted the mental attitude of the poor and lowly so far as to murmur at the unfairness of certain bunkers into which his best shots found their way. I could not help reflecting how tersely he would once have received such complaints, but I expressed the deepest sympathy and felt it.

It is sometimes said that every officer should serve some time in the ranks in order to know and understand what the private soldier is thinking. It might be similarly argued that the good golfer should graduate through the ranks of the long handicapped to learn the fiery but often unspoken indignations of the humble. As a rule he has begun too young for such knowledge and has forgotten the time when the bunkers seemed hopelessly far away. It was pathetic to find Mure of all men attaining to it in his old age.

For myself, if I may for a moment be wholly egotistical, I incline to think that the game gave me up in what seemed a hard way and yet may in reality have been a merciful one. I could still play not too outrageously ill when arthritis made so sudden and rapid an attack that the descent from two rounds to one, one round to nine holes and then to just a few practice shots was rapid too. Vanity had little to endure and no excuses were needed for that which was obvious. The practice shots can still be played now and then and give pleasure even though a rather painful one, and if vanity dies so hard that it prefers them in solitude, that is an innocent and forgivable weakness. Even as I write, I am looking forward to a few of them within sound of the sea.

And so "avay vith melincolly" and let me count the blessings of giving up. They are not to be despised and are reasonably free from the reproach of sour grapes. At least some of the fun, much of the companionship and all the friendliness remain. There is great pleasure in watching, though it must be owned that golf drives a harder bargain with the retired than does any other game. He cannot sit at his ease in the pavilion or on a stand, but must pursue the players over a broken and difficult country. He comes to watch more and more on inner lines of communication. He resigns himself to the knowledge that the holes at the far end of the course are not for him; he must be content with ghoulish hopes of an agonizing finish about the sixteenth and seventeenth greens. If he inclines to be censorious in his comments he cannot be put to the proof; no one can say to him in effect, "Go and do better yourself." I do not think, however, that he does grow fiercer but rather milder. His judgment is apt to err on the side of admiring very ordinary strokes, since it is tinged by his knowledge that he can no longer make any strokes at all. It is so hard to maintain a wholly impersonal standard of criticism. He falls unconsciously into a second childhood of making pyrotechnic noises at any normal drive. The fact that he could once make such a drive himself may be obvious to him from well-known landmarks on the course but he does not believe it for all that. It is an excess of humility and not of arrogance that makes him a less and less trustworthy judge of others. He is so humble as to mistake anything that glitters, however faintly, for gold. I would put little faith in him now as a chooser of teams.

There is no great comfort in that to be sure, but in some other compensations there is very real comfort. For the retired warrior there are no anxieties, no agonies, no thwarted ambitions, no wretched little jealousies, no bitter regrets. Never again will he toss and tumble, thinking of the match that is before him on the morrow. No black demon of a missed putt from the match that is past will crouch beside his pillow to arouse him at midnight. He will not watch his conqueror going on gaily from round to round and murmur to himself that that is where he ought to be. There will be no penitence for having been cross, for as far as the game is concerned he need never be cross anymore; no miserable pretense of being a good loser, for there is nothing to lose.

On the morning of the match the course had always a hard, unsympathetic look. The greens so beautifully trim and smooth seemed like places of public execution made ready, on to which the criminal must step out with a show of bravery at the appointed hour. The very flags blowing out straight from their sticks spoke to him of the wind as a personal enemy. Fate still hangs brooding heartless over the course but him she cannot touch. The voice of the starter is no longer the voice of doom. There will be heaps of slain ere the bloody day is out, but he will still be alive in inglorious security.

Gone too are those frantic inquisitions into wrongdoing, that last-minute searching for a remedy. The retired, like the King, can do no wrong and so does not want to find out what he had been doing wrong. Once upon a time he could scarcely bear the thought of the morrow, to say nothing of the intervening night, unless he had exorcised the devil of error. He must light on a new device before darkness inexorably fell. The gathering dusk still found him hunting feverishly while the lights began to twinkle in the clubhouse, and all the sane people had long since gone home. It was so essential to peace of mind to finish with a good one; the risk of just one more was so terrible and yet something stronger than himself drove him on.

The wear and tear of those researches was great, alike for body and mind, and yet I incline to think that they are what he misses most. Practice shots are now but a pleasant recreation; they have no serious object in view and so can have no ending of triumphant relief. He can still say to himself that he now knows what he was doing, that he has got it at last, but all too soon comes the thought, "After all what's the use?" The instinct to end with a good one is not to be eradicated (good is a relative term) but it is only an instinct, unsupported by reason. There is this consolation; it is now possible to study a new work of instruction on the game without seizing the fire-irons to test the author's doctrines. Let AB be the intended line of flight and let CD be anything it pleases! He can read the stuff, not without a certain detached interest, but as tranquilly as he would the *Pons Asinorum* itself.

I have made the best case I can for giving up, and there really does seem something, not much perhaps but something, to be said for it.

Superfluous lags the vet'ran on the stage,

but people are wonderfully kind in not telling him so, and he is happily stupid enough not to find it out for himself.